THE
CLASSICAL
MODEL

THE
CLASSICAL
MODEL

Literature and Knowledge in

Seventeenth-Century France

H ARRIET S TONE

Cornell University Press

Ithaca and London

Selections from Michel Foucault, *The Order of Things: An Archaeology of the Human Sciences,* trans. Alan Sheridan (New York: Vintage, 1973), are copyright © 1966 by Éditions Gallimard. Reprinted by permission of Georges Borchardt, Inc., and Routledge (Tavistock) for the author.

First published 1996 by Cornell University Press.

Printed in the United States of America

⊗ The paper in this book meets the minimum requirements of the American National Standard for Information Sciences— Permanence of Paper for Printed Library Materials, ANSI Z39.48–1984.

Library of Congress Cataloging-in-Publication Data

Stone, Harriet Amy, 1953–
    The classical model : literature and knowledge in seventeenth-century France / Harriet Stone.
      p.   cm.
    Includes bibliographical references and index.
    ISBN 0-8014-3212-X (alk. paper)
    1. French   literature—17th   century—History   and   criticism.   2. Classicism— France.   3. Literature and science—France.   4. Knowledge, Theory of.   I. Title.
PQ245.S78   1996
840.9'004—dc20   95-52449

For Jonathan Stone
and Melissa Stone

Contents

Preface

In this book I situate literature as an equal partner in the search for knowledge that developed in seventeenth-century France under the watchful eye of the absolutist court. I take seriously literature's capacity to order a view of the world, detecting in the vision of things offered by writers of fiction a key to understanding how meaning is fashioned. In the crafting of literature's forms, in the display of its art, there exists a legitimate science. This is not the science of discovery but the science of representing what is known. Thus by *science* I am referring to the *scientia* of the classical period, the paradigms that order knowledge.

Classical science combined what today are the separate disciplines of philosophy (logic, epistemology) and science (the observation, identification, description, experimental investigation, and theoretical explanation of natural phenomena). It is thus consistent with the history of the classical period to invoke the term *science* to describe the possibilities for structuring knowledge. Although I posit a link between literature and science, I do not intend to establish literature as a vehicle for communicating scientific findings. I do not highlight in literary texts explicit references to life on the moon, discoveries in anatomy, or the like. Instead I focus on the formal composition of literary works in an effort to determine how these texts explore possibilities for ordering ideas. I propose to analyze the epistemology of textual relations, that is, the logic or system (*logos*) established by a given text to organize the information that constitutes its knowledge (*episteme*).

[ix]

By knowledge I refer to all the meanings produced by a text, whatever its truth claims. Truth denotes an objective, verifiable, and comprehensive understanding of the world. It corresponds to science's goal of a completed table of elements, an absolute order of things. Truth, however, remains an ideal, since there are always more facts to be uncovered and classified, whereas knowledge refers to the information actually conceived en route to this goal. Knowledge is the sum of information pieced together by representation. I argue that knowledge includes not only the particular identities established by the text but also the critical perspective that the text self-reflexively provides about the process of representation. I show fiction, like science, to inform our idea of how knowledge is constituted in and as representation.

The primary aim of literature is arguably to please and not to inform. Yet, as I demonstrate, literature extends the experiment with method that flourished in France's scientific community in the seventeenth century. Method here refers specifically to the Cartesian formulation of an analytic protocol for scientific investigation and, more generally, to all similar attempts to know the world through the logic of analytic systems. Applied to literature, method underscores the process through which the author organizes the various elements of his or her text into a unified whole. I use the term *model* to refer to the formal apparatus—the whole of the text's design—responsible for this process.[1]

To interpret a work of literature one must be aware of the disposition of its elements. What is left onstage and what is removed from it; what is present at court and what is excluded from it; what is privileged by the characters and what is silenced by them are so many indicators of the epistemological practice through which meanings

---

[1] A text can be said to embed in its own functioning a discourse, or internal map to signification, that explains how it fashions signs and positions them in such a way as to produce a unified representation. My term *model* refers to this embedded discourse. It is interesting to compare this notion with David Porush's comments on the interrelation of science and literature in the modern period: "Descriptions of any intelligent system (and the Universe is obviously one; fictional texts create others) in order to achieve epistemological potency must include accounts not only of how the system is regulated and organized, and of how it communicates among its own parts, but also of how it knows and describes itself. In other words, any epistemologically potent system must include a discourse that enfolds its own intelligence" ("Voyage to Eudoxia: The Emergence of Post-Rational Epistemology in Literature and Science," *SubStance* 71/72, Special Issue: *Epistémocritique* [1993]: 45). Porush's claims for the modern emphasis on contextualization are equally valid for the classical period: "No significant communication can be calculated, let alone deciphered, apart from the disposition of the system of meaning in which it is embedded. Indeed, as the literary text always signals, information is context" (44).

are identified and negated. In literature, moreover, we see that representation is fundamentally an art of contextualization. That is, the designation of a specific *context* is responsible for establishing and evaluating a particular *content*. In my readings of classical texts I study representation as a framing device, akin to a scientific taxonomy, through which meanings are identified and classified. My particular focus, however, is the shifting of contexts, the slippage out of the frame of representation, which occurs in classical texts.

This focus is intended to challenge the very notion of unity implicit in the classical ideal. I seek to problematize the concept of representation as a whole, integral system and to offer in its place a theory of a far more complex and more uncertain rendering of the world. I show literary texts first to establish, then to subvert, the model through which they order information. These texts indicate how meanings are continually multiplied, elided, tested, and reconstructed. For this reason it is necessary to understand representation as an ongoing process, an indefinite becoming, if we are to grasp the full implications of the formulation of knowledge in the classical period. Literature can be said to exploit the tension that exists in science between a coherent method, a belief in the possibility of constructing a unified and totalizing knowledge, on the one hand, and a fragmented reality and the need to parcel information, to accumulate it piece by piece, on the other.[2]

I do not propose an exhaustive treatment of seventeenth-century French literature. Instead I offer detailed readings of individual works that span the century: Rotrou's *Véritable Saint Genest*, Corneille's *Horace*, Racine's *Andromaque* and *Bérénice*, Molière's *Amphitryon*, La Rochefoucauld's *Maximes et Réflexions diverses*, Lafayette's *Zaïde* and *Princesse de Clèves*. In the final chapter I connect the study of literary representation to the science of Descartes's *Discours de la méthode*, Furetière's *Dictionnaire universel*, and Pascal's *Pensées*. Pascal's poetic yet highly systematic—and thus, paradoxically, "scientific"—deconstruction of the taxonomic model serves as a final exemplar of the interplay of science and literature in the classical period.

The scope of the present study is, I believe, sufficiently broad to

---

[2] For a succinct analysis of the question of classification as it specifically relates to the increased specialization of knowledge in the classical period, particularly in the natural sciences, see Lorraine J. Daston, "Classifications of Knowledge in the Age of Louis XIV," in *Sun King: The Ascendancy of French Culture during the Reign of Louis XIV*, ed. David Lee Rubin (London: Associated University Presses, 1992), 207–20.

justify the assumption that grounds this work, namely, that literature does speak to us about knowledge. Literature proves an interesting testing ground for epistemological relations because, to the extent that each work—or, in the case of La Rochefoucauld and Pascal, each individual fragment—constitutes a whole of representation, it offers in concentrated form a study of the relations that science explores as part of an infinite representation. A literary text has the potential for being entirely regular in its patterning. Such perfection is its art. It is all the more striking, therefore, to note the persistent failure of a classical literary text to contain all of its elements within the limits that it has prescribed for itself. Through its production of this something more, the literature studied here displays how classical science, in its efforts to inform a view of the world through the determination of a rigorous classification system, similarly comes to occupy the indefinite but evocative space between description and observation, language and the real, conjecture and certainty.[3]

The task of conceiving a place for classical literature within the tradition of scientific investigation may well appear daunting. Although this work does not fall within the purview of the philosophy of science per se, my investigation into literature's role in the epistemological practice of seventeenth-century France challenges the viability of any theory of knowledge that would exclude literature. My primary concern is not with exposing, in New Historicist fashion, a broad spectrum of archival documents that shed light on literature. With the exception of Descartes's *Discours,* I do not analyze even those texts that record the history of science. Nevertheless, the New Historicists' contention that to know a particular period in history we need to cross the boundaries between disciplines has echoes here. My efforts to articulate how science and literature mirror each other reflect the New Historicist idea that humanists can in fact participate in inquiries formerly left to experts in the social sciences and the sciences.[4]

Critics now stress the whole nexus of discourses—scientific, histor-

---

[3] I thank my colleague Randolph Pope for suggesting that the lack of a perfect fit between observation and experiment, as between methodical and persistent doubt, is what drives science, not the application of well-known facts. The latter, he astutely notes, is not science but technology.

[4] For more on New Historicism, see Stephen J. Greenblatt, *Renaissance Self-Fashioning: From More to Shakespeare* (Chicago: University of Chicago Press, 1980); *Shakespearean Negotiations: The Circulation of Social Energy in Renaissance England* (Berkeley: University of California Press, 1988); and H. Aram Veeser, ed., *The New Historicism* (New York: Routledge, 1989), and *The New Historicism Reader* (London: Routledge, 1994).

ical, and literary, but also economic, religious, political, juridical, moral, aesthetic, and even culinary—which govern a particular culture. Such research implies that much is to be gained from considering a given discipline as contextually related to another, as forming part of the composite cultural mosaic for the society under study.[5] Consistent with this approach, I interpret the history of the consolidation of power in the classical age within the context of the larger body of cultural representations that mark the rise of absolutism. Representations emanating from the court are not ranked above, hierarchically, but on a par, synchronically, with those produced by science and the arts.[6] Knowledge is therefore understood to be a function of the creation and manipulation of signs common to all the master craftsmen of the classical age: the king, philosophers, and literary authors. In seventeenth-century France the court regulated the flow of information not only through its own legislation and propaganda—the force of law as elevated into the cultural icon of the Sun King—but also through the founding of academies and the patronage system, which fostered the artist's dependence.[7] This was the method that guaranteed its power. By association with the authors of his realm, however, the king's unique privilege is in turn recontextualized—

[5] Of course, all of these cultural forms are ordered through language. No more than the authors themselves, we cannot step outside of discourse to a purely objective understanding of the world, one that is not itself formed in language. Thus, when I refer to the formation of knowledge in classical texts, I am analyzing what is actually a subset of discourse, a particular cultural construct as conceived within the larger "grammar," or linguistic apparatus, in which all thoughts are shaped, irrespective of time or place.

[6] The nonhierarchical approach toward culture that I adopt in this study follows work on the seventeenth century by Timothy J. Reiss and Erica Harth. See Timothy J. Reiss, *The Discourse of Modernism* (Ithaca: Cornell University Press, 1982); *The Meaning of Literature* (Ithaca: Cornell University Press, 1992); and Erica Harth, *Ideology and Culture in Seventeenth-Century France* (Ithaca: Cornell University Press, 1983), and *Cartesian Women: Versions and Subversions of Rational Discourse in the Old Regime* (Ithaca: Cornell University Press, 1992).

[7] For more on the king's image, see Georges Balandier, *Le pouvoir sur scènes* (Paris: Balland, 1980); Louis Marin, *Le portrait du roi* (Paris: Minuit, 1981); Jean-Marie Apostolidès, *Le roi-machine: Spectacle et politique au temps de Louis XIV* (Paris: Minuit, 1981); Peter Burke, *The Fabrication of Louis XIV* (New Haven: Yale University Press, 1992); and Mitchell Greenberg, *Subjectivity and Subjugation in Seventeenth-Century Drama and Prose: The Family Romance of French Classicism* (Cambridge: Cambridge University Press, 1992). For an analysis of the effects of royal patronage on the development of the sciences, particularly the need for utilitarian research that served the needs of the state, see Harth, *Ideology*, chap. 6; and Alice Stroup, "Louis XIV as Patron of the Parisian Academy of Sciences," in *Sun King: The Ascendancy of French Culture during the Reign of Louis XIV*, ed. David Lee Rubin (London: Associated University Presses, 1992), 221–40. Both authors include extensive bibliographical references.

problematized—and the relation of power to knowledge revitalized. For in representation the formulation of knowledge is never final, never completely stable, never totally mastered, and thus never entirely coincident with the will of man to rule his world.

No knowledge, we freely admit today, occurs in a vacuum.[8] Even science, the rigors of its proofs notwithstanding, is subject to the weight of culture, to the pressures of the historic moment, and to the interests of the particular society in which it develops. For these cultural "givens" create expectations—expectations that inevitably shape the progress of scientific research.[9] Contemporary philosophers of science hold that science itself is a cultural artifact, a product of diverse cultural influences. Scholars now consider science to inscribe the values of the communities in which it develops. That is, science is seen to be inextricably bound to cultural norms, to the organization of society as determined by gender, to the distribution of wealth and power, and so on.[10] In this new, antitraditionalist view, therefore, science is no longer held to be an objective and disinterested field of investigation. Rejecting the earlier belief that the scientific method isolates, neutralizes, and objectifies, recent studies instead point to the method's own dependence on the larger cultural fabric.

So we see that in seventeenth-century France the gradual separation of science from religion does not produce an entirely independent and neutral knowledge. Much of science posits an order that resembles the divine order, an indication that all ties with religion have not

---

[8] Cf. Porush's discussion of cybernetics: "In its relatively naive attempt to formulate a mathematics of information, science discovered something that all literary acts express tacitly: information cannot be understood in a vacuum" (44). My study intends to make explicit some of literature's tacit, or implicit, assumptions.

[9] This is one of the principal arguments made by Helen E. Longino, *Science as Social Knowledge: Values and Objectivity in Scientific Inquiry* (Princeton: Princeton University Press, 1990).

[10] Thomas S. Kuhn argues that science is not impersonal and objective; scientific "truths" are relative, dependent on the paradigm—what today we might call the cultural context or discursive environment—in which science develops (*The Structure of Scientific Revolutions*, 2d ed. [Chicago: University of Chicago Press, 1970]). Studying the effects of the traditional male-dominated system of values on scientific research, Evelyn Fox Keller discovers in Kuhn's work the origin of much contemporary thinking about the interdependence of science and ideology (*Reflections on Gender and Science* [New Haven: Yale University Press, 1985], 4–5). For a discussion of how feminists extend the debate about science undertaken by Kuhn, Popper, Hanson, and others, see H. Longino, chaps. 1–2.

been severed. To the extent that it does function as a new order, classical science assumes a weighty power in making knowledge the product of method, its own ability to classify information. The establishment of a taxonomy is itself a complex process that, although it aims at objectivity, is not unambiguous. Categories for ordering information are not created ex nihilo. The knowledge that is shaped by science may reflect not only what one discovers but also what one already knows.[11] The scientific method does foster discovery and facilitate man's ability to predict and control the natural world. Nonetheless, it reflects a problem inherent in all knowledge systems, namely, the inability to establish identities independently of prevailing codes. Science generates meaning only in terms of its own paradigms: "The mirror that scientists hold up to nature is the mirror their science has devised."[12] No information, no "fact," exists independently of the system that conceives it. Classical literature clearly shows the "vicious" quality of all representation: it exposes not only how representation controls the production of meaning but also how it does so as a function of its own codes. For this reason literature can always be said to model more than it intends.

Because it understands all knowledge to be an approximation, science does not perceive the ambiguities of classification as constituting an epistemological collapse. There is no intellectual, moral, or technological failing in the fact that knowledge is acquired and refined over time. Although scientists are aware that future discoveries will

[11] A case in point is Descartes, who "sought to discover the laws of nature by deductively inferring them from some 'a priori' or 'necessary' truths. The justification of the laws thus derived was, therefore, granted, without any need for a posteriori, or empirical, testing. To be sure, an important role was given to observation in Descartes' scientific method; in order to derive a statement about a particular event or phenomenon, one has to include among the premises statements describing the observed initial conditions of the particular process, as well as statements expressing laws of nature. However, these predictions could not serve as tests for the laws of nature since the latter drew their validity from the a priori truths from which they were derived." Aharon Kantorovich, *Scientific Discovery: Logic and Tinkering* (Albany: State University of New York Press, 1993), 63.

[12] David Locke, *Science as Writing* (New Haven: Yale University Press, 1992), 34. Locke further notes: "The constructs of science—its models, its laws, its explanations—are conceived within their own frameworks, their own patterns of thought, their own paradigms . . . and they have, in effect, no meaning outside those frameworks, those patterns, those paradigms" (197). Locke's study lucidly and persuasively demonstrates how contemporary literary criticism clarifies the language of science to show that it, like literature, is imaginative, expressive, and context-driven.

require a reassessment of what is known, knowledge is still advancing. In the seventeenth century findings in astronomy lead to improved navigation and cartography; studies in anatomy and botany bring about better medical treatments; attention paid to military, agricultural, and manufacturing equipment has numerous practical applications.[13] But when we step back and consider how in this period such knowledge is produced within the larger frame of a history dominated by the controlling presence of the monarchy, which in the seventeenth century founds and sustains the Académie française (1635) as well as the Académie royale des sciences (1666), we are struck by the degree to which the responsibility for creating the tools of knowledge implies the concomitant responsibility for applying them judiciously. All authors, whether scientists or writers of fiction, know that to write is to exercise power; that to assign identities to things is, finally, to control them. In this context ambiguity indicates a failure to exert control. Exploiting language's potential for nuance and multiple meanings, classical literature signals the potential for disorder. The consolidation of knowledge and the consolidation of power are parallel operations, and these texts show that there is no easy harmony to be found in this connection. What one loses on the side of certitude, however, one gains in the expansion of knowledge. The indefinite results can be said to enrich rather than diminish the body of information that representation produces.

This book is not the first to argue the relation between science, either early or modern, and literature. Indeed, the exploration of links between these disciplines is now a legitimate professional subgenre.[14] Nor is my work the first to discover in literary texts a meaning that elides or somehow extends that conveyed by the author's carefully wrought paradigms. But what makes the focus on seventeenth-century French literature so important, aside from what it reveals about individual works of this period, is that this prolifera-

[13] For a more detailed enumeration of the Académie des sciences's research interests, see Stroup, 230. See Harth, *Ideology and Culture*, chap. 6 for a discussion of the Académie's utilitarian pursuits.

[14] Locke attests to the growing importance of this research: "For long a minor, barely tolerated sidebar to 'serious' literary study, the field of literature and science has in the decade of the 1980s virtually exploded. Testimony to the newfound popularity of this area was the formation in 1985 of the Society for Literature and Science, along with the growing number of conferences and publications dedicated to the field and to specific subsets within it" (20). He provides an elaborate bibliography to document this trend (215n59).

tion of meaning occurs despite the explicit efforts of classical authors to prevent it. If subversive relations can be found to exist in the very period dedicated to resisting them, in the age dedicated to creating a cultural monolith centered on the image of the absolutist king, then it is a sign that the knowledge generated in representation is fluid, indefinite, subject to change. Experimentation in the classical period has the upper hand over method, this privileged product of France's scientific, political, and artistic economy.

Earlier versions of Chapter 2 appeared in "Beyond the Promise: Racine's Andromaque," *Symposium* 43 (Winter 1989–90): 284–303; and "*Bérénice: Les voiles du pouvoir*," in *Ordre et contestation au temps des classiques*, ed. Roger Duchêne and Pierre Ronzeaud (Paris: Biblio 17, 1992), 225–33. Chapter 4 includes material from "Reading the Orient: Lafayette's *Zaïde*," *Romanic Review* 81 (March 1990): 145–60; and "Exemplary Teaching in *La Princesse de Clèves*," *French Review* 62 (December 1988): 248–58. I thank the presses concerned for permission to use these materials here.

I also thank Cambridge University Press for permission to reprint translations from *The Philosophical Writings of Descartes*, trans. John Cottingham, Robert Stoothoff, and Dugald Murdoch, vol. 1 (Cambridge, 1985), copyright © Cambridge University Press, 1985; Georges Borchardt, Inc., and Routledge (Tavistock) for permission to quote from *The Order of Things: An Archaeology of the Human Sciences*, trans. Alan Sheridan (New York: Vintage, 1973); and the University of Minnesota Press for permission to reprint passages from Louis Marin, *Portrait of the King*, trans. Martha Houle (Minneapolis, 1988). All other translations, deliberately literal, are my own.

Many individuals have helped to make this book possible. I am most grateful to Gerhild Williams for her careful reading of the manuscript. I thank Julia Simon for her commentary on the text and for sharing the eighteenth century with me. Adelheid Rundholz-Weihe offered much encouragement for this project by following my ideas so attentively in class and beyond. David Ingram provided important information for the Introduction. Randolph Pope generously read and helped to refine Chapter 5. This book owes much to Mitchell Greenberg's critique and to the example of his own work. I am indebted to Timothy Reiss, whose queries and comments have guided the manuscript into its final form. Heartfelt thanks are due as well to Emily Guignon for her assistance with the translations, and to Pascal Ifri for critical service in this domain. I greatly appreciate the generous support of Norris Lacy and the Department of Romance Languages and Literatures at Washington University. Last, but by no means least, I thank Bernhard Kendler and the Cornell University Press staff for their careful nurturing of the manuscript.

HARRIET STONE

St. Louis, Missouri

THE
CLASSICAL
MODEL

Introduction

Modeling a Classical Discourse

In the privileged circles of intellectual activity in seventeenth-century France, the identities of philosopher, scientist, and poet are often blurred. Descartes's writing bears witness to this phenomenon. The traditional triad of academic disciplines—philosophy, history, and poetry—is collapsed in the *Discours de la méthode*, where the philosopher introduces a new science, a rational model for the study of the world. Descartes's account of his scientific method is constructed much like a literary narrative, complete with intercalated stories and plot digressions, and with Descartes himself featured as the hero of the discovery he chronicles. The philosopher simultaneously plays the parts of researcher and poet.[1] Moreover, Descartes's science of representation—his method—is closely allied with the formal mastery displayed by authors of fiction in designing their texts.

Whether it be a document such as the *Discours de la méthode* which records an experiment or a tragedy that offers a moral lesson, representation is always a construct; it offers a particular interpretation of the world by framing events in a deliberately schematic way. In both the scientist's and the fiction writer's texts we can detect the framework, or organizational structure, through which discrete elements of perceived experience are filtered into recognizable patterns of thought that originate meanings.[2] I therefore take as my premise

---

[1] I examine the role of Descartes's autobiographical persona in the *Discours* more closely in Chapter 3.

[2] There is no origin to meaning in the absolute sense, since language clearly pre-

the idea that the bond linking science and literature is representation as a closed system for organizing ideas. It is my contention that literature participates in the shaping of knowledge in the seventeenth century to the degree that it, too, demonstrates knowledge of living beings, of the laws of language, and of the century's prevailing philosophical discourse. Michel Foucault evokes these same categories in *Les mots et les choses* (published in English as *The Order of Things*), a seminal work whose analysis of classical science in many ways grounds the present study.[3] Foucault uses these concepts to define a structure for evaluating the organization of thoughts in the classical period, the order of language that he calls the "classical episteme."[4] Influenced by Foucault's work, Timothy Reiss in *The Discourse of Modernism* studies the contribution of science fiction and utopias to the formation of knowledge in the classical period. His more recent study *The Meaning of Literature* attempts to develop a concept of literature that reflects what he terms the "multicultural environment" originating in seventeenth-century Europe and extending through the nineteenth century. The specific contribution of literature to the French classical episteme remains to be analyzed, however. I mean to emphasize how literature that has no explicit scientific content plays a role in the seventeenth century's experiment with method. In a departure from the history that subordinates literature to science, my investigation of

cedes any effort by an individual author to inform a view of the world. Rather, texts can be said to originate meaning to the extent that they construct a particular identity. Here *origin* refers to the author's elaboration of a specific model for contextualizing the various elements within representation.

[3] Michel Foucault, *Les mots et les choses: Une archéologie des sciences humaines* (Paris: Gallimard, 1966). Translations are from *The Order of Things: An Archaeology of the Human Sciences*, trans. Alan Sheridan, (New York: Vintage, 1973). Unless otherwise indicated, all references to Foucault throughout the text are to this work. Parenthetical citations give first the page of the translation then the page of the French edition.

[4] Foucault describes not the content of works but the structuring of ideas that results when a diverse body of texts on the human sciences is studied together in order to discern the set of organizing practices that govern the texts: "I am not concerned, therefore, to describe the progress of knowledge towards an objectivity in which today's science can finally be recognized; what I am attempting to bring to light is the epistemological field, the *episteme* in which knowledge, envisaged apart from all criteria having reference to its rational value or to its objective forms, grounds its positivity and thereby manifests a history which is not that of its growing perfection, but rather that of its conditions of possibility; . . . what should appear are those configurations within the *space* of knowledge which have given rise to the diverse forms of empirical science. Such an enterprise is not so much a history, in the traditional meaning of that word, as an 'archaeology' " (xxii/13).

classical culture exposes a rationalism that is no more exclusively scientific than the art of writing is exclusively literary.

Descartes serves as the cultural icon of the history I explore. Although he benefited from a long evolution in scientific research which extended back many decades, Descartes has come to symbolize the classical period's new science. He thus serves as primary exemplar of the relations I explore in this book. In the chapters that follow I refer to Descartes not only as the author of specific texts which I analyze but also as the figure who, in modeling the seventeenth century's fascination with method, exposes both the clarity of axiomatic thinking and the ambivalences of textual relations.

Science and Literature

In important respects science and literature are uncommon bedfellows. By definition, fiction offers an imaginary idea of things, a nonobjective interpretation of the world. Conversely, science endeavors to posit the truth; it means to establish facts devoid of any human partiality, that is, exclusive of all opinion, all subjective judgment. In the classical period scientists such as Descartes conducted experiments in optics and perspective that dealt expressly with the subject of images and illusions. As the object of scientific study, however, illusion does not have the same status as in fiction. Descartes's experiment with the stick that appears bent when immersed in water, the interest in anamorphic art, and the studies of the rainbow—to name just the most celebrated cases—all treat illusion as part of real experience. But there is another illusion at work in classical science which links it closely with literature. Science is dedicated to perfecting a method that makes possible the positive identification of all things in the world, an absolute order of things. Like literature, however, scientific writing resonates. Meanings are fixed; categories are developed and information is filtered into them. But the results are less than certain. This is not to say that either scientists or literary authors are unaware of the difficulties of representing their discoveries and the complications inherent in classification. Rather, it is to emphasize how in both kinds of writing more meanings are made available to the reader than are solidified by the text's careful disposition of elements into a unified pattern. I believe that literature best illustrates this aspect of representation.

How, specifically, does one assess literature's contribution to the formulation of knowledge? What does one use to measure the knowledge-producing capacity of a work of literature? I have been suggesting that the answer lies in the text's formal relations—the repetitions, oppositions, inversions, and exchanges that pattern the text and provide a framework for interpretation. These discrete operations constitute a system that I call the text's *model.*[5] The model is the grid of resemblances, differences, permutations, substitutions, and the like that allow the text to communicate its content to us. It is easier at first to consider the model as a particular sign—mirror, Orient, law— rather than as a logical system. For example, *Horace* and *Bérénice* are both patterned through a concept of law that is expressed formally as a metaphor for Rome. Roman authority depends on the suppression of all foreigners, the elimination of all who are different. The formal operation that orders the texts is thus the exclusion of opposites. But the texts are not the same. Neither, moreover, signifies uniquely in terms of the model that it erects. It is precisely this overriding of the model that provides a focus for my study.

I am referring here to a certain slippage of meaning that merits elaboration. The meaning that I describe as overriding the text's model is, like all other meanings that we discern, produced through this model. There can be no meaning that is not generated by the text, no meaning that is not an effect of the modeling process that the author establishes. Some meanings, however, cohere with the model, whereas others cannot be explained uniquely in terms of the model's functioning. For example, both of the plays just cited create a Roman model through which to define and expel an Other. Yet my readings of these works suggest that their full significance depends on a concept of alienation that is tantamount to seeing the Other in Rome. That is, the alienation of Rome is such that it cannot be erased even when the foreign identity is defeated, as it is in Corneille's play, or banished, as it is in Racine's. Unlike the identities that the plays' model succeeds in naming as either Roman or as foreign, this final "excess" meaning cannot be positively differentiated through reference to the model as a device for containing knowledge, in the restrictive sense of isolating and limiting identities.

In its elaboration of a model to fix identities, literature consistently

---

[5] My concept of the model relates most directly to what Foucault defines as the "general grammar," the science of signs through which writers organize individual perceptions and pattern the continuous flow of their thoughts (73/88).

gives life to a knowledge that it endeavors to suppress. The reader/
spectator sensitive to the art of representation registers not only the
text's patterns, the recurrent forms that shape the text, but also the
text's patterning of information, the *how* of its representation. The
patterns predict that only conforming, classifiable types will be projected into the future, that only these have a role in advancing knowledge. The actual effect—the final knowledge produced by a text—is,
however, less than predictable. We register even meanings that flow
through the grid which the author has devised to fix identities. We
recognize the sexually ambivalent, the Other, the marginal, the repressed, the masked, the elliptical. We retain in our minds impressions of all that the text does not name: all that the absolute monarchy
negates in order to affirm its own invincible law; all that is but cannot
be shown. Thus, despite authors' efforts to express an ideal order
through the conventions of unities, proprieties (*bienséances*), and ver-
isimilitude, literary texts cannot be adequately explained in terms of
a coherent design. To appreciate how literature shapes knowledge,
we must consider not only how its constituent parts are unified
through a central model but also, more importantly, the inadequacies
of this model for explaining some of the more profound meanings
embedded in the text.[6]

Literature and History

Before we consider the formal dynamic, it is useful to consider how
seventeenth-century texts actively engage in the subversion of meaning as part of the historic process. In an influential study of literature's
social function as an instrument in the service of the state, Alain Viala
describes how the talents of individual writers are used by the monarchy to idealize, and thereby enhance, its authority. He refers to what
he terms the duplicity of texts, which he cites as evidence that "har-

---

[6] Although it is certainly true that exclusionary activity is contained by the text (part
of what it creates), it is not enough to posit, as Timothy J. Reiss has, that all querying
by the system is contained by it (*The Discourse of Modernism* [Ithaca: Cornell University
Press, 1982], 51). Any drama that includes a conflict (and they all do) can be said to
contain both sides of the argument, that is, to include these polarized elements within
the same space of representation. I mean to show the intricate relation through which
the text, in setting up an opposite to be excluded, makes this Other available to the
reader in such a way as to conflate the terms of the opposition. What is contained is
the Other, but this Other can no longer be adequately described simply as opposite;
for it is never entirely negated, devalued, excised.

monious classicism" is but a myth: "Duplicity implies a dual meaning and, eventually, a lie; it is inscribed within the problematic of the euphemism. A text signifies by the way it gives shape to a process of generating meanings and as soon as two divergent meanings appear (simultaneously, in succession, or alternately), its meaning becomes triple: it signifies both meaning a, meaning b, and their coexistence."[7] Now, when Viala writes about duplicity, he is concerned with content and not form—problems with censorship and the need to write a text that functions on several levels at once, thereby allowing its author to avoid prosecution. But if one translates these remarks epistemologically—if one thinks not of double entendres and equivocation, or the genius of satire and parody, but rather how resemblances and differences order meaning—one begins to understand that the frame structure of the text is subject to a peculiar tension. More specifically, in the literary texts under study I uncover a process that I describe in Chapter 1 as the "breaking of the frame" of representation, whereby elements that are not contained or identified through the text's model nevertheless continue to signify.

If duplicity is understood in this context to mean the obfuscation and indirection of the text's modeling process, then the classical episteme is exposed as contestatory at its very core. The failure to specify and maintain distinct identities is as integral to the order of classical discourse as is its celebrated power to make language the "completely adequate and transparent representation" of the things in the world.[8] We find contestation in the history of the classical period: the strife of the Fronde; the bourgeoisie's ties to the crown; the wars that considerably empty the royal coffers; the divisions between Catholics and Protestants; scientific findings that threaten religious beliefs; and so on. So, too, within a single work the tension between authorized and unauthorized, identified and negated, similar and different, controlled and evolving signals a gap in representation. The reader/spectator's knowledge is not restricted to the "official" discourse celebrated by the text through its consolidation of elements into a synthetic whole.

---

[7] Alain Viala, *Naissance de l'écrivain: Sociologie de la littérature à l'âge classique* (Paris: Minuit, 1985), 297.

[8] Reiss, *Discourse*, 36. The coincidence of word and thing as elaborated by the *Logique de Port-Royal* has been explored by Foucault (see especially his discussion of the transparency of language, 58/72) and by Louis Marin, *La critique du discours: Sur la "Logique de Port-Royal" et les "Pensées" de Pascal* (Paris: Minuit, 1975).

This difference is important, for, as I argue, what occurs in the seventeenth century, beyond the specific achievement of science in developing a rigorous method for analysis, is a concentration of intellectual activity in interpretation as it extends to an awareness, or factoring in, of these other elements. Interpretation here implies both the active structuring of meanings in conjunction with a set of values and, significantly, an understanding of how views that conflict with such values are suppressed. Interpretation is opposed to revelation, the discovery of the preestablished, immutable order of things. Knowledge is not just the product of representation as it molds meanings that cohere with a particular model. For such meaning does not pass uncritically in the mind's eye. We also feel the effects of, and thus can be said to know—even if our knowledge is in part implicit or unconscious—the method through which the model governing representation is itself constructed: representation *as* representation. And here is the rub. We recognize not only what the text values but also how it assigns value. We see the author's hand as he or she writes, and this knowledge intrudes on our sense that the knowledge represented is adequate or complete.

This question has particular significance for the age of absolutism, where the making of knowledge is inseparable from the genius of statecraft and the court's pivotal role in the development of both the arts and the sciences. If the text's consolidation of meaning can be said to reflect, as content, the imposition of official discourse and the role of the court as arbiter of truth, then the text's fuller knowledge as it connects to an awareness of representation as representation must be considered a challenge to any arbitrary order. A study of the process of representation reflects the tension between the containment or consolidation of meaning on the one hand and the transformation or expansion of meaning on the other. It allows us to appreciate the classical age not only for the monarch's will to power, not only for the crown's desire to establish through the ubiquitous image of the king an absolute frame of reference for interpreting events. We also note the seventeenth century's sustained inquiry into all that resists an idealized and thus false knowledge. Rejecting the appearance of truth, Descartes insists that anything that is not clearly identified as true should be dismissed as false rather than erroneously assigned a place in his taxonomy. Literature—and in this designation I include the elements of scientific texts which perform a meaning in excess of the explicit content that they model—extends science's conceptualization of representation.[9] Literature exposes the process through which the text's model is in turn modeled, and thus recontextualized, as part of the cumulative process of interpretation.

The Classical Model

To situate this problematic, let me offer as an emblem for the classical period, a first model of the classical model I propose, Descartes and Louis XIV as two faces of a Janus figure. Unable to see each other across the classical episteme's glass, each face is nonetheless the unsuspecting mirror image of the other. In this image we see two heads of a state that was as much a state of mind (measurable in its ability to control and manipulate thoughts and language) as a political entity. Originally believed to be the god of light who opened the sky at daybreak and who closed it at sunset, Janus eventually came to preside over all beginnings and endings, as over all entrances and exits. It is Descartes who opens the century at daybreak, ushering in a revolution in science. His writings document the dawn of a science based as much on logic, the long chain of associations, as on the pure mathematical formulation of all that is measurable.[10] Descartes faces away from the king not only because he wrote before Louis came to majority but also because the king may have been personally responsible for banning the teaching of Descartes's works in French universities.[11] Presiding over the latter half of the century, Louis assumed for himself the power of light. Reflected in this image of the Sun King is the glory of the man who was able to transform himself into an immortal figure signifying ineluctable authority.

Nevertheless, much binds philosopher and king together despite a history of antagonism and separation. It was during Louis's majority

[9] In this context I use the terms *literary, rhetorical, poetic,* and *occulted* writing interchangeably.

[10] Robert Mandrou, *Des humanistes aux hommes de science: XVIe et XVIIe siècles,* vol. 3 of *Histoire de la pensée européenne* (Paris: Seuil, 1973), 163.

[11] Peter Burke, *The Fabrication of Louis XIV* (New Haven: Yale University Press, 1992), 131. L. W. B. Brockliss is more specific: "Louis XIV demanded that professors of philosophy on several occasions in the late seventeenth and early eighteenth centuries stop teaching a number of Cartesian positions. . . . However, it was always a question of aspects of Cartesian dualism that seemed to threaten Catholic orthodoxy. No attempt was ever made to stop professors offering mechanical explanations of natural phenomena" (*French Higher Education in the Seventeenth and Eighteenth Centuries: A Cultural History* [Oxford: Clarendon, 1987], 446n4).

that Descartes's influence was most strongly felt. Descartes's launching of the scientific method, moreover, showed him to be, like the king subsequently, taking power away from religion.[12] Descartes does leave a place for God in the *Discours*, but this space, as his contemporaries were quick to note, is independent of the method that he champions. Faith is explained not by recourse to methodical doubt and critical examination, as is the case for other experience. The proof of God instead extends from an analysis of the idea of perfection: my idea of a perfect being must have been placed in me by a nature more perfect than my own. Science, then, if explicitly intended *not* to take over for God, does nonetheless seem to function independently of the Creator.[13] The consolidation of power under the monarchy echoes science's affirmation of knowledge that conflicts with religious doctrine. Although church and state remained separate, the court in the seventeenth century celebrated the priestly with the secular as a way of extending its authority.[14] Louis was believed to be a sacred ruler whose touch had the power to heal. The court's control thus reflects a turn-

[12] Timothy Reiss argues that by the end of the sixteenth century religion was already "in the service of state power and . . . it could no longer provide any monolithic comprehension of human existence or singular guide to human action" (*The Meaning of Literature* [Ithaca: Cornell University Press, 1992], 65). The very emergence of scientific discourse as a domain distinct from theology, moreover, suggests that by the seventeenth century, religion's sphere of influence, while still considerable, had been altered. Brockliss notes that in this period the teaching of natural sciences diverged significantly from the teaching of moral and metaphysical sciences. Instruction in experimental physics and practical medicine, although still in its infancy and still maintaining ties to Aristotelian metaphysics, had come to represent change. French academic institutions for the natural sciences were "dynamic and up-to-date" centers of learning. Moreover, by the 1690s emphasis was placed on a mechanistic ideology, which held, in opposition to Aristotle's doctrine of the permanence of matter, that motion stemmed from a physical, if invisible, pressure. In contrast, the teaching of ethics and metaphysics remained part of a "history of stasis" (441). Basing his conclusions on university curricula, Brockliss argues that science came to win out over both church and state because it gained a certain independence (445–46).

[13] My point here is not to deny the conflict surrounding the role of God in Descartes's writing, a subject that continues to provoke much critical discussion even today. Rather, I argue that the mere fact that Descartes has been seen by some to separate out a scientific system from religion is a sign of the changes that were taking place as these two domains became more distinct and less easily reconciled to each other's principles.

[14] For an extended treatment of this issue as it connects to the theory of the king's two bodies and to the power of the king as image, see especially Ernst H. Kantorowicz, *The King's Two Bodies: A Study in Mediaeval Political Theology* (Princeton: Princeton University Press, 1957); Louis Marin, *Le portrait du roi* (Paris: Minuit, 1981); Jean-Marie Apostolidès, *Le prince sacrifié: Théâtre et politique au temps de Louis XIV* (Paris: Minuit, 1985); and Burke.

ing away from traditional religion, which was centered uniquely on the priestly function, and toward a new kind of faith in man's ability to cultivate knowledge and control its dissemination.

If the eighteenth century would eventually fight the monarch who assumed power, it would not reinstate the cause of religion. Already in the classical period the common link between Descartes and Louis was the very human desire to be master of the world, the claim to omnipotence that the mildly restrictive "almost" (*quasi*) fails to disguise in the philosopher's discourse: "I have almost never encountered a critic of my views who did not seem to be either less rigorous or less impartial than myself" (Je n'ai quasi jamais rencontré aucun censeur de mes opinions, qui ne me semblât ou moins rigoureux, ou moins équitable que moi-même).[15] King and scientist were united by the same glorification of the master subject. The Janus model invites a felicitous joining of science and history: "I think, therefore the state is me" (Je pense donc "l'état c'est moi"). Peter Burke affirms that if Louis "did not say [the state is me], at least he allowed his secretaries to write in his name that 'when one has the state in view, one is working for oneself' [quand on a l'état en vue, on travaille pour soi]."[16] Descartes and Louis were both products of a cultural evolution, a turning away from a belief that much of what ordered the world surpassed man's capacity to understand and to manage it. Conceived within this more secular orientation of ideas, man's most productive devotion was arguably to his participation in the organization and reformulation of his world.

Still, the opposed positions of Descartes in Holland and Louis XIV seated in the center of Versailles suggest a fundamental tension which it is my intent to explore. Holland, a country where the inhabitants "had the reputation of being more concerned with their own affairs than they were curious about those of others," afforded Descartes the peace of mind necessary to write.[17] In Versailles, whatever the lasting effects of the Fronde, the concentration of political, social, and artistic

---

[15] René Descartes, *Discours de la méthode pour bien conduire sa raison*, in *Descartes: Oeuvres et lettres*, ed. André Bridoux (Paris: Gallimard, 1953), 173. The translation of Descartes is from *The Philosophical Writings of Descartes*, trans. John Cottingham, Robert Stoothoff, and Dugald Murdoch, vol. 1 (Cambridge: Cambridge University Press, 1985), 146. Unless otherwise specified, all subsequent translations of Descartes are from this edition. In parenthetical citations, the page number of the English translation precedes that of the French edition. Quotations of Descartes are from the *Discours* unless otherwise stated; these are cited in the text.

[16] Burke, 10.

[17] André Bridoux, ed., in *Descartes: Oeuvres et lettres*, (Paris: Gallimard, 1953), 11.

life under the penetrating gaze of the Sun King reflected the monarchy's efforts to control its subjects by controlling the flow of information.[18] Descartes, moreover, represents a subjectivity that makes every man, if not equal to every other, equally capable of the "good sense" that allows him to reason.[19] The rational subject, I contend, sees not only what is but also the process—the method of ordering and measuring—through which this thing is identified and comes into being. Translated into the historic domain, this subject would be sensitive to the propaganda machine that is the state's potent weapon for hiding the man who is king behind his kingly image. The monarch symbolizes the monolithic quality of a history elevated to mythic status through association with ancient Roman gods and heroes. In this tension between greater and lesser, inclusion and exclusion, legitimation and negation, we see the classical model set in motion.

One is moved to inquire here how two such masters as Descartes and Louis XIV can coexist, how these faces can be perched on the single body of Janus. This underrepresented body/*corps* reflects not just the body politic of those who followed the king's example but the entire intellectual corpus of the classical period. What we see is the strained reason that situates the idealized representation of Louis beside the representation of the "good sense" which permits us to recognize this ideal as an image willfully and arbitrarily created by the court. One must ask, therefore, whether an awareness of the process through which monoliths are created, an understanding of the inner workings of the state as a symbol-producing apparatus, does not affect one's view of these monoliths. That is, one cannot but wonder whether one's knowledge of the workings of the system, of representation as representation, does not in the final analysis serve to challenge the efficacy of the signs produced.[20]

[18] Joan DeJean refers to Versailles as "the palace intended to keep the French aristocracy together in one community and under one roof, and to keep its principal members permanently under the king's surveillance" (*Tender Geographies: Women and the Origins of the Novel in France* [New York: Columbia University Press, 1991], 63).

[19] Descartes writes: "The power of judging well and of distinguishing the true from the false—which is what we properly call 'good sense' or 'reason'—is naturally equal in all men" (La puissance de bien juger et distinguer le vrai d'avec le faux, qui est proprement ce qu'on nomme le bon sens ou la raison, est naturellement égale en tous les hommes [111/126]).

[20] For a clear analysis of propaganda and the "making of the monarchy" under Louis XIV, see Burke's study of what he terms the "fabrication" of symbols designed to promote the king. It is important to note that my own examination of representation does not depend on a determination of whether challenges to the ideal that texts model are consciously undertaken by the public. Presumably some contemporaries were more

To take a specific example, does the public's understanding that classical theater erects a tribute to the king, its recognition of the elements that come together in this celebration, simply reaffirm the king's authority? Or does the theater, in its dramatization of the king's authority, make the audience somehow sense the arbitrariness of his rule by exposing the trappings of power, the statecraft that ensures monarchic control? Spectators obviously do not forget what occurs during the four acts and several scenes that precede the restoration of monarchic order in the tragedy's denouement. The perfection of the model of the king's power, moreover, stands in sharp contrast to the imperfect society that survives at the play's end. Thus Racine's Thésée, mourning the death of his son, Hippolyte, and the collapse of his family—a loss measured for him in both personal and political terms—endures with Aricie. He is moved to adopt this former enemy because her connection to Hippolyte makes her the last vestige of family, and because, we suspect, he has come to appreciate at some level how the real enemy resided inside the family unit and not with a foreign power.[21] Although in its most dramatic artistry the play asks the audience to obliterate certain impressions (those of the belea- guered Thésée) in favor of others (the favorable elimination of Phè- dre's threatening presence), Racine's text establishes various layers of meaning that reverberate after the fall of the final curtain. The text functions as a palimpsest, and as such it mirrors the larger problem of contextualization which I have been outlining. Today we say that certain ideas are not lost but repressed, hidden from consciousness but still factors in our behavior. Similarly, some elements of the trag- edy enacted onstage are layered, positioned away from the model, yet

---

aware of the methods of science, the machinations at court, and the techniques of literary representation than were others. These individuals were possibly more cognizant of the values implicit in certain advancements within these disciplines. It is not my purpose, however, to evaluate the actual critical capacity of the viewing public, to test Descartes's notion of the universality of good sense. As I discuss later, in showing how literary texts resist containment within a fixed analytical structure, I point to the ways in which our knowledge exceeds the boundaries of the model, or logical framework, responsible for ordering information. What matters is how representation shapes a view of the world—how such a view is etched, whether consciously or not, in the mind's eye of the reader/spectator.

[21] For a discussion of the role of the family viewed in conjunction with the monar- chy's power and seduction, see Mitchell Greenberg, *Subjectivity and Subjugation in Sev- enteenth-Century Drama and Prose: The Family Romance of French Classicism* (Cambridge: Cambridge University Press, 1992), 141–73.

still capable of exerting an effect on the audience. That is, these elements are not filtered systematically into the categories delimited by the model, but neither are they entirely lost to meaning.

To see this alternative view is not to deny the efficacy of the king's image that the drama constructs. I do not deny that this image restores order in the wake of Phèdre's negative influence. But this perfected form represents the arbitrariness of choice, the imbrication of values. Significantly, the other view is not explained by the knowledge evoked through the play's careful modeling of the king's paternalism. It is distinct from all that we know about the law from Thésée's last appearance onstage. Phèdre's evocative performance also shows the negative effects of a culture that denies difference, that is, the untenable consequences of a law that condemns both a woman and her stepson to ignore desire. One can further discover in this denial a possible explanation, or first cause, for the deaths of Phèdre and Hippolyte. Both characters are guilty of betraying Thésée's law.[22] But it is likewise apparent that Hippolyte's death, to the extent that it is an error resulting from Phèdre's deceit and Thésée's own lack of judgment, suggests an innocence that in turn complicates our understanding of Phèdre herself. If Hippolyte is unjustly punished, or punished for the wrong crime—not for loving Aricie but for supposedly seducing Phèdre—can we find justice in the father's law, the law that condemns stepmother and son to the same fate? This second reading does not negate but rather extends and recontextualizes the first. We see the symmetry of Racine's artistry, how he closes the text by purging society of all elements deemed unfit for its survival. But we also see the corruption of what survives.[23] Literature thus captures the other face of Janus: the beginning that marks every ending, the opening that qualifies every act of closure.

[22] The law that prohibits Hippolyte from marrying Aricie because she is a descendant of the previous royal family is, of course, distinct from the law that prohibits Phèdre from committing adultery/incest with her stepson Hippolyte. It is not the content of specific laws that concerns me here, however, but rather law's symbolic function as the ordering principle for the play. Underlying each law as tailored for a specific crime is the common principle through which society attempts to inhibit the desire of the individual and thereby protect the needs of the community. Broadly defined as a mechanism for ordering behavior according to prescribed standards, law here correlates directly with the model ordering knowledge.

[23] For a fuller treatment of these issues, see Harriet Stone, *Royal DisClosures: Problematics of Representation in French Classical Tragedy* (Birmingham, Ala.: Summa, 1987).

Expanding the Foucauldian Model

Configured in this manner, the classical model studied in the chapters that follow shows the rigid coordinates of the Cartesian system, understood metaphorically as the closed frame of representation, to be realigned. It is necessary to account for the slippage of the subject who, like Phèdre, is identified (positively) as a renegade (negative). We must explain the subject who is excluded from speech through death, exile, imprisonment, yet who still speaks to us, still informs our knowledge.

To situate my study I turn to Foucault, who in *Les mots et les choses* underscores a shift in the seventeenth century away from the world of objects and toward representation. Foucault elaborates how in the classical period the identity of things reflects their position relative to other things within the model elaborated by science. If this emphasis on representation as the locus of knowledge serves to ground my notion of seventeenth-century science, a few cautionary remarks about my agenda with regard to Foucault are nonetheless pertinent here. My use of *Les mots et les choses* is at once heuristic and contestatory. I invoke Foucault's analysis because he proposes what is arguably the most extensive account of the structural foundations of method, the logic governing thought in the classical period. I intend to expand Foucault's definition of the classical episteme to include the whole of ordered knowledge as figured not only in the sciences but also in literature. I do not, however, refer to Foucault with the intention of adopting his controversial theory of historic ruptures.[24] We can appreciate his elucidation of science, what he articulates about the function of representation, without returning to the theory that radical breaks—paradigm shifts—occur before and after the classical period. Indeed, I completely release my study from the period structure of Foucault's work. I pare back the scope of his definition of *classical,* which he sees as extending from the mid-seventeenth through the eighteenth centuries, to look exclusively at seventeenth-century texts, beginning with a baroque play by Rotrou. I include the baroque in my discussion of literature not because of an arbitrary division of history into centuries, but because I believe that the baroque offers a fundamental principle for understanding—

---

[24] Although this theory is commonly associated with Foucault, one does well to note that he acquired it from Bachelard via Canguilhem.

and not, as is commonly done, for contrasting—classical representation.

I do not attempt to situate Foucault's early theorizing in *Les mots et les choses* with his later research, in which he retreated from some of his initial ideas about classical representation. Nor do I attempt to apply directly Foucault's analysis of the classical episteme to literature, to extract from his examination of the sciences a method for interpreting fiction. I do call into question some of the assumptions that found Foucault's analysis of science. I refute the idea that scientific texts produce the meanings that they claim to produce and only these. My purpose in resurrecting Foucault's analysis, however, is not to dismiss it again but rather to extend it another step. Through my study of literature I mean to develop a portion of the cultural material that Foucault elides and in this way to establish a more viable notion of the classical episteme.

Foucault shows that a reliance on mathematics allows philosophers such as Descartes to conceive of the world in terms of specific categories that are subject to calculation and manipulation. A complex thing might be subdivided into its various components, and these components in turn compared and recombined to form an even more complex compound. All identical elements are understood to be interchangeable, while all other elements can be ordered in such a way as to specify their difference from the "similar" elements as well as from all the other "different" ones. What distinguishes the classical episteme, therefore, is its capacity to reformulate or reconfigure elements within representation. Underlying my study is the notion that Descartes's emphasis on the need to divide a complex problem into its component parts and to simplify by degrees has its corollary in literature's framing of meaning.[25]

Drawing attention to the tension that occurs within the model that it erects, literature is perhaps most revealing of the actual practice of science as it gathers and classifies information. Classical scientists do not ignore the problems inherent in taxonomic systems. They know well the arbitrariness of the order assigned to things, the incongruity of the fixed category and the constantly changing world. They understand the benefits of arranging elements in such a way that they can be profitably studied, classified, and, as necessary, reclassified. Un-

---

[25] See the second and third precepts of Part 2 of the *Discours* as well as Descartes, *Règles pour la direction de l'esprit*, in Bridoux, *Descartes*, xiv.

derlying their work, however, is a belief in the absolute coherence of the knowledge they produce. Although he argues that classificatory systems are provisional, Descartes indicates that each system directly contributes to a unified body of knowledge. Lorraine Daston notes that Descartes considers encyclopedic studies an antidote to the dangers of increased specialization. Yet he is confident that, whatever a scientist's specialization, whatever his point of entry into research, he will make his way to the unified whole of knowledge by following a single set of rules:

> Classificatory schemes could only be matters of temporary convenience, provisional maps to guide the investigator by revealing the principal lines of connection that would eventually make the whole cohere. Above all, disciplinary divisions were artificial and ultimately an obstacle to the progress of knowledge, for they blinded scholars to the network of interconnections that bound the sciences together at the deepest level.... Descartes's confidence that almost all of human knowledge could be deduced from a single set of axioms provided French savants with an implicit rationale for specialized research. The order of the propositions which compose the system is not absolutely fixed: given the axioms and a minimal set of basic propositions, it was possible to start at many different points and, with sufficient diligence, still eventually produce the system in its entirety.[26]

Descartes's faith in the efficacy of representation contrasts markedly with Diderot's commentary in the *Encyclopédie* in the next century. Following his articulation of the process of making stockings, Diderot remarks on the limits of even the most meticulous representation. His careful attention to all of the machine's various parts and operations notwithstanding, Diderot is painfully aware that his text fails to render his object adequately:

> We see, after what I have just said about the shape and the connections between the parts of the stocking loom, that we were wrong to believe that we would acquire some knowledge of the entire machine without entering into the details and the description of the parts: but they are so numerous that it seems that this work must exceed the limits that we

[26] Lorraine J. Daston, "Classifications of Knowledge in the Age of Louis XIV," in *Sun King: The Ascendency of French Culture during the Reign of Louis XIV,* ed. David Lee Rubin (London: Associated University Presses, 1992), 209.

assigned ourselves, both for the whole of this text and for the quantity of plates. *Besides, where should we start this text? How should we have the plates made?* The connections between the parts would require us to say and to show everything at once, which is not possible, neither in the text, where things necessarily follow one another, nor in the plates, where the parts overlap.

On conçoit, après ce que je viens de dire de la liaison & de la forme des parties du métier à *bas*, qu'on se promettrait en vain quelque connaissance de la machine entière, sans entrer dans le détail & la description de ces parties: mais elles sont en si grand nombre, qu'il semble que cet ouvrage doive excéder les bornes que nous nous sommes prescrites, & dans l'étendue du discours, & dans la quantité des planches. *D'ailleurs, par où entamer ce discours? comment faire exécuter ces planches?* La liaison des parties demanderait qu'on dît & qu'on montrât tout à la fois; ce qui n'est possible, ni dans le discours, où les choses se suivent nécessairement, ni dans les planches, où les parties se couvrent les unes les autres.[27]

Diderot acknowledges the difficulty of using language to translate experience. He is frustrated by the problems associated with the need to capture on paper the fluidity of motion and the unity of the machine whose composite parts he can articulate and design independently. In the eighteenth century the limits of knowledge are thus clearly articulated even as information is displayed and accumulated in the encyclopedia. It is perhaps not merely an accident of history that Diderot and other distinguished writers of the Enlightenment divide their interests between science and literature. I do not intend, however, to advance the argument that it is literature which gives rise to the later science. I am suggesting that literature helps to clarify the complexities of representation to the extent that it mirrors both the efficacy of method as championed by Descartes and the inherent problems of classificatory systems as articulated by Diderot.

All meaning, I argue, is context-dependent—dependent on the particular frame in which it is conceived. In the classical period representation puts this process *en abîme*. Literature shows clearly how a shift in the frame structure is responsible for a shift in meaning. Timothy Reiss's study of science fiction and utopian literature of the sixteenth and seventeenth centuries offers a view of epistemological

---

[27] Denis Diderot, "Bas," in *Oeuvres complètes*, ed. Herbert Dieckmann, Jacques Proust, and Jean Varloot, 33 vols. (Paris: Hermann, 1975–), 6:76–77; my emphasis.

practices which helps to clarify this process. Following Foucault, Reiss analyzes how one dominant discourse, or episteme, comes to be replaced by another. Arguing that such major transitions are most evident in the classical period and again in our own time, Reiss describes what he terms the occulting practice "composed of widespread activities (although the phrase is awkward) that escape analysis by the dominant model." These undetected elements "do not acquire 'meaningfulness' " in terms of the dominant model and "are therefore in the strictest sense *unthinkable*."[28] Reiss contends that the practice through which meaning is occulted gradually renders the primary theoretical model inoperative, resulting in the emergence of a new discourse. My own analysis is consistent with Reiss's to the extent that it depicts a similar transitional structuring of meaning, a similar slippage from the established paradigm. But by locating this slippage inside all of the works that I study, I refer not to Foucault's idea of a radical rupture at certain historic points, or to the more gradual rise of a particular class of discourse which Reiss terms analytico-referential. I mean instead to emphasize a pervasive tension throughout the classical period. This tension reflects the difference between a faith in the perfectibility of method on the one hand and the sustained experiment with method on the other.

Foucault argues rather schematically that in the classical period resemblances no longer ground the ordering of knowledge except to the extent that they help us to perceive differences (68/82). It is tempting, in accord with Foucault's emphasis on the shift from similarities in the Renaissance to the positing of identities and differences in the classical period, to find in seventeenth-century literary texts further evidence of a shift away from analogy. Regulated through the activity of inclusion and exclusion, the identification and valorization of elements in these texts depends on the act that isolates and expels the Other. Difference there is, but the classification of this difference is a complex and, I believe, uncertain process. Indeed, we find that indifferentiation, a concept that Mitchell Greenberg invokes to account for the ambivalent sexual identities of the cross-dressed characters in *L'Astrée*, is by no means unique to sexual identities or to this early novel.[29] In later works the shift to what might be described as

---

[28] Reiss, *Discourse*, 11.

[29] Greenberg locates d'Urfé's text at the crossroads of preclassical and classical epistemes: "Situated precisely at that moment of transition between the world of the Renaissance and the Classical universe, at that moment Foucault so eloquently describes

an absolute difference is never realized. Like *Phèdre,* the texts studied in the chapters that follow demonstrate that the exclusion of difference is never total. In order to account for these uncertain identities, one needs to look more precisely at the division of the space of representation into same and different, to observe how, within the frame of representation, it becomes impossible to identify with certainty all characters through a single model.

In his preface to *Les mots et les choses* Foucault distinguishes between this work and his earlier attempt to write a history of madness. *L'histoire de la folie* (*The History of Madness*) offers what he terms the history of the Other, a history of difference, or, more precisely, the rejection of difference. In contrast, the "history of the order of things" is, he claims, a history of the Same: "of that which, for a given culture, is both dispersed and related, therefore to be distinguished by kinds and to be collected together into identities" (xxiv/15). Identities and differences are determined; then all things sharing certain features, or "marks," are grouped together in the same class. But literature, I contend, testifies to the sustained existence of an Other that is not epistemologically "mad," unavailable to us through representation. This Other is not Foucault's Other, whose voice has been suppressed by history; it is not the human subject expelled ("so as to exorcize the interior danger") or imprisoned, shut away inside representation ("in order to reduce its otherness" [xxiv/15]). Certainly there is a political Other in these texts—characters who are excluded because their religion, sex, or race marks them as a threat to a stable political order. The text's Other can be said, moreover, to mirror the real Others of the seventeenth-century monarchy—the Frondeur, the foreign power, the Oriental, the women who challenge the court in their salons as well as on the battlefield.[30] I am referring specifically, however, to the Other that underlies these historic relations, to the Other that is a product of the text's own representation. The example of

---

in *Les mots et les choses* as the moment of transition between two epistemological systems through which and by which the human subject defines the world and his own place in that world, at the interstice of that never possible differentiation, the *Astrée* stands as their partition, their parturition, separating and connecting, differentiating and eliding all difference, in that impossible moment that is at once a beginning and an end, the birth of one world order and the death of another" (*Subjectivity,* 27–28).

[30] For more on the singularly influential challenge to Louis's authority exerted by women in their political activity and in their writing, see DeJean, *Tender Geographies,* chap. 1.

Phèdre suffices to suggest how literature's Other is expelled without being negated, exposed as different yet not eradicated.[31]

The texts that I study consistently emphasize the inseparability of power and control; they model the reinforcement of state ideology at the expense of other values, a key element in Foucault's theorizing about the institutionalization of power. I argue that in these works all that appears to lack a name and a place is also integral to the establishment of meaning. Although we are accustomed to associating the concepts of Otherness and difference with Derrida, the same "logic of deconstruction" underlies much of Foucault's own theory. Arguably, what most opposes the two philosophers is the emphasis on historical context in the case of Foucault, and the emphasis on the metaphysical in the case of Derrida. Throughout this book the investigation of *scientia*, the structuring of knowledge, is framed within a Foucauldian effort to analyze the actual epistemological praxis of seventeenth-century France as it extends from science to literature. If a Derridean approach to a marginalized presence likewise informs my analysis of the function of texts, this influence is perfectly compatible with that of Foucault, provided that one applies his claims for the history of the Other to the epistemology of classical texts. That is, in these works the Other who is a character must also be perceived as a function holder within representation. Each character represents a piece of knowledge, an element within the taxonomy that the author constructs. Without denying the historical import of these works, the importance of the characters as agents of the depicted history, I mean to accentuate how as part of the cultural history of the seventeenth century the marginalized elements in representation come to signify.[32]

Literary representation plays out the will to power that subtends the

---

[31] Some have argued that outside *Les mots et les choses* Foucault himself provides us with a way of reading texts so as to know the Other. H. D. Harootunian suggests that Foucault's approach to interpretation is "a way of experiencing and externalizing alterity, and [we] come to recognize that those who have been absented from the practice of historical narrative have empowered the story that has been told. Yet, the move to resituate the Other, and to propose that discourse permits the articulation of a field consisting of a variety of subject positions, questions narrative's claim to representation and closure" ("Foucault, Genealogy, History: The Pursuit of Otherness," in *After Foucault*, ed. Jonathan Arac [New Brunswick: Rutgers University Press, 1988], 112).

[32] In Chapter 5 I will return to a discussion of why, in the particular historical context framed by this study, although one cannot speak of a reconciliation between Foucault and Derrida, one can point to a certain compatibility between these philosophers with regard to the formation of knowledge in the classical period.

classical emphasis on the absolute as an ultimate control, a complete and therefore empowering knowledge. Still, the text's ordering of information—its fundamental division of elements into identities and differences—is shown in the chapters that follow to be blurred by the very system, or taxonomy, that it establishes to affirm identities. The model that would group these identities and these differences fails to offer a finite knowledge. For any name—good/bad; included/excluded; present/absent—the text has us invoke to classify its elements is exposed as arbitrary. The more deeply embedded textual strategy makes us see each name in terms of some connection, if not resemblance, to the other. Reiss explains that classical science, in establishing itself as a master discourse to be emulated by all other discourses, offers its own continuity in place of the discontinuity of objects.[33] Yet scientific writing cannot be restricted to a single, equivocal meaning any more than literature can. The knowledge represented by science corresponds with meanings as they are fixed within a taxonomy. But this knowledge is inseparable from the process through which the taxonomy is developed over time, that is, the testing of the method itself. Demonstrating the provisional nature of any model that appears to afford continuity, literature points us back to science as it confronts the difference between its efforts to order a unified knowledge on the one hand and, on the other, the fragmentation both of the real and of representation itself.[34]

A determination of the limits of the model developed by literary texts, an analysis of the frame structure that organizes them, is the easy part of any investigation into the epistemological groundings of classical literature. I would not be proposing this study if my sole intent were to rehearse the patterning of unities that scholars have traditionally celebrated in the literature of the Grand Siècle. Examining selected works extending from Rotrou's *Véritable Saint Genest* through Lafayette's *Princesse de Clèves*, I analyze the space of representation as it evolves from the beginning of the century to its close. What the geometry of this unfolding reveals is how the mirror of the text that reflects in the early part of the century through the baroque's

---

[33] Timothy J. Reiss, "Cartesian Discourse and Classical Ideology," *Diacritics* 6 (Winter 1976): 23.

[34] I do not here disagree with Reiss. This parceling is arguably a continuous process. Nonetheless, it is important to note that any continuity must be measured against the discontinuity of knowledge that is consolidated bit by bit over time and, at critical junctures, reconfigured.

mises en abîme comes finally to refract in the ellipses, as Joan DeJean has labeled them, of a woman's inimitable example.[35] In this shifting space the ultimate knowledge of classicism begins to emerge. The baroque theater's duplication of a single model, its play of mirrored forms, is displaced by the novel's championing of meanings for which no model exists, its celebration of the unrepresentable. By following this progression we see that knowledge, the positive identification of things, gradually gives way to a more encompassing process of knowing the limits of the knowledge that writers construct through their models. The readings that follow are intended to show what lies behind classicism's perfected forms, to discover in literature the truth of the other side of representation, the other face of the knowledge reflected in the text.

In my concluding chapter I return to the issue of science and literature in a reading of Descartes, Furetière, and Pascal. I mean here to recontextualize Foucault himself, to underscore the occulted meaning of his text. My aim is not to "deconstruct" Foucault so much as to situate him anew within the context afforded by my emphasis on literature's role in ordering knowledge. Focusing on the functioning of taxonomies in the *Discours de la méthode*, Furetière's *Dictionnaire universel*, and the *Pensées*, I mean to position the episteme developed by Foucault within the larger, revalorized context of a cultural discourse that molds even the process through which scientific knowledge, like Foucault's episteme itself, is fashioned.

I hope to affirm through this focus on literature's contribution to the scientific experiment of the seventeenth century a more complex understanding of classicism than either science or literature alone can provide. Although the founding of the Académie française and the Académie royale des sciences would appear to signal the historic severing of the arts from the sciences, the focus on classification suggests the complementarity of these disciplines. Literature benefits from science's methodological underpinnings; these foster an appreciation of form, in general, and of the logic of systems, of the literary text as an ordered structure, in particular. I believe that literature can in turn be used to illumine the contextualization process through which all representation—scientific as well as literary—orders meaning.

It should be clear, however, that my intent is not to deny important distinctions between the divergent goals and practices of science and

[35] Joan DeJean, "Lafayette's Ellipses: The Privileges of Anonymity," *PMLA* 99 (October 1984): 884–902.

literature, but to stress for the classical period in France how and to what extent all writing contributed to a cultural identity. Indeed, the entire question of contextualization that I highlight reflects the larger issue of interpretation that motivates all critical inquiry. Three centuries after Descartes, on another continent, and in another discipline, the question of making knowledge is still open, and is still, I believe, a compelling focus for scholarly attention. What we find in the classical period are not simply the roots of modernity but the very consistent process through which a culture develops a body of knowledge that exceeds what can be represented by even its most perfect models, a process that leaves something residual, something other, but something unquestionably significant, for future generations to fashion.

I now begin where Foucault begins, with his articulation of classical representation based on his interpretation of Velázquez's *Las meninas*. Rather than follow Foucault's path, however, I mean to turn away from science and toward literature, not joining them with him again in a sustained discussion until the end of my project.

Chapter One

Frame Theory:
Foucault, Rotrou, and Corneille

Foucault opens *Les mots et les choses* with a compelling analysis of Velázquez's *Las meninas* (see Figure 1).[1] An example of seventeenth-
century naturalism, this painting is "not essentially a device for
describing the world as it is but, rather, for revealing a higher order
of visual and intellectual relationships."[2] We are drawn into the illusion of this painting, whose meaning depends on the elaborate play
of framed representations that are included self-reflexively in the composition: a rear view of the supports of a canvas, numerous paintings,
a mirror, a doorway, windows. It is a painting about the artful construction of a painting, the *mise en abîme* of the elements of signification. The fact that many of the frames contain images that are
invisible or otherwise difficult to discern suggests, moreover, that the
act of framing itself—and not any specific content or narrative regarding the formal portrait of the royal couple, King Philip IV and
Queen Mariana—tells the real story of how the painting structures
meaning.[3]

---

[1] Painted by Velázquez in 1656, this life-size work is also titled *Portrait of the Royal
Family*; it was renamed *The Maids of Honor* in the nineteenth century.

[2] Julius S. Held and Donald Posner, *Seventeenth- and Eighteenth-Century Art: Baroque
Painting, Sculpture, Architecture* (Englewood Cliffs, N.J.: Prentice-Hall, 1979), 184.

[3] Held and Posner note that in the nineteenth century, consistent with a new emphasis on narrative, two interpretations were offered: Princess Margarita and her entourage have entered the room where a portrait of her parents, King Philip IV and
Queen Mariana, is being painted; or, conversely, the princess is being painted as the
royal couple enters the room (184).

Figure 1. Diego Rodriguez Velázquez. *Las meninas*. Museo del Prado, Madrid, Spain.
Photograph: Alinari/Art Resource, New York.

The room depicted is large, and presumed to be Velázquez's own studio. On the left side the artist—that is, his double as represented in a self-portrait—stands behind his easel. The artist's gaze is fixed on his model, and on us, since the viewer of Velázquez's masterpiece stands in the same space as the king and queen who pose for the artist's double. At the rear of the room hangs a series of dimly lit paintings. Near the center of this far wall we distinguish a mirror in which the reflection of the royal couple appears. At the back of the room, to the right of the mirror, a marshal holds open a curtain in a doorway that connects to a passage. Posed with his feet on different steps and with one knee bent, this figure suggests movement. Yet we cannot know whether he is coming or going. On the right-hand side of the composition more paintings are hung between two windows. These paintings and the windows are visible primarily as frames, since they are situated at right angles to the viewer. Foucault calls attention to the fact that the window on the extreme right, which is the light source for the painting, illuminates both the studio depicted in the painting and the unrepresented area in front of it in which the king and queen are presumed to be posing for the artist (5/21). In the foreground of the painting, extending from the easel to the far right, is a group of spectators which includes the young Princess Margarita, who is positioned between two maids of honor. The one to the left is offering the Infanta a glass of water. Behind the attendant on the right appear two additional court figures. In the lower right-hand corner of the painting are two dwarfs, the smaller of whom, a boy, stands playfully under the window with his foot resting on a dog in the foreground. Examining the painting from left to right, we can therefore distinguish three primary focal points: the painter; the royal couple reflected in the framed mirror; and the spectators in the foreground. A fourth area depicts the marginalized presence of the inscrutable marshal who observes the scene from the rear of the studio as he enters/leaves, seen only by the real king and queen and not by any of the figures in the painting. The significance of his position is one that I will highlight in a manner intended to cast Foucault's own analysis in a somewhat different light.

What is striking about Velázquez's work is that the royal couple, who are ostensibly the model for the entire composition, appear nowhere in it. The king and queen are invisible, although they constitute the painting's anecdotal subject, its raison d'être from the point of view of narrative. Only the couple's reflection in the mirror and the many glances turned toward them as they stand outside the painting affirm their presence. Foucault identifies the image in the mirror on the far wall as the direct reflection of the king and queen, who pose in the space beneath the frame. H. W. Jansen suggests that this image could also be a reflection of what is on the canvas that we cannot see.[4] Such ambiguity, however, merely supports Foucault's thesis that the significance of the painting lies in its own play of images and not in any verifiable relation between representation and history, that is, between what is depicted in the painting and the actual event of the royal couple's posing for the artist.

Nearly all the figures in Velázquez's painting are engaged in contemplating either the royal couple directly or, in the case of the two maids of honor, the Infanta, who stands symbolically at the center of the painting under her parents' mirrored reflection. Still, the real presence of the king and queen—their position outside the painting and the perspective that it affords—fails to unify the composition. Posing for the painter, the king and queen occupy the same space as both Velázquez when he contemplates his canvas and the spectators who view his work. Foucault explains that the viewer function is diffused in the painting, split into three separate angles of vision which extend from the painter (who doubles Velázquez), the mirror (which doubles the royal couple), and the courtier on the stairs (who doubles the spectator). As a result, the organizing gaze—the perspective that informs the painting—is occulted. The "invisible center" occupied by the royal couple outside the painting fails to provide a single line of vision through which to explain the disposition of elements. The sovereign vantage point, as this implies both the king's position with respect to the scene depicted in the painting and the privileged access that this position denotes in terms of knowledge and power, does not clarify either the canvas being painted by the artist or the paintings hung on the walls of the artist's studio. The center outside the painting fails, moreover, to explain why Velázquez chooses not to expose what the artist has painted on his canvas and why all glances are not directed at the royal family (one of the courtesans and the boy dwarf look at neither the king and queen nor the princess). This "invisible" center does not indicate why so much attention has been placed on the spectacle of representation, the act of framing the painting, rather

---

[4] H. W. Jansen, *History of Art: A Survey of the Major Visual Arts from the Dawn of History to the Present Day* (Englewood Cliffs, N.J.: Prentice-Hall, 1973), 433. Jansen believes that the artist paints a full-length portrait of the entire royal family: the princess, who has just posed for him, and her parents.

than on the spectacle of the court. Why is the king's presence eclipsed and the painter's own figure displayed so prominently? Does this ellipsis confirm the theory that even in real life the king functions less as a man than as a symbol?[5]

Although he does not treat the question of the historic importance of the king's image directly, Foucault informs us that meaning in the painting does depend on the artist's ability to shift our focus away from the real model and into representation itself:

> Perhaps there exists, in this painting by Velázquez, the representation as it were, of Classical representation, and the definition of the space it opens up to us. And, indeed, representation undertakes to represent itself here in all its elements, with its images, the eyes to which it is offered, the faces it makes visible, the gestures that call it into being. But there, in the midst of this dispersion which it is simultaneously grouping together and spreading out before us, indicated compellingly from every side, is an essential void: the necessary disappearance of that which is its foundation—of the person it resembles and the person in whose eyes it is only a resemblance. This very subject—which is the same—has been elided. And representation, freed finally from the relation that was impeding it, can offer itself as representation in its pure form. (16/31)

Knowledge is shown to be a function of the internal organization of elements in the painting and not the presumed mimetic relation between image and model. With the founding (actual, imitable) subject—the real king and queen—evacuated from the scene of representation, the model *in* representation, the "painterly image," becomes necessarily the model *of* representation. That is, Velázquez's painting models how knowledge is structured in symbolic language. Meaning is regulated through the ordering of signs rather than through an act of imitation intended to establish a relation of similarity with the real. The actual royal couple has been replaced by an image, a reflection in the mirror. The function of this image is measurable not in terms of the accuracy of its likeness, for in the couple's absence such a judgment cannot be made, but rather in terms of its relation to the other elements of the painting. Knowledge is therefore shown to originate in representation itself.

The artist's easel, the paintings hung at the back and on the right-

---

[5] See Introduction, note 14.

hand side of the room, the framed mirror and the window frame, like the gazes that point into and beyond the painting, are all signs which inform Foucault's theory of the representation of representation. Placed *en abîme*, these elements maintain a relation of similitude with the painting that contains them.[6] We recognize that any similarity between these elements and the real outside representation is less significant than their order within representation. Foucault distinguishes between Dutch painting of the period, which often includes a mirror whose reflection literally re-presents the various objects displayed in the painting, and Velázquez's painting, where "the mirror is saying nothing that has already been said before" (7/23). Referring to Foucault, Lucien Dällenbach further observes that in *Las meninas*

> the mirror faces the observer as in Van Eyck's painting. But here the procedure is more realistic to the degree that the "rearview" mirror in which the royal couple appears is no longer convex but flat. Whereas the reflection in the Flemish painting recomposed objects and characters within a space that is condensed and deformed by the curve of the mirror, that of Velázquez refuses to play with the laws of perspective: it projects onto the canvas the perfect double of the king and queen positioned in front of the painting. Moreover, in showing the figures whom the painter observes, and also, through the mediation of the mirror, the figures who are observing him, the painter achieves a reciprocity of gazes that makes the interior oscillate with the exterior and which causes the image to "emerge from its frame" [*sortir de son cadre*] at the same time that it invites the visitors to enter the painting.[7]

The expression "to emerge from its frame," implying that an image should stand out from the painting, comes from Velázquez's master, Pachero. Velázquez, Foucault notes, has reversed the formula (8/24). Indeed, as Dällenbach clarifies, Velázquez appears instead "to make the model [the posing subjects], and with it, the spectator, enter the painting. Théophile Gautier's exclamation upon seeing the painting ('But then where is the frame?') translates this oscillation well."[8]

Velázquez's mirror does not imitate what *is* in the studio: it does not reproduce the easel, artist, Infanta, and her attendants. The mir-

---

[6] See Lucien Dällenbach, *Le récit spéculaire: Essai sur la mise en abyme* (Paris: Seuil, 1977), 18.

[7] Ibid., 21.

[8] Ibid., 21n2.

ror does imitate what is *not* there: the royal couple, and the generations of spectators who assume the couple's place before the painting. This doubly uncertain relation between the actual model for the painting and the signs within it establishes an ambivalent signifying space.

This ambiguity proves crucial to our understanding of how knowledge is ordered in literary representations of the classical period. Still playing with the expression "to emerge from its frame," we discover a new tension in the reciprocity of inside and outside, inclusion and exclusion, that resonates within Velázquez's work. For this tension marks not only the space opened up between representation and the founding model (the space between the painting and the actual presence of the king and queen) which Foucault underscores but the internal organization of the painting as well. The latter is modeled by the marshal "framed" ambivalently in the doorway, caught in a motion for which there exists no definitive interpretive context. In an explanation so speculative as to accentuate the precariousness of the marshal's position, Foucault formulates various narrative possibilities that would justify the inclusion of this figure in the painting:

> Against this background, at once near and limitless, a man stands out in full-length silhouette; he is seen in profile; with one hand he is holding back the weight of a curtain; his feet are placed on different steps; one knee is bent. He may be about to enter the room; or he may be merely observing what is going on inside it, content to surprise those within without being seen himself. Like the mirror, his eyes are directed towards the other side of the scene; nor is anyone paying any more attention to him than to the mirror. We do not know where he has come from: it could be that by following uncertain corridors he has just made his way around the outside of the room in which these characters are collected and the painter is at work; perhaps he too, a short while ago, was there in the forefront of the scene, in the invisible region still being contemplated by all those eyes in the picture. (10–11/26)

No single perspective clarifies the marshal's role. As I noted earlier, he can be seen neither by the painter, whose presence organizes the majority of elements within the painting, nor by the other spectators in the painting. He is visible to the royal couple as they sit for their portrait. But he is seen by them, and by the spectator of Velázquez's painting, only in profile. To the extent that the marshal is integrated into the composition, it is as a figure whose obscurity ominously reflects the fragility of all that the painting identifies. For Foucault he is a presence that "repeats on the spot, but in the dark reality of his body, the instantaneous movement of those images flashing across the room, plunging into the mirror, being reflected there, and springing out from it again like visible, new, and identical species. Pale, minuscule, those silhouetted figures in the mirror are challenged by the tall, solid stature of the man appearing in the doorway" (11/26).

How do we explain this challenge to the images in the mirror without explaining it away? The marshal is perhaps sufficiently removed from the scene for his gaze to encompass the painter's easel and the real king and queen modeling for him, and, by extension, our own presence as we study Velázquez's composition. Through his unspecified yet, owing to its range, empowering glance, he invites us to penetrate deep into the painting. He urges us to look behind all that can be explained through the art and the act of representation—the celebration of a work that offers itself, the act of painting, as its own spectacle—and toward an awareness of all that this representation produces but cannot identify with certainty. Occupying an indefinite space within the painting, the marshal conveys the uncertain passage from frame structure to meaning. For this reason he serves as a crucial placeholder in my theorizing about the ordering of knowledge in the classical period.[9]

I submit that in the seventeenth century, knowledge can be explained by the double break "from the frame of representation." Knowledge is the product of the external break with the real, with the founding model, as emphasized by Foucault. Significantly, however, knowledge as signified by the marshal in Velázquez's work is also the product of an internal rupture, a process through which representation elides its own explicit logic. Some elements "emerge from" the master or primary model that representation erects to order experience. In the discussion that follows, I introduce the idea that classical representation models a knowledge which is far less certain than is

---

[9] It is interesting to note that Foucault's depiction of the marshal's position, as it accentuates a tension between presence and absence, identities and differences, center and margins, is consistent with a Derridean orientation. The same can be said for all the figures whom the marshal models in the present study: Genest and Camille; Andromaque and Bérénice; the gods in *Amphitryon*, the autobiographical subject of the *Discours*; amour propre in La Rochefoucauld; the Oriental subject of *Zaïde*; and the Princesse de Clèves. Chapters 2 through 4 will show that all of these subjects "supplement" the text's primary representation in ways consistent with Foucault's interpretation of the marshal's ambiguous role in the painting.

implied by either the reciprocity of Velázquez's multiple *mises en abîme* or the notion of control implicit in the act of framing. In making this claim I am building on a number of points that Foucault makes in reference to the disposition of elements within the painting, and, in particular, to the openness of the space of representation. Rather than synthesize these elements, however, I mean to focus on the fact that within representation another elision occurs that is no less important in determining how the classical period lays the groundwork for knowledge.

In the cited passage which concludes his interpretation of *Las meninas*, Foucault claims that, by excluding its subject (the posing king and queen), representation here offers itself in its purest form as representation. Considered in light of its own arrangement of signs, however, representation does more than point to the absent subject outside its frame. It reveals at the periphery of the model that it constructs another void in which the most profound meaning of the text conveys itself to us. The marshal stands before a secondary light source, in a doorway which, although it fails to illumine the artist and the other spectators, provides a key to interpreting the painting. The primary light source, the window, gives life to the artist at work as he is surrounded by the tools of his profession and the courtesans who validate his art, all signs that ensure the integrity of the illusion that Velázquez creates. We have seen that most of the images in the painting speak self-reflexively of representation's capacity to originate meaning, to occult all sources of signification external to it. Yet the marshal in the doorway leads us beyond this ideal of perfection and completeness. By virtue of his remoteness and obscurity, the marshal models an even more complex and compelling challenge to the concept of mimesis.

As in Velázquez's painting, French classical literature reveals the capacity of representation to order meaning in the absence of a founding model. For example, the theater never depicts the court of Louis XIV directly, preferring instead to magnify the royal presence through references to ancient, biblical, and mythological sources. Literary and historical models do, of course, exist for classical works, but the knowledge they order is less dependent on these precursors than on contemporary notions of statecraft. Still, even the model of the seventeenth-century monarchy does not go unchallenged. Literary texts consistently create a fissure in the frame that would assign all identities in a manner consonant with state ideology.

Authors frame a representation of representation that is at the same time something more. As my discussion of Rotrou's play *Le véritable Saint Genest* (The veritable Saint Genest) and Corneille's *Horace* will illustrate, the meaning modeled through the text's recurrent patterns is incomplete. The marshal in Velázquez's composition does nothing to undermine completely the authority of a painting ordered through images and gazes. He, too, suggests the power of a gaze that registers the sovereign presence of the king and queen; he, too, fosters the reciprocity of subject and object positions in the painting. He is seen by the royal couple and thus models within the painting the viewing relation that they model outside it. To focus on the marshal's marginalized presence, therefore, is not to decenter the painting. Indeed, Foucault has located multiple centers: the painter, the princess, the mirrored image, as well as the space that extends beneath the bottom frame where the actual model/spectator is located. But the marshal's ambivalent status as the figure exiting/entering the studio, as the beginning/end of its narrative, that is, as the liminal experience of what can and cannot be identified, allows us to see that in Velázquez's painting "excess" also has a place in the structuring of knowledge.

We cannot take in all the figures of the painting in one glance. Not only do the life-size proportions of the painting preclude such an appreciation, but also the fact that the heads of the figures are turned in different directions means that our gaze is deflected. The painting communicates through images which, in order to be understood, must thus be considered in sequence, one after the other, in the context of a history that is still unfolding. It is a history that is still unframed, even in this painting composed of frames within frames.

As a real, corporeal presence, the marshal, more than even the mirror image of the royal couple, impresses on us the limits of such representation. As much as the painter and his tools, he offers a perspective for knowing how meaning is crafted. From his place at the rear of the room, the marshal lets us identify the painter as origin, as the primary model for this portrait without a royal subject present in it. But the marshal makes us see the painter as an origin that is arbitrarily chosen from among other options. Out there where the marshal stands, another history is taking shape; other models for knowledge are ready to be constructed. And this fact allows us to see not the uncertainty of what has been achieved within representation, for the marshal in the doorway is a witness to this production, but its incompleteness. If we understand the classical episteme to refer to all the possibilities for knowledge dominant in this period, we cannot afford to ignore what slips through the frame of representation.

By re-presenting Foucault's representation of Velázquez's painting in this way, I am not setting up the argument that Foucault's claims for science as a representation that breaks with its model are wrong, and that literature, which internally redoubles the act of breaking from the frame, is right. The relation between the two discourses is far more subtle and supple. Witness the fact that Foucault in his study of Velázquez assigns the label "classical" to a form of artistic expression whose literary counterpart is "baroque." We know that the distinction between baroque and classical within the literary tradition is by no means absolute.[10] Jean Rousset insists that these concepts are neither opposite nor identical:

> One says: order, measure, reason, rule, and it is classicism. One will thus say: disorder, excess, fantasy, liberty, and it will be Baroque. Cosmos and chaos: equilibrium and vital surge [*jaillissement vital*]. This is true and it is false. . . .
>
> One risks, moreover, distorting the issue in making the Baroque an exact counterproof of the classical and in constructing the history of the seventeenth century as the simple play of opposites. The Baroque and the Classical see each other as enemies, but as one does within a family; they oppose each other in a fraternal way.[11]

Arguably, this uncertainty within critical discourse as it applies to literature only underscores its imperfections with regard to the more rigorous scientific taxonomy studied by Foucault. If I invoke this problem here, however, it is not to cast aspersions on the classification system used by literary scholars. I mean to suggest that we have something to learn by reconciling Foucault's analysis of *Las meninas*, which, as I shall establish, offers a virtual blueprint for reading a ba-

---

[10] For an excellent introduction to the imprecision of the term *baroque*, see Timothy Hampton, "Introduction: Baroques," *Baroque Topographies: Literature/History/Philosophy*, ed. Timothy Hampton, *Yale French Studies* 80 (1991): 1–9. Jean Rousset draws attention to the opposition between the baroque perceived ahistorically, as a series of stylistic attempts to approach a linguistic ideal, and the baroque as a historical period, "the baroque age." Attempting to reconcile these diverse perspectives, he argues: "Instead of having one century perceived in terms of a progressive and monochrome evolution, many parallel seventeenth centuries would be seen to emerge" (*La littérature de l'âge baroque: Circé et le paon* [Paris: Corti, 1954], 9). Hampton's reading of this passage has particular resonance for the present chapter's emphasis on frame theory: "The seventeenth century becomes a kind of historical fresco that is both unified (within a frame) and multiple ('several seventeenth centuries'), both static and mobile, both spatial and narrative, both monstrous and familiar" (6).

[11] Rousset, *Littérature*, 242–43.

roque play such as *Le véritable Saint Genest,* with his own dismissive remarks about the baroque:

> Similitude is no longer the form of knowledge but rather the occasion of error, the danger to which one exposes oneself when one does not examine the obscure region of confusions. . . . It is the privileged age of *trompe l'oeil* painting, of the comic illusion, of the play that duplicates itself by representing another play, of the *quid pro quo,* of dreams and visions; it is the age of the deceiving senses; it is the age in which the poetic dimension of language is defined by metaphor, simile, and allegory. (51/65)

The Baroque Model: *Le véritable Saint Genest*

Acts 3 and 4 of *Le véritable Saint Genest* are devoted to the performance of a play, *Le martyre d'Adrian* (The martyrdom of Adrian) for an imperial audience that includes the Emperor Diocletian along with his daughter, Valerie, and her future husband and co-emperor, Maximin. The play within the play enacts a glorious moment from Maximin's past: the conversion to Christianity of Adrian, a distinguished Roman soldier, and the death sentence issued to him by Maximin. During his performance of *Le martyre,* Genest, who plays the part of Adrian, is touched by divine grace. He ignores the script to enact his own conversion to Christianity. Thus in Rotrou's play, as in Velázquez's painting, illusion gives way to the truth. Here, too, meaning originates in representation that elides its founding model, a fixed subject outside representation. The imitation of history is limited to the script of *Le martyre d'Adrian,* the text that Genest is to perform in his role as actor but which he abandons in his role/identity as a new Christian. Genest's actual performance, his passage from feigning to becoming, is depicted as a conversion from ignorance to knowledge. Exceeding his role, he completes an act of self-mastery: "He was rehearsing his Role and he wanted to surpass it" (Il repassoit son Roole et s'y veut surpasser).[12] Here the theatrics of role-playing become an example of what J. L. Austin has labeled the performative speech-act. Minus the staging, minus the alterity of dramatic recitation in which one speaks the words of another, Genest's recitation of his role is the perfor-

---

[12] Jean Rotrou, *Le véritable Saint Genest,* ed. E. T. Dubois (Geneva: Droz, 1972), 2.2.452. All subsequent quotations from *Le véritable Saint Genest* are cited in the text.

mance through which he renounces his profession and the theater's celebration of imperial power in order to realize his self-knowledge, his true identity before God:

> No, Marcele, our Art is not of such importance
> That I have promised myself much reward from it;
> The favor of having had Caesars for witnesses,
> Has acquired too much glory for me, and has overpaid my efforts;
> Our wishes, our passions, our night watches and our pains,
> And finally all the blood that flows from our veins,
> Are for them tributes of duty and love,
> Where Heaven binds us, in giving us life;
> So, too, have I, since I drew my first breath, always
> Made wishes for their glory and for the happiness of the Empire;
> But where I see it as a question of a God's welfare,
> Much greater in Heaven than they are in this place;
> Of all the Emperors, the Emperor and the Master,
> Who alone can save me, as He gave me life;
> I justly submit their Throne to His Altars,
> And against His honor I owe nothing to the mortals.

> Non, Marcele, nostre Art n'est pas d'une importance,
> A m'en estre promis beaucoup de recompense;
> La faveur d'avoir eu des Cesars pour témoins,
> M'a trop acquis de gloire, et trop payé mes soins;
> Nos voeux, nos passions, nos veilles et nos peines,
> Et tout le sang enfin qui coule de nos veines,
> Sont pour eux des tributs de devoir et d'amour,
> Où le Ciel nous oblige, en nous donnant le jour;
> Comme aussi j'ay toûjours, depuis que je respire,
> Fait des voeux pour leur gloire et pour l'heur de l'Empire;
> Mais où je voy s'agir de l'interest d'un Dieu,
> Bien plus grand dans le Ciel, qu'ils ne sont en ce lieu;
> De tous les Empereurs, l'Empereur et le Maistre,
> Qui seul me peut sauver, comme il m'a donné l'estre;
> Je soûmets justement leur Trône à ses Autels,
> Et contre son honneur, ne dois rien aux mortels.

> (5.2,1547–62)

The slippage from illusion to reality is completed by the martyr's death. As Jacqueline Van Baelen notes, "Genest . . . only *becomes* Genest by the death that destroys the feint: 'And that he fully wanted, by his impiety / In dying, to make a truth of a feint' ['Et qu'il a bien voulu par son impiété, / D'une feinte, en mourant, faire une vérité'].''[13] Thus, all the elements of the play conspire to extract a final meaning from the spectacle that becomes history. The re-presentation of the representation that is Genest's performance in his own name is an example of Foucault's representation of representation, of a knowledge grounded not in history (Adrian's defeat by the Romans) but in the model that representation itself offers as it strips itself of its mimetic function and locates truth in performance.

By comparing the play within the play to the frame motif of Velázquez's painting, I am, of course, insisting on the importance of a spectacle that calls attention to itself as spectacle. The same self-reflexivity evident in the painting's easel, framed paintings, and so on is apparent in the repeated attention given to theatrical performance in Rotrou's play. The hero's discussion with the designer about the set decorations; the spectators' comments about the performance; the rehearsals; the visibility not only of the stage but of the wings of the theater within the play; Maximin's delight upon seeing himself onstage; and discussions about the actors' role in service to the emperor all rehearse the play motif within the play.

Moreover, just as in Velázquez's work the gaze is divided into three separate functions—the artist, the image, and the spectator—so, too, *Saint Genest* refracts the gaze of the historical, extratextual model by creating three distinct gazes within the play: that of Genest as director attending to the troupe's production; that offered through the play within the play as it mirrors history; and that of the imperial audience attending the performance. As director of *Le martyre d'Adrian*, Genest holds a place in representation similar to that of the artist in *Las meninas*. Like the painter, the director "frames," or provides a context for, the imperial image through his production of the play. The mirror function, which is introduced as a centerpiece through the play within the play, can be defined more narrowly as the image of Maximin as depicted by the actor Octave. Unlike the royal couple in the Spanish painting, Maximin *is* figured in representation, present onstage as spectator to the troupe's performance. Still, the function of the mirrored image, here the actor's role, similarly conveys the alterity of the couple's reflection to the degree that the role performed by

---

[13] Jacqueline Van Baelen, *Rotrou: Le héros tragique et la révolte* (Paris: Nizet, 1965), 162. Van Baelen cites *Saint Genest* 5.7.1749–50.

Octave is not that of Maximin, spectator "sitting" before the stage like the royal couple before the artist, but rather that of Maximin, distinguished military figure in a history that predates the actual performance.

Perhaps more than any other aspect of the drama, the fact that the performance is interrupted conveys the discontinuity between model and representation that Foucault has underscored in relation to the function of the mirror in Velázquez's work. As performed before the play's internal audience, the play within the play is the theatrical equivalent of Velázquez's elision of the royal couple posing for the artist. For in abbreviating the performance, Rotrou literally abandons his internal model, the script as it imitates history, which serves as the play's external model. That is, the scripted performance of Adrian's martyrdom for the imperial audience is the mirror in the text that reflects the "what is there" of the historical events that frame the drama. The actual performance of the play, however, also reflects "what is not there" in the actors' script, namely, Adrian's own example as it is exchanged for Genest's. In this ambiguous relation of representation to the model, we note the same distancing from history evident in Velázquez's masterpiece by the absence of the king and queen.

We can also isolate a counterpart to the marshal's function. Genest in the role of Adrian fills this ambivalent space that marks the passage from the inner frame, that of the play within the play, to the outer frame story of Rotrou's drama. Like the marshal, Genest is a spectator to the action to the extent that his role as performer (Adrian) is intended to separate him from himself (the pagan Genest). The marshal's ambivalent status in the painting is mirrored in the tension provoked by Genest's role, as is apparent in the question "Hallo, who is minding the Play?" (Hola, qui tient la Piece? [4.7.1298]). This uncertainty is reinforced by the obstacle that Genest in this transitional moment presents to the internal spectators' expectations that they see their own history mirrored in his performance. That is, the relationship that Foucault highlights in terms of the interrupted gazes that order *Las meninas* is parallel to the complex relations through which Rotrou's audience, in response to Genest's emergence as a historical figure in his own right, interprets the events onstage. Diocletian and his entourage see Genest's conversion to Christianity as a betrayal of history as it did occur and as it is supposed to be reenacted onstage. And they also view the performance as a challenge to Roman authority in the present. Conversely, Rotrou's own Christian audience can be expected to approve the martyrdom. Cynthia Skenazi argues persuasively, moreover, that the Frondeurs in the audience would not respond positively to the much-lauded self-made men who determine the outcome of events, Diocletian and Maximin: "For a seventeenth-century audience, such praise corresponds to the admission of a downfall that evokes the situation of the 1640s: the Fronde will not be fought by self-made men; it will be exploited by a *noblesse de sang* that can only scorn these common heads of state [*roturiers*], imitated by a handful of poor devils like Genest."[14]

To appreciate fully Genest's position in representation, we need to consider Rotrou's overall design. The performance of *Le martyre d'Adrian* mirrors the play's frame story to the extent that both establish representation itself as the sole criterion for knowledge. The opening scene describes Valerie's initial concern that her father will not allow her to marry Maximin—a concern she expresses after dreaming that she has been wed to a shepherd. Her fear that Maximin, a former shepherd, will be judged an unfit husband are allayed by her father's revelation that he himself is of humble origin. The couple's marriage at the close of the play thus confirms that dreams do, as Valerie affirms, function like oracles. More precisely, a dream is a representation that not only informs us of the truth but also can be said to inform the truth, to make knowledge, to the degree that it is validated by men's actions. This relation is implicit in Valerie's insistence that the power to realize, to "make a truth" (*faire une vérité*) of her dreams resides with her father, who legitimates the story of the shepherd's rise to power through his approval of the couple's marriage.[15] Viewed from this perspective, the play within the play as performed by Genest, particularly when he steps out of his role, mirrors rather than negates the relations through which the frame characters acquire knowledge. All the characters act to make themselves other than what history prescribes them to be. In this reflection of opposites, this refraction of the mirror function, we note a further parallel with the many unsynthesized gazes of Velázquez's painting which Foucault takes as primary evidence of representation's power to break away from the founding model.

The thematics of Rotrou's play indicate that if the historical model

---

[14] Cynthia Skenazi, "La représentation du théâtre dans *Le véritable Saint Genest* de Rotrou," *Papers in French Seventeenth-Century Literature* 17, no. 32 (1990): 79.

[15] In a blanket acknowledgment of her father's power, Valerie insists that the truth value of her dream rests with Diocletian's actions (1.1.71–80).

has been elided, it is only to make room for the sacred.[16] Viewed from within this religious context, representation evidences the more traditional (preclassical, in terms of Foucault's epistemology) effort to imitate in art the essence of the world created by God. The theater here serves the mediating function of a larger history, that of the transcendence of all human knowledge in the divine.[17] Still, the formal structure of the play invites us to see Genest's conversion as an effect realized through representation, occurring as it first does in language. Genest hears through a heavenly voice that he will not be performing in vain (2.4.421–24). His situation is thereby distinguished from that of the character whom he plays, for Adrian is motivated by the example of other men.[18] This moment of self-awareness is no Cartesian cogito; the angel's voice is external to Genest. But the hero's conversion is, significantly, shown to begin prior to his hearing the angel: "In effect, as in name, I find myself to be another; / I pretend to be Adrian less than I become him" (D'effet, comme de nom, je me treuve estre un autre; / Je feints moins Adrian, que je ne le deviens [2.4.402–03]). In the most literal sense, therefore, the text's "I feign less" is the representation in which Genest's self-knowledge generates, proof of his "veritable" existence: therefore he is (*donc il est*). Rehearsing his part, Genest begins to conceive his final identity as a Christian. That he does so is proof of the divine power upon him; how he does so is every bit a celebration of the theater's power to signify.

I have traced these relations somewhat schematically in an effort to maximize the parallels with Foucault's analysis. My intent is not to offer a new reading of Rotrou's play but to read Foucault against Foucault, as a representation of his own representation. Specifically, I mean to reconcile Foucault's theory that the classical period locates truth in the representation of representation with his apparently contradictory, albeit "classic," position that the baroque, in so many words, is nothing but trompe l'oeil. As the example of Velázquez

[16] For more on the importance of the religious significance, see Robert J. Nelson, *Immanence and Transcendence: The Theater of Jean Rotrou, 1609–1650* (Columbus: Ohio State University Press, 1969); Jacques Morel, *Jean Rotrou: Dramaturge de l'ambiguïté* (Paris: Armand Colin, 1968); and Van Baelen.

[17] Cf. Nelson: "The aesthetic of imitation could not express more dramatically God's seeming transcendence of the world Genest leaves and Rotrou's seeming transcendence in this moment of his own theater of immanence! Genest rejects *both* art and the nature it reflects for the sake of the truth that is opposed to them" (33).

[18] See Nelson, 30–31.

shows, the theory of classical representation can be elaborated from a study of the function of the *mise en abîme*, a consummately baroque effect. If, moreover, we separate out a thematics of illusion from illusion as a formal device, we find a theoretical model for both the representation of representation, as defined by Foucault, and the representation within representation, as I have defined it here.

The thematics of illusion cannot be said to have a place in the epistemology of the classical period; fantasy per se (as distinct from optical illusions and similar phenomena studied by science) is frivolous, erroneous, and has no bearing on the ordering of knowledge. But as a formal device, illusion connotes the separation of representation from the external model; it is the reality produced through representation, as distinct from the real history of lived events. There are two such founding models in Rotrou's play: the Roman defeat of Adrian and the contemporary French attitude toward Genest's own conversion. Significantly, neither model is represented in representation. Adrian's history is in part elided. And the French spectators, as we have seen, affirm a knowledge that in terms of both religion and politics negates the view of the internal audience.

Within representation illusion can be considered a formal device whereby the secondary "emergence from the frame," Genest in his marshal-like position, structures a meaning even though this meaning is not reflected in the drama's frame structure. We can speak of "illusion," a truth created within representation, because Genest, like the marshal in the doorway, cannot be positively identified by the Roman model that the play establishes to identify his conversion. Illusion here thus corresponds not so much with the error of a false identity as with the ambivalent identities that the model orders.

This affirmation is intended not to challenge Genest's Christian identity or the positive connotations of his sainthood, but to focus on the ways in which this identity is figured within the Roman context that seals the play. With regard to Velázquez's painting, Foucault specifies that the internal audience—the Infanta and the other members of the court included in the foreground of the painting—cannot see the painter, the king and queen's image in the mirror, or the marshal standing on the stairs (10–13/26–28). Similarly, in Rotrou's play the subject is divided between Genest as director, Genest as Adrian, and Genest as saint. The audience does not see Genest as director when he performs as Adrian; and it loses sight of Adrian when Genest begins to feel the effects of divine intervention and moves away from his character. In the disunity of this gaze, in the multiple glances that

shatter the model symbolizing the triumph of Roman history, we uncover a representation whose illusion, or performance, opens itself up
to the real word of God.[19]

Genest serves as a placeholder between two representations, the
Roman and the Christian, and between two spectator functions, the
Roman disapproval and the contemporary Christian recognition of
the "veritable" hero. This slippage has resonances for Velázquez as
well as for classical literature, despite its concentrated efforts to contain such excesses. By emphasizing the indeterminacy of elements
ordered within representation, we are able to isolate Foucault's negativity concerning the baroque as restricted to a thematics of falseness
and invention rather than to form and method. At the same time, we
are able to reserve those "baroque" aspects of his analysis that point
to the unresolved tensions in Velázquez's painting—its occulting of
the gaze, its multiple centers, its mirroring of an absent subject—for
a more expansive theory of the epistemological underpinnings of the
classical period as reflected in literature. If, according to the traditional criteria, the classical emphasizes containment, the tightness of
a structure that eliminates all that does not conform to the meaning
framed by the text, it is equally dependent on a most baroque pro-
pensity for what Jean Rousset terms a "vital surge," and which we
might connect with Foucault's borrowing of the expression "to
emerge from its frame." What we must reject is the facile dismissal of
the baroque as false, illusionary, untenable in an epistemological system.

Perceived within the frame of the classical, the very baroque excesses acquire the seriousness needed to capture the attention of
Foucault, who is intent on affirming the power of representation to
fix an order of things independent of its connections to the real.
Foucault nevertheless underplays the threshold experience, the rep-

---

[19] A comparison with Corneille's *Illusion comique* suffices to suggest that the emphasis
on the spectacle of representation as a source of knowledge is not limited to drama
with a religious theme. As the chronology of these plays indicates, the classical moment
that I am defining cannot be restricted to the later parts of the century, as is traditionally
done. My attempt in this chapter is to establish a continuum from the baroque through
the classical. I do not mean to deny the political changes, scientific advancements, and
aesthetic reorientation that mark the years separating these plays from those discussed
in Chapter 2, or what distinguishes them from one another. Rather, I mean to suggest
that what changed did not negate but rather extended the baroque's focus on excess.
For more on the history of change, see Timothy J. Reiss, *The Discourse of Modernism*
(Ithaca: Cornell University Press, 1982), and *The Meaning of Literature* (Ithaca: Cornell
University Press, 1992).

resentation within representation that simultaneously locates meaning inside the frame inserted within representation and, like the marshal in Velázquez's painting, outside this frame. As the example of Corneille will demonstrate, it is in the liminal space that representation establishes the profound significance of its most marginal subject.

The Classical Dilemma: *Horace*

Horace represents the quintessential classical ideal of order. Restricting the flow of meanings to binary opposites—Rome/Albe; state/family; duty/passion; male/female—Corneille frames his text within a traditional logocentric system whereby one meaning can be derived from its opposite. By the end of act 5, Albe is eliminated as a political opponent; family values are subjugated to the interests of the state; passion is sacrificed to the hero's duty; and Camille's resistance to her brother is overridden by the force of his hand, which kills her, and the king's words, which vindicate him.[20] Representation is therefore carefully designed to contain knowledge within the very specific limits of Roman authority. The second term of each opposition is suppressed in order to assert the (truth) value of the first; the play's symmetries are unbalanced to favor the hierarchical extension of Roman law as it reaches from daughter to wife to husband, hero, king, and gods. It is not without relevance to Foucault's theory that the Roman claim to absolute authority mirrors that of the contemporary French monarchy, although contemporary history is not figured directly onstage.

Corneille's tragedy specifically shows the signifying power of representation to function through an act of framing that is, as befits a play about war and aggression, more a censoring than a mirroring device. History is represented in such a way as to affirm the monarchy's power to write itself into law. In this self-contained mirroring, however, something important is left for dead and buried. In his final speech Tulle brings closure to the crisis affecting society by first excusing Horace, arguing that the hero's murder of his sister is ultimately of less consequence than his military value to the state, and then by ordering that Camille be placed in the tomb with her lover:

---

[20] I argue later in this chapter that vindication is distinct from exculpation.

I pity her, and to offer her cruel fate
What her amorous mind might wish,
Since on the same day the ardor of the same zeal
Completes her lover's destiny and her own,
I want the same day, witness to their two deaths,
To see their bodies sealed in the same tomb.

Je la plains, et pour rendre à son sort rigoureux
Ce que peut souhaiter son esprit amoureux,
Puisqu'en un même jour l'ardeur d'un même zèle
Achève le destin de son amant et d'elle,
Je veux qu'un même jour, témoin de leurs deux morts,
En un même tombeau voie enfermer leurs corps.[21]

The play would appear to admit no excess, to seal every last detail within its Roman frame. Every challenge to Roman law, depicted through the metaphor of sameness, seems to be buried with Tulle's final command that Camille be entombed beside her lover. In a perceptive analysis of how the patriarchal system functions, Mitchell Greenberg points specifically to the promotion of the ideology of the state through a repression of affect, as depicted by the women's preoccupation with family rather than civic duty. He sees in Camille's burial an indication that her identity is ultimately subject to male authority, reinscribed within its law: "The tragedy of origins and difference, of symmetry and State, ends in the establishment of a new, triumphant order of the same. Camille is put where she did not want to be, in the same place/grave as Curiace. The two are made One."[22] According to this reading, Camille is recuperated by the state, integrated into the "oneness" of law that functions through the exclusion of all difference. In an earlier study I take issue with this interpretation, and I would like to return to my position briefly in order to frame my application of Foucault's analysis of classical representation to Corneille's tragedy. Disputing Greenberg's claim that all excess is eradicated with Camille's burial, I argue instead that Tulle in fact commemorates her revolt against the system that has oppressed her:

---

[21] Pierre Corneille, *Horace*, in *Oeuvres complètes*, ed. André Stegmann (Paris: Seuil, 1963), 5.3.1777–82. All subsequent quotations from *Horace* are cited in the text.

[22] Mitchell Greenberg, *Corneille, Classicism, and the Ruses of Symmetry* (Cambridge: Cambridge University Press, 1986), 87.

Entering the paternal metaphor only after her life is spent, Camille is never really one with those who would make her the same (*même*). To be recognized after death by the system whose law threatens her identity—to be ceremoniously honored by society's leader—assures, moreover, Camille's sustained presence in history. The play's final scene is less a sacrifice of her difference than a tribute to it. Entombed with her lover, Camille represents the violation of all synthesis, the triumph of diversity and dissension within a tradition of arbitrary oneness.[23]

My interpretation of Camille's privileged status as Other is based largely on the notion that the symbolism of the burial is sufficient to memorialize her, and thus to identify her difference to the audience, both internal and external. To make, quite literally, a place for her in history, even a place of burial, is to stop short of negating her. What the concept of the representation of representation, particularly as it incorporates the notion of "emerging from the frame of representation," allows us to appreciate more fully is the how and the why of this affirmation of the heroine's role. For though it offers no *mise en abîme* except as the battle scenes are rehearsed by witnesses onstage, this play is likewise structured through a second representation: Horace's defeat of Curiace is replayed in his murder of Camille.[24] Indeed, if it is remarkable for its symmetrical pairing of Horaces and Curiaces, Romans and Albans, masculine identities and feminine identities, the play is equally striking for its failure to respect the unity of action. And if Camille has wounded Horace's pride, source of the provocation that moves him to strike her, she has arguably done the same to her creator, Corneille. In his oft-quoted *Examen*, the playwright admits to weaknesses of his play that result from the second death, which accords too much importance to the latter half of the drama:

> This death produces a double action by representing the second danger into which Horace falls after escaping the first. The unity of a hero's danger in the tragedy is responsible for the unity of action; and when he is saved from it, the play is finished, if the escape from this danger

[23] Harriet Stone, *Royal DisClosure: Problematics of Representation in French Classical Tragedy* (Birmingham, Ala.: Summa, 1987), 31.

[24] Suzanne Gearhart likewise stresses the importance of Camille's role by situating her performance within the context of Hegelian philosophy and the question of ethics (*The Interrupted Dialectic: Philosophy, Psychoanalysis, and Their Tragic Other* [Baltimore: Johns Hopkins University Press, 1992], chap. 3).

does not by necessity engage him in another one, such that the connection and the continuity between the two make for only one action; which does not occur here, where Horace returns triumphant with no need whatsoever to kill his sister nor even to speak to her; and the action would be sufficiently ended with his victory. The fall from one danger into another, with no cause, here creates an effect that is all the worse because the hero falls from a public danger, where the entire State is at risk, into a private danger, where it is only a question of his own life, and, moreover, from an illustrious danger, where he could fall victim only gloriously, into one from which he cannot escape unscathed. Add to this . . . that Camille, who occupies only a secondary role in the first three acts, where she yields the primary role to Sabine, assumes the primary role in the last two acts.

Cette mort fait une action double, par le second péril où tombe Horace après être sorti du premier. L'unité de péril d'un héros dans la tragédie fait l'unité d'action; et quand il en est garanti, la pièce est finie, si ce n'est que la sortie même de ce péril l'engage si nécessairement dans un autre, que la liaison et la continuité des deux n'en fasse qu'une action; ce qui n'arrive point ici, où Horace revient triomphant sans aucun besoin de tuer sa soeur ni même de parler à elle; et l'action serait [suffisamment] terminée à sa victoire. Cette chute d'un péril en l'autre, sans nécessité, fait ici un effet d'autant plus mauvais que d'un péril public, où il y va de tout l'Etat, il tombe en un péril particulier, où il n'y va que de sa vie, et, pour dire encore plus, d'un péril illustre, où il ne peut succomber que glorieusement, en un péril infâme, dont il ne peut sortir sans tache. Ajoutez . . . que Camille, qui ne tient que le second rang dans les trois premiers actes, et y laisse le premier à Sabine, prend le premier en ces deux derniers.

(*Examen* 248–49)

Horace's murder of Camille is a far more equivocal act of heroism than is his defeat of Curiace. Even though Camille betrays the state's interests in denying the glory of Horace's military conquests, Tulle ultimately condemns the hero's response to her. Nonetheless, critics—notably Serge Doubrovsky—have favored "Corneille the creator" over "Corneille the critic," defending the unity of action as "one unique movement in two stages." According to this logic, Camille's challenge is even more trying, and more appropriately taxing to a hero than Curiace's, since as a sister she represents a greater assault on his need to assert himself against all sentiment and sentimentality.[25] That is, precisely because she is a blood relation, an "other self" (*autre soi-même*), Camille represents the greater obstacle to the hero's aspirations. This reading allows us to see in Camille's murder a *mise en abîme* of the frame story about the hero's ability to sacrifice himself for his country. But it is likewise this event as it breaks the frame of representation—as a sign of what is absent from the hero's performance—that contributes to the ordering of knowledge here.

This view becomes clearer if we note that the play can be effectively graphed according to the same compositional structure that Foucault emphasizes in Velázquez's painting. Tulle makes the ultimate determination to pardon the hero and to bury the sister he murdered. Maker and keeper of law, the king can thus be said to occupy the space of the painter. Horace as hero functions like the royal image reflected in Velázquez's mirror. Camille duplicates the marshal's position in the framed doorway. Le vieil Horace, Valère, and Sabine, all participants in Horace's "trial," as critics frequently refer to act 5 on account of its juridical tone, assume a role comparable to that of the Infanta and her entourage: they are an internal audience to the king's pardon. From this arrangement of the characters we begin to uncover the process through which Corneille shows the state to affirm its own power as spectacle and the limits to knowledge incurred from such deliberate and self-conscious representation.

In order to discover what new resonances the text reveals to us about the conditions that make knowledge possible in the classical period, it is necessary to look beyond the grid linking creator, mirror, and spectator and to focus on the relations implied by this organization of elements. Specifically, the concept of spectacle as part of the historic process through which the seventeenth-century monarchy projects its image of absolute power must be analyzed along with the ways in which the spectator, subject to this projection, processes the information ordered through the play. Indeed, in self-consciously demonstrating how representation functions as a representation of its own power to make meaning—to encode meanings in conjunction with a particular set of values—Corneille's drama reveals the question of knowledge to be far more complex than is implied by a reading that seeks to harmonize the conclusion. That is, the notion of tragedy

---

[25] Serge Doubrovsky, *Corneille et la dialectique du héros* (Paris: Gallimard, 1963), 154, 155.

is implicit in the way in which the play problematizes the knowledge gained if we work back from a tally of who is left standing when the curtain falls: Tulle and Horace rather than Camille and Curiace.

Camille could have been dispensed with in considerably less generous ways. Granted, if no mention of her were made at all, there would be a loose end to the story, which would violate classical standards for regular drama. But if Camille had, for instance, been ordered buried with an insistence that the burial occur on the Alban side of the line, or buried not with "her lover" (*son amant*) but with "the enemy," or if Tulle had not expressed his own pity and sympathy, the honors accorded the hero for his service to the state would be more complete. It is in the very double aspect of the final tribute, paid first to Horace and, in the same speech, to Camille, that the "putting to rest"—the entombing or enclosing of her revolt within the frame of representation—achieves its full stature. I submit that of the two images that close the play—the brazenly Roman Horace and the frustrated revolutionary Camille—hers is the more remarkable. Camille locked in the tomb with her lover is the more potent image not in terms of the actual, factual power represented by the drama, but precisely because it works there where it is supposed to be suppressed. The attention paid to Camille does not override the state's affirmation of the hero, but it nonetheless influences our understanding of Horace's triumph, his incursion into the sublime. Buried, Camille is still lodged provocatively in the margins of representation. As I shall show, she represents a knowledge broadened by the capacity of the text to recontextualize the hero's rise to power. Our indirect, perhaps subliminal, awareness of the importance of Camille's revolt as triggered by her burial must be factored in with his sublime if we are to account fully for the knowledge that the text produces.

Representation establishes the hero as primary symbol, product of the state's official discourse. In much the same way that Velázquez's painting celebrates representation in the medium of painting, and *Saint Genest* in the medium of spectacle, in Corneille's drama it is Rome's representation of its own statecraft that is put *en abîme*. It is important to note that in *Horace* what we witness is not simply the state's exercise of power but the representation responsible for creating that power. This representation is centered in the function of the hero as sign, a body whose physical accomplishments are more than matched by its ability to represent the power of Rome to memorialize its imperial dreams.

The hero functions like the mirror image of the royal couple in

Velázquez's painting to the extent that`the founding model, the cor-
poreal presence of the soldier on the battlefield, is separate from the
identity of the hero as it functions within the symbolic order governing Rome. On the battlefield what enables Horace to encircle the
enemy and defeat him is his superior physical and strategic skill. In
the witnesses' accounts of his military accomplishments, Horace is inscribed as a hero within the law, and thus fashioned according to
Rome's own imperial designs. Like the king and queen in Velázquez's
portrait, however, these battle scenes do not really order representation; the rules governing the unity of time and place preclude their
being enacted onstage. As a sign of Rome's glory, moreover, Horace
is poised precariously on the edge of the mirror's frame, whose protective enclosure he comes close to shattering when he strikes Camille.

Horace never recants his stated belief that heroism requires him to
repress all that binds him to his family and to Albe, his birthplace.[26]
After the battle, the only reference that he makes to his family is to
its honor, as distinct from any love; he exults in vengeance achieved
against the enemy:

> My sister, behold the arm that avenges our two brothers,
> The arm that alters the course of our opposed destinies,
> That makes us masters of Albe; and, finally, behold the arm
> That alone today determines the fate of two States.
> See these signs of honor, these proofs of my glory,
> And express what you owe to the happiness of my victory.

> Ma soeur, voici le bras qui venge nos deux frères,
> Le bras qui rompt le cours de nos destins contraires,
> Qui nous rend maîtres d'Albe, enfin voici le bras
> Qui seul fait aujourd'hui le sort de deux Etats.
> Vois ces marques d'honneur, ces témoins de ma gloire,
> Et rends ce que tu dois à l'heur de ma victoire.

> (4.5.1251–56)

This speech echoes Horace's earlier pronouncement that his engagement in war represents a calculated effort to suppress all that inter-
feres with the mission to serve his homeland and his king:

---

[26] "Albe is your origin: stop and consider / That you are carrying the sword into
your mother's breast" (Albe est ton origine: arrête et considère / Que tu portes le fer
dans le sein de ta mère [1.1.55–56]).

Against whomever it may be that my country uses me,
I blindly accept this glory with joy;
That of receiving such commands
Must stifle in us all other feelings.
Whoever, ready to serve his country, considers other things,
Prepares himself like a coward to do what he must;
This saintly and sacred duty breaks all other ties.
Rome has chosen my arm; I examine nothing.
With a gladness that is as full and sincere
As that with which I married the sister, I will fight the brother
And, to cut short this superfluous speech,
Albe has named you; I no longer know you.

Contre qui que ce soit que mon pays m'emploie,
J'accepte aveuglément cette gloire avec joie;
Celle de recevoir de tels commandements
Doit étouffer en nous tous autres sentiments.
Qui, près de le servir, considère autre chose,
A faire ce qu'il doit lâchement se dispose;
Ce droit saint et sacré rompt tout autre lien.
Rome a choisi mon bras, je n'examine rien.
Avec une allégresse aussi pleine et sincère
Que j'épousai la soeur, je combattrai le frère
Et, pour trancher enfin ces discours superflus,
Albe vous a nommé, je ne vous connais plus.

(2.3.491–502)

Refusing to see in Curiace anything but "an other self," a challenge to kill what is his and hence a welcome test of his own ability to sacrifice, Horace enters the battle having repressed his emotion. If he projects a heroic image that all but subsumes the physical demands of the conflict, however, he proves vulnerable to new attacks—not to his person this time but to his persona, his heroic identity.

In the scene that precipitates his attack against Camille, Horace responds to her taunting challenge to the very standards that frame his glory. She attempts to invalidate Rome, its sublime, as a criterion for judging her brother. She refuses to recognize the code of honor that exempts the hero from having to behave as a man:

Rome, the sole object of my resentment!
Rome, for whom your arm has just sacrificed my lover!

Rome, who saw your birth, and whom your heart adores!
Rome, whom I hate because she honors you!

Rome, l'unique objet de mon ressentiment!
Rome, à qui vient ton bras d'immoler mon amant!
Rome qui t'a vu naître, et que ton coeur adore!
Rome enfin que je hais parce qu'elle t'honore!

(4.5.1301–4)

What has happened from the first to the second stage of the drama, therefore, is not only that the killing has moved closer to the core of representation—we see all but Camille's actual murder—but also that Horace has been thrust out of society's protective imaginary register, the frame that transforms mortal flesh into a transcendent ideal.[27] Protected from the constraints of lesser needs, from the emotions that attach him to others, the hero in this speech is allowed to transcend normal, mortal limits. The problem, of course, is that his sister, for all her flagrant scorn of Rome's imperial mission, is of too weak a flesh—female and unarmed—to be a worthy opponent. She represents a serious challenge to Horace's ability to maintain his elevated place within the symbolic order framed by representation.

It falls to Tulle to mediate this crisis. The king recognizes, in a programmatic way, the needs of the state over the needs and desires of the family. But whereas the hero can repress to the point of blindness these same needs and desires, Tulle states emphatically that Horace's vengeance against his sister is a crime:

This shocking action made practically before our eyes
Outrages nature *and wounds even the gods.*

---

[27] For reasons of proprieties (*bienséances*), evidence of the murder is only heard from offstage: "Oh, traitor!" (Ah, traître! [4.5.1321]). Corneille distances himself from a production that would have the murder occur onstage. If, as he argues in the *Examen*, Camille's death "spoils the ending" (*gâte la fin*) of his play, it is not his fault: "This death is seen onstage; which would be more the actress's fault than my own, because when she sees her brother put the sword in his hand, fright, so natural to her sex, must cause her to run away, and to receive the blow behind stage, as I indicate in this printing" (On voit cette mort sur la scène; ce qui serait plutôt la faute de l'actrice que la mienne, parce que quand elle voit son frère mettre l'épée à la main, la frayeur, si naturelle au sexe, lui doit faire prendre la fuite, et recevoir le coup derrière le théâtre, comme je le marque dans cette impression (*Examen* 248).

That such a crime is produced through an initial, impulsive movement
Could not serve as a legitimate excuse for him:
The least severe laws agree on this point,
And if we follow them, he deserves to die.

Cette énorme action faite presque à nos yeux
Outrage la nature, *et blesse jusqu'aux Dieux.*
Un premier mouvement qui produit un tel crime
Ne saurait lui servir d'excuse légitime:
Les moins sévères lois en ce point sont d'accord,
Et si nous les suivons, il est digne de mort.

(5.3.1733–38; my emphasis)

Tulle here privileges the state over both familial and, dramatically through a reference to the gods, even religious and ethical concerns. He does not hesitate or equivocate, expressing through his "if" a royal privilege to sidestep these "inferior" laws as they reinforce the traditional family structure at the expense of the state. The hero is now answerable only to the monarch, who acts to protect the empire by securing its military interests.

The king chooses not to impose the law that would sentence Horace to death. He does not, however, ignore the law. The result is the same as if Tulle had either blamed Camille or dismissed Horace's action as warranted by her offensive, treacherous behavior. Horace is exonerated: "Live then, Horace, live you too generous warrior, / Your virtue puts your glory above your crime" (Vis donc, Horace, vis guerrier trop magnanime, / Ta vertu met ta gloire au-dessus de ton crime [5.3.1759–60]). Nevertheless, the new order established when Tulle superimposes the power of the state onto the family structure represents an important epistemological shift. Rather than disguise his motivations, the king exposes and then deliberately lays aside the old standard in favor of his own. Power resides not in the simple exercise of will but in the state's re-presentation of Horace's mortiferous acts, its statecraft. Tulle's pronouncement affirms the truth not by hiding Horace's crime and placing blame elsewhere but by championing the image of an imperial Rome. This image is further enhanced through Tulle's likening of Horace's situation to that of Romulus, founder of Rome. Romulus' fratricide against Remus makes him an apt model for Horace's deed and, more important, for the state's decision to forgive but not deny the crime:

Enough good subjects in all the provinces
With impotent promises release themselves from their obligations to
    their princes,
All can love their kings, but all cannot
By illustrious deeds assure their States.
Both the art and the power of making crowns strong
Are gifts that heaven grants to few persons.
Such servants are the kings' strength,
And such men are also above the law.
Let the laws thus now be silent, let Rome dissimulate
What since her birth she saw in Romulus:
She can well overlook in her liberator
What she was able to suffer in her first author.

Assez de bons sujets dans toutes les provinces
Par des voeux impuissants s'acquittent vers leurs princes,
Tous les peuvent aimer, mais tous ne peuvent pas
Par d'illustres effets assurer leurs Etats,
Et l'art et le pouvoir d'affermir des couronnes
Sont des dons que le ciel fait à peu de personnes.
De pareils serviteurs sont les forces des rois,
Et de pareils aussi sont au-dessus des lois.
Qu'elles se taisent donc, que Rome dissimule
Ce que dès sa naissance elle vit en Romule:
Elle peut bien souffrir en son libérateur
Ce qu'elle a bien souffert en son premier auteur.

                                        (5.3.1747–58)

The effect of Tulle's analogy with the founder of Rome is to impose
a distinction between Rome's silencing of Romulus' and Horace's
crimes on the one hand and Horace's own deliberate suppression of
what he has known and loved on the other ("I no longer know you").
To dissimulate as Tulle does is not to fail to see ("she saw in Romulus"), not to fail to know. Rather, Tulle substitutes another identity
for the experience that the law has already succeeded in naming:
fratricide. If Rome has learned to exchange one code of law for another, it does not fail to recognize the implications of its action. This
is its art, "the art and the power" to strengthen crowns; it is the representation through which the state empowers itself. Seeing therefore grounds a greater knowing. And we see the king lay the ground,
literal and figurative, for Camille's burial just after we witness his

protection of the hero. In this act, as I shall explain shortly, we come to understand the greater knowledge ordered through representation.

Identifying the murder as a crime, Tulle, in a paradoxical juxtaposition, asserts his superior authority by demonstrating the same double standard that Camille earlier invoked to Sabine:

> Speak more sanely of your pains and mine,
> Each person sees others' sorrows with an eye other than he sees
> >   his own,
> But if you look carefully at those where heaven plunges me,
> Next to theirs, yours will seem to you to be a dream.
> Only Horace's death is something for you to fear.
> Brothers are nothing compared to a husband,
> The marriage that attaches us to another family
> Detaches us from the one in which we lived as girls.

> Parlez plus sainement de vos maux et des miens,
> Chacun voit ceux d'autrui d'un autre oeil que les siens,
> Mais à bien regarder ceux où le ciel me plonge,
> Les vôtres auprès d'eux vous sembleront un songe.
> La seule mort d'Horace est à craindre pour vous.
> Des frères ne sont rien à l'égal d'un époux,
> L'hymen qui nous attache en une autre famille
> Nous détache de celle où l'on a vécu fille.

> > > > > > > (3.4.877–84)

Camille puts a woman's duty to her husband's family above her obligations to her own family. She distinguishes between similar emotions—fear of losing a loved one—by citing a higher authority: traditional law rooted in the paterfamilias as this law sustains authority through male descendants. Logically it is only one step beyond this exchange, this substitution of one standard for another, to the privileging of the state which the king enacts at the play's close at the expense of the family. Tulle, in effect, evokes an executive privilege whose logic is consistent with Camille's own.

I am not suggesting through this association of Tulle and Camille that the family is held at the same level as the new state authority. Rather, I mean to emphasize how, in repressing the crime only after it is named, in bringing into representation and then rejecting a particular "truth" about history, Tulle consolidates his power without erasing from memory how that power has come into being. Ultimately, the significance of Camille's burial with Curiace is as a marker of this process. Along with her lover, Camille comes to signify the tension of the representation within representation. The invocation of her name marks the deferral and suspension that models not the exercise of state law, which would bury all difference, but the power of representation to substitute new meanings and new values for existing ones, as exemplified by Tulle's defense of his decision. The apology that the king offers supports a law that would exclude Camille, that would bury her difference under the weight of a hierarchy subjecting women to men, men to heroes, heroes to the king, and family to the state. Tulle protects society through this strategic military defense; he protects the family by sublimating its desires to the greater cause of statehood.[28] By interring Camille, however, the king doubles the representational register, for he puts the heroine's revolt *en abîme*. Significantly, at the precise moment when the state consolidates its power in a new symbolic order—an order rooted in all that is uniquely and inviolably Roman—it breaks the frame of this representation by giving a permanent place to Camille's revolt.

The proposed burial is, as Greenberg has convincingly argued, an act of repression to the extent that society is asked to dismiss Horace's crime. Still, one is moved to ask how Tulle intends to accomplish this task by burying Camille. He does so, if not with full public honors (he does not glorify Camille as he does Horace), then in full public view. Certainly repression is implicit in Tulle's own defensive strategy as well as in the displacement that occurs as attention is shifted from familial to state power. But the juxtaposition of bodies laid to rest—like that of heroic and criminal murders perpetrated by Horace, like that of the double ceremony that honors the hero and the sister he has killed—serves to open the space of representation. Like Velázquez's marshal, Camille continues to signify what cannot be identified in representation. Indeed, in this case she can be said to signify because she is unrepresentable. To be unrepresentable is to be absent, to be placed under the earth and out of view. Nonetheless, Camille's burial replicates her earlier challenge to her brother's honor, and it doubles the moment at the close of the play that is intended to seal his glory. Tulle's generosity toward the heroine thus has the effect of re-presenting as memory, as a secondary image offered to the spectators,

[28] For more on sublimation, see Greenberg, *Corneille*, chap. 3.

her own revolutionary engagement with the hero. Camille emerges as the symptom of the repressed history, a presence that signifies, paradoxically, by means of its own nonrepresentability within the new order of discourse manifest in Tulle's final speech.

If Tulle links himself to Camille in the end, therefore, the effect is not just to purge society by putting to rest her revolt once and for all. In her burial we discover representation's own *mise en abîme* of its epistemological praxis. The belief in the drama's synthetic close, which negates Camille's revolt, assumes that the audience of Corneille's play will erase, or repress, the impressions of one scene as it is succeeded by another. Yet this compression of the signs displayed in representation is inconsistent with the divine presence as invoked by Tulle. Camille's burial forms part of a larger ritual enacted to appease the gods:

> But we owe the gods a sacrifice tomorrow,
> And we would have heaven unfavorable to our wishes,
> If our priests, before the sacrifice,
> Did not find the means to purify him [Horace].
> His father will take care of this; it will be easy for him
> At the same time to appease Camille's spirits.

> Mais nous devons aux Dieux demain un sacrifice,
> Et nous aurions le ciel à nos voeux mal propice,
> Si nos prêtres, avant que de sacrifier,
> Ne trouvaient les moyens de le [Horace] purifier.
> Son père en prendra soin, il lui sera facile
> D'apaiser tout d'un temps les mânes de Camille.

> (5.3.1771–76)

If we consider that the gods themselves are held in contempt when Tulle in the lines quoted earlier overrides even the religious law condemning the hero—"This shocking action made practically before our eyes / Outrages nature and wounds even the gods"—then the return to the religious context at the end is less decisive than it first appears. Tulle's invocation of the gods opens the space of representation as it brings the history of Horace to a close. The sacrifice is meant to bring back the gods' support after Camille's offense. But is it not an offense to the gods to ignore their law, to fail to recognize Horace's crime of fratricide as punishable by death? It is in this uncertain space, created by Tulle as he means to draw society under his control, that Camille is buried. Indeed, the affirmation that the king orders Camille's burial can be read with an accent on *king* as well as on *burial.* Whereas the latter shows the triumph of a classicism that would contain all identities within a model of the same—within the metaphor of Rome that excludes all revolt, all difference—the former implies an act of recognition, the naming of the deed at the precise moment when it is to be repressed.

Entombed with her lover, Camille does not negate the power of representation to exclude her. Rather, she represents precisely by her marginal position in representation the critical notion that representation is established around a void: in the space produced when the founding model, here Horace as hero, fails to unify the work. From her position outside the law, Camille represents a fuller knowledge. She informs us how knowledge is, like the paintings within the painting and the play within the play, represented within representation. For all its efficacy, therefore, the law that restores political order is separate here from the order of things perceived by the spectator. The final knowledge structured by the play is a function not only of the meanings framed by representation—the hero's triumph as authorized through Tulle's apology—but also of all that is evacuated from this frame: Camille in her too masculine revolt, and Curiace in his too feminine sentimentality.[29] These other meanings, these ambivalences, are not erased completely; rather, they are memorialized by Camille. By its ambivalence her burial with her lover marks the limits of knowledge as it is sanctioned by the state.

Just as the marshal stands before a secondary light source which does not occult the primary light source for the painter, his model, and their audience, Camille's final entombment does not supplant the more dominant closure provided through the play's representation of the king's authority and the idea of Rome as a unique and totalizing power. But Camille appears to deny the single focus of the spectator who would assimilate her to an ideal of monarchic power. Her burial, like the king's defense in which Horace is named a hero, joins her to an act of commemoration. To remember is to re-present, to sustain the juxtaposition of opposites. Meaning does not reside exclusively in this excess as depicted by Camille, in the marriage of enemy camps in death.

[29] The pairing of the couple in death represents the union of lovers, each of whom was too identified through the other sex to fit comfortably into the system that Tulle affirms as uniquely Roman. For more on the role of sexual indifferentiation in the play, see Greenberg, *Corneille,* chap. 3.

But Camille does by her marginal status within the drama show the value of what has been excluded. She informs us that if representation is the starting point for meaning—if, in the state's self-promotion of its symbolic register, it imposes a particular order of things—this is not the only possible starting point for knowledge. To account for this larger, more comprehensive understanding of the ordering of information within the play, we must recognize the critical function of Camille as marking the space between an arbitrary (restricted, Roman) and a more comprehensive knowledge acquired by the spectators who do not erase earlier scenes from memory. Corneille's audience does not process the events of the play in such a way as to obliterate the original paradigm of family law once it recognizes the new state law. Rather, the final perspective is always doubled, always more than can be taken in with one glance. Any perception of the unity founded within the text is inevitably coupled with the perception in the play's final moment that Camille is invoked, identified, along with Horace.

The image of the heroine, perhaps buried deep in the unconscious of Corneille's audience, nonetheless survives as a vestige of the knowledge-making capacity depicted by the play. The spectators know that their own king's authority rests precisely with his ability to establish an absolute control over the state apparatus. Camille, therefore, is more than just a sign of what the state has repressed. She is a challenge to what the state affirms, onstage and off, a challenge to the absolute state of the knowledge of the state spectacle (*spectacle d'Etat*) that is the state's representation of itself as representation.

Velázquez, Rotrou, and Corneille all represent the act of representation as the contextualizing process through which meanings are conceived and reconceived. In his emphasis on the mirror in Velázquez's painting which reflects the absent subject, Foucault distinguishes a representation that functions as a mirror of a predetermined order from a representation whose mirror is angled to reflect the inward movement through which it certifies its own power to signify in the absence of any external model. But it is in highlighting the marshal's function that Foucault has created a subject for the present study of classical literature. The mirror suggests the perfectibility of a self-contained representation that re-presents its own functioning. The indeterminacy of the marshal's position instead suggests a challenge to this eminently classical order of things. In Chapter 2 I pursue the structuring of this other meaning by examining the techniques of recontextualization utilized by Racine.

Chapter Two

Perspectives on Knowledge:
Andromaque and *Bérénice*

The heroines whose names adorn Racine's tragedies *Andromaque* and *Bérénice* achieve a pride of place. These plays inform a view of the world by excluding the heroine. Yet Andromaque and Bérénice both make their mark on a text that would construct an edifice for meaning at their expense. Without the heroine's sacrifice there would be no loss, no tragedy. Andromaque's loss punctuates the history of the play before it begins: the death of her husband, Hector, sends her into grief before the opening scene. In the course of the events dramatized onstage, however, Andromaque wins out against her captor, Pyrrhus, and saves the life of her son Astyanax. Although qualified by Hector's absence, which continues to pain her, this final success crowns a drama dedicated to exposing the heroine's resourcefulness. Bérénice follows the opposite path, from triumph to adversity. She comes to Rome the adored lover of Titus, the dead emperor's son; in the end she leaves Rome as Titus rises to power after having agreed to pay the price of separating from her. Despite these differences, the two heroines serve much the same function within the epistemology explored by Racine. The roles enacted by these characters impose within representation a dramatic shift in perspective: they effectively reconfigure the play's model for knowledge.

Beyond the Promise: Andromaque's Struggle for Meaning

The heroine's loss and sacrifice seem unpromising subjects for tracing how the epistemological field is expanded in the classical period. On the surface of things, both loss and sacrifice represent what is negated by the model that the text uses to assign identities. Yet by focusing on Andromaque's unique position within the society that imposes her loss, I argue in this chapter that she is a highly competent figure whose role it is to open up the process of signification. In her performance we discover meanings other than those ordered by the model that Racine sets in place to frame her loss. Intended to vindicate the Trojans at the expense of the Greeks, this eminently classical model is based on patriarchal rule and the privileging of the Same. For the Trojans, Sameness refers to the past as it shapes the present: the father as he bequeaths a heritage to the son; the hero as he defends his traditions against those of the enemy. Andromaque, her own pain notwithstanding, can be seen to represent the possibility of formulating a new knowledge within this old order of things.

This model imposes a rationalist perspective on the drama. The term *rational* refers both to the concept of a logical discourse and, more specifically, to the Trojans' efforts to contain the disorder represented by their Greek oppressors. On the Greek side, Hermione and Oreste succumb to psychic distress before the play's end, and Pyrrhus flouts his princes' command to return Astyanax. The emphasis on perspective is appropriate because in *Andromaque* the opposition between order and disorder, system and accident, is directly connected to Racine's organization of visual space, and hence to point of view as it provides a context for organizing the discrete elements of the drama.

Racine's audience would be expected to condemn the excesses of passion realized in Hermione's frenzied call for Pyrrhus' murder and to recognize failure in Oreste's derangement following the assassination. Nevertheless, it is difficult to interpret the striking image of Andromaque as queen with which Racine ends the history of her struggle against Pyrrhus. This moment signals Andromaque's reign and the elimination of the threat against Astyanax, Troy's ultimate promise for the future. Although history did see the death of this child, and Racine could assume that his spectators would know this history, he is careful to end the play with the child still alive and the mother not only protected but in a position to pass on to him the values defended by Hector.[1] Racine presents a window into history which at the same time serves as a window away from history. The contradictory expectations regarding Astyanax's fate in Epire and the divergent points of view that such expectations set in motion are inconsistencies that the drama sustains from beginning to end. The drama appears to solidify the monocentric vision that sees Troy model a future whose achievements resemble those of the past. Racine's defense of Andromaque's position can nonetheless be shown to take her outside the protective limits of this model of knowledge. In the discussion that follows I illustrate why much of the significance of the aftermath of Pyrrhus' death escapes the rationalist perspective which orders the heroine's safe passage from captive to queen.

Jean Starobinski's eloquent description of the problematics of the gaze in Racine's theater affirms the impossibility of equating knowledge—what one sees—with the avoidance of tragedy: "The Racinian gaze is not blinded to the point of being unable to uncover the truth. But for this gaze not being blinded is a worse condition: all the truths that the gaze uncovers are evil; all the confessions that it provokes . . . will have mortal consequences."[2] It would appear, however, that much of the play is structured to counter the negative effects that Starobinski underscores. The spectator's gaze reflects the indelible patterning of a society intolerant of acts that would change its understanding of the world, a society that condemns all permutations of its ordering system. This self-perfectionism actually defines a self-protectionism. On Racine's stage the events that can be assimilated to prevailing ideological structures are sanctioned, while exceptional behavior is condemned as irrational. Viewed from this perspective, what one sees is order. Yet the question of a rational order, like that of exemplarity

---

[1] Reinhard Kuhn cites tradition, particularly Astyanax's death in the *Iliad*, as the only context for interpreting Racine's tragedy ("The Palace of Broken Words: Reflections on Racine's *Andromaque*," *Romanic Review* 70 [1979]: 336–45). But as Richard Goodkin argues, the extant version of the play removes Andromaque from the stage at the end, whereas the original 1667 version, consistent with Euripides' model, had her appear and affirm her subjugation: "Twice a widow, and twice the slave of Greece" (Deux fois veuve, et deux fois l'esclave de la Grèce). Racine's 1676 preface appears to refute his insistence in the original preface that his characters are portrayed exactly as in antiquity. In the later version he claims that only Hermione's character is borrowed from Euripides. Racine can thus be said to move away from earlier models and toward a new interpretation of history. Richard Goodkin, "A Choice of Andromache's," *Yale French Studies* 67 (1984): 225–27.

[2] Jean Starobinski, *L'oeil vivant* (Paris: Gallimard, 1961), 86.

(the capacity to determine future actions based on a given model), is a vexing one for representation. On the one hand, representation assumes a pre-given knowledge in its emphasis on the authority of the past: Hector, although dead, arguably motivates all the actions of the play. On the other hand, the reliance on tradition as law, and, by extension, on established epistemological categories for processing information, is insufficient to explain Andromaque's performance. In the first case, knowledge implies the power of the rational subject to imitate past examples, to re-present the glorious deeds of the past so as to ensure a comparable future.[3] In epistemological terms, the order of things is the prevailing order of things; all representation is a re-presentation. Any new meanings are collapsed into existing paradigms. When experience cannot be classified in this way—that is, when meanings cannot be identified through existing categories for ordering knowledge—the extension of the subject in history is presumed to be impossible. The subject's inability to follow established examples and respect the codes of the past thus reflects, to adopt Starobinski's phrase, the "mortal consequences" of an empirical collapse. Negation is the inevitable consequence of the failure of the rationalist perspective to account for problems that cannot be explained by its paradigms.[4] Still, to recognize that some experience is excluded from representation is to suggest that the knowledge acquired by the audience concerns not just the knowledge produced by the text's model as it supports tradition and Hector's authority, but also the function of representation as this includes the text's overwriting of its own paradigms.

Andromaque's performance exposes this other meaning. Andromaque not only "deceived the ingenious Ulysses" (trompa l'ingénieux Ulysse) by substituting another child for Astyanax.[5] She also confounds the spectator's discerning glance as she maneuvers to protect her son from Pyrrhus. Andromaque serves as the agent of the perspective whereby the whole of our understanding becomes possi-

---

[3] Georges Poulet argues, therefore, that only one time exists in Racinian drama, that of the past as it patterns both the present and the future. Regarding *Andromaque* he observes: "No work has ever expressed more completely the repetitive power of enduring time [*la durée*]" (*Etudes sur le temps humain*, vol. 1. [Paris: Plon, 1952], 152).

[4] Such is the nature of all logical systems. See especially Thomas S. Kuhn's analysis of scientific paradigms which exclude problems not reducible to normative standards (*The Structure of Scientific Revolutions*, 2d ed. [Chicago: University of Chicago Press, 1970], 37).

[5] Jean Racine, *Andromaque*, in *Oeuvres complètes*, ed. Luc Estang (Paris: Seuil, 1962), 1.1.74. All subsequent quotations from *Andromaque* are cited in the text.

ble. But she is also the agent whereby our understanding gives way to uncertainty. For in her performance the established order of things yields to something more. Racine's artistic achievement in *Andromaque* can, therefore, be considered an effect of trompe l'oeil.

A Significantly Silent Space

The tragedy constructs a paradigm of Trojan glory centered on Hector's image. In the hero's military victories the Trojans recognize not only prowess on the battlefield but also the positive effects of a soldier's loyalty to his country and his sense of duty. This identity is so pervasive as to continue to influence the fate of Troy after Hector's death. Racine depicts a widow's efforts to keep alive the hero's values through her own fidelity and her veneration of his name. Viewed from this perspective, the re-presentation of Hector in Epire which constitutes Andromaque's performance, this imitation of history, is the life principle through which Troy extends itself over time. Inexhaustible in its potential for repetition, representation implies that, like a death that influences no new course of action, a death from which nothing survives, all that exceeds its limits is pure negation. Under the category of negation fall not only the Greeks' actions to suppress the Trojans but also all that resists enactment, all that cannot be figured onstage. To leave representation is to deny memory, to refuse all bonds with the past. It is to weaken Troy by weakening the conventions that give it meaning. The drama posits a direct link between physical absence and the failure to signify. Were Andromaque incapable of eliciting Hector's memory, were she unable to extend his presence in Epire through her own acts and commemoration, the integrity of Troy as a nation would be undermined and the superiority of its culture denied. Yet, as we shall see, Andromaque achieves no greater competence, no greater mastery of the world and her place in it, than when she refuses to re-present. The heroine's competence depends on her capacity to reject the models for knowledge available to her and to penetrate a space outside representation—a space offstage that exists beyond the limits of even the Trojan perspective—in which she achieves an independent identity. She not only rejects Pyrrhus' challenge to Hector's memory but also defies the play's own model for ensuring continuity and coherence.

The focus for the present study is the crucial moment in which Andromaque decides to save both her husband's honor and her son's life by contracting a marriage whose only consummation will be her suicide. The moment cannot easily be recalled, for the event is not actually represented; Andromaque's decision takes place off-stage between acts 3 and 4. Pyrrhus has presented Andromaque with an ultimatum: either marry me and accept my promise to protect Astyanax from the Greeks, or refuse my offer of marriage and agree to sacrifice Astyanax. Andromaque tells her confidant Céphise at the close of act 3, scene 8 that she will go to Hector's tomb to determine the appropriate course of action; she does not announce her intentions until act 4, scene 1. Andromaque's response is thus inscribed between two acts. It occurs in a silence and in a space replete with meaning: she penetrates the experience of death without succumbing to negation.

In Andromaque's resistance to Pyrrhus we discover both the tragedian's construction of a logical perspective and his obscuring of such a perspective. Refusing Pyrrhus, Andromaque fights the usurper of the Trojan identity. Pyrrhus would ally himself with Hector by protecting Astyanax; Andromaque refuses to concede this victory over time and tradition. Her tenacity, however, is anything but clear proof of a singular, consolidated point of view. The heroine's presence off-stage is an absence whose silence speaks loudly against Troy's rational, monocentric view of the world to the extent that it denies the completeness of this order of things. On the one hand, Andromaque's resistance to the renegade Greek hero exposes the fallacy of his logic, the fault of his disloyalty to his own country's law. On the other hand, she personally suffers the effects of the Trojans' inability to guarantee her survival. Nor is this pain the simple result of a political defeat. The same logic that would have her reject Pyrrhus as the enemy, as Other, would also have her negate her own difference within the Trojan economy which makes her Other to Hector's Same. Within Trojan society she is a lesser subject than he. In the end, however, Andromaque survives not by marginalizing her difference but by capitalizing on it. She accomplishes this act of self-determination without sacrificing her beliefs in her country, her husband, her child, or, most significantly, herself.

The specific language of Pyrrhus' ultimatum—"This I say to you: you must either perish or rule" (Je vous le dis: il faut ou périr, ou régner [3.7.968])—suggests that Andromaque's resistance to his overtures has had its effect. In the two terms of this opposition the elision of "to live, to take pleasure" is significant. Neither the option to marry nor the option to refuse marriage represents fulfillment for the heroine. In the first case Andromaque would save Astyanax at the cost of infidelity to Hector. In the second she would preserve their love by sacrificing Astyanax, the child to whom she is bound as a mother and who represents the last trace of the hero's glory and his love for her. Interestingly, what occurs in act 3 prior to Andromaque's taking her leave of Céphise to consider her options before Hector's grave is a defense of the normative position for a woman. It is to be distinguished from what Andromaque determines between acts, a decision that she symbolically attributes to Hector. That is, Andromaque's defense of the Trojan point of view occurs prior to her visit to Hector's grave, suggesting that what she concludes in the course of her imaginary dialogue with her dead husband, though it allows her to remain faithful to him, is something more than a defense of the hero.

Céphise finds a source of optimism in Pyrrhus' ultimatum. She cautions Andromaque against exhibiting too much fidelity: "Madam, this is enough of a show of fidelity to your husband. / Too much virtue could make you a criminal" (Madame, à votre époux c'est être assez fidèle. / Trop de vertu pourrait vous rendre criminelle [3.8.981–82]). Céphise's defense of Troy is based on the exigencies of the present. Yet it is precisely the idea of a present disconnected from the past that Andromaque finds so offensive, for this discontinuity contradicts the tradition that underwrites the prestige of Troy. Céphise's claim that Pyrrhus has separated himself from Achille's deeds provokes Andromaque's emotional vindication of her own position: "Must I forget them [Achille's deeds] just because he no longer remembers them?" (Dois-je les oublier, s'il ne s'en souvient plus? [3.8.992]). Pyrrhus would be a rebel, ignoring his ties to the Greeks and his historic opposition to Hector and Troy: "Madam, tell me only that there is some hope, / I will return your son and will serve as his father; / I will instruct him myself to avenge the Trojans" (Madame, dites-moi seulement que j'espère, / Je vous rends votre fils, et je lui sers de père; / Je l'instruirai moi-même à venger les Troyens [1.4.325–27]). Because of her faith in a power structure rooted in the son's identity with the father—the hierarchical command that extends from father to son—Andromaque, however, sees only outrage and offense in Pyrrhus' conscious decision to ignore his father's murderous deeds. She equates order with the obligation to remember and respect what has been. What occurs offstage is another matter.

Twice in the course of act 3 Racine treats the subject of Andromaque's impending decision to take her own life with ironic foreshadowing. In Pyrrhus' ultimatum, "You must either perish or rule," the substitution of "to perish" (*périr*) for *to see Astyanax perish* (*voir périr Astyanax*) links the notion of death to the Trojan widow's choice.[6] Similarly, Céphise affirms: "I had predicted as much, that in spite of Greece / You would still control your own destiny" (Je vous l'avais prédit, qu'en dépit de la Grèce / De votre sort encor vous seriez la maîtresse [3.8.977–78]). Although unavailable to the characters in this scene, the irony of these speeches prepares Andromaque's momentous resolve to die on the marriage altar, which she announces in act 4 after her visit to Hector's tomb. Her action is momentous because she decides to do more than remember.

Andromaque changes the terms of Pyrrhus' proposition. Either you marry me and I save your son, he posits, or you refuse to marry me and I relinquish your son to the Greeks. Neither A nor B, she determines, but rather a C of my own invention. I marry you, thereby securing your promise to defend my son, then I take my own life, thereby remaining faithful to Hector:

> Since I must sacrifice myself, I am thus going
> To assure the remainder of my life to Pyrrhus;
> In receiving his vows on the altars, I am going
> To bind him to my son by immortal ties.
> But immediately afterwards my hand, deadly to me alone,
> Will cut short what remains of an unfaithful life;
> And, saving my virtue, will return what I owe
> To Pyrrhus, to my son, to my husband, and to myself.

> Je vais donc, puisqu'il faut que je me sacrifie,
> Assurer à Pyrrhus le reste de ma vie;
> Je vais, en recevant sa foi sur les autels,
> L'engager à mon fils par des noeuds immortels.
> Mais aussitôt ma main, à moi seule funeste,
> D'une infidèle vie abrégera le reste;

---

[6] This line allows for some ambiguity as to whether "perish" cannot also refer metaphorically to Andromaque's reaction at the thought of Astyanax's death or to Pyrrhus' extension of the death threat to Andromaque herself. The consistent object of Pyrrhus' frustration, however, is Astyanax: "The son will compensate me for the mother's scorn" (Le fils me répondra des mépris de la mère [1.4.370]).

Et, sauvant ma vertu, rendra ce que je doi
A Pyrrhus, à mon fils, à mon époux, à moi.

(4.1.1089–96)

Recognizing that sacrifice is imposed by both of Pyrrhus' options, Andromaque accepts the idea of death with a certain neutrality. Yet she insists in the end on what she owes not only to Pyrrhus, to Astyanax, and to Hector, but to herself as well. The solutions proposed by Pyrrhus negate the possibility of her personal satisfaction. Andromaque's introduction of a third term into Pyrrhus' dialectical argument liberates her from the constraints of his power. That is, by challenging the binarism of his logic and by reconceiving his proposition in her own terms, Andromaque effectively reconceptualizes herself and reconfigures the spectator's knowledge.[7]

Pyrrhus would substitute himself for Hector in the Trojan family triangle, thereby assuming the father's pivotal position with regard to son and mother. His resolution contrasts with Hector's own provisions for his son. Should Hector die, Andromaque is to become the extension of his life, not merely his substitute: "I leave you my son as a pledge of my faith: / If he loses me, I claim that he shall find me again in you" (Je te laisse mon fils pour gage de ma foi: / S'il me perd, je prétends qu'il me retrouve en toi [3.8.1023–24]). Hector's proposal that Andromaque take his place is thus to be distinguished from Pyrrhus' desire to appropriate Hector's role. Pyrrhus would transform himself, abandoning the role of enemy for that of protector. The profane violator would become the sacred father/lover. Andromaque, however, insists that blood ties alone ensure the hopes for continuity expressed in Hector's speech.

The effects of Andromaque's proposal to take her life and to join Hector are significant. Though the enemy might well be accepted as a father figure by his adopted son, and though Pyrrhus might well raise Astyanax to identify himself proudly as Hector's descendant, both Pyrrhus and the Trojan child would need to confront Andro-

---

[7] Although he similarly locates in Andromaque's decision to take her life a refusal of the play's binarism and a resistance to the idea of closure, Goodkin insists that "non-choice" is never an option for the heroine: "Having a choice between choice and non-choice is itself a choice, and thus closes out non-choice as a viable option. The longer Andromaque stays onstage, the more apparent it becomes that the choice is hers" (239). Goodkin concludes that Racine takes Andromaque offstage to prevent her from making a choice, a line of reasoning that ultimately places the heroine in a more passive role than I assign her.

maque's rejection of the would-be Hector for the real hero. Directly quoting Hector's words to her upon his departure for battle, Andromaque in act 3 appears to act out his vision; she extends the Trojan heritage by keeping his words alive. Nevertheless, by act 4 she has positioned herself against Hector as well. Andromaque's decision to distinguish between the fulfillment of a promise to Hector and the fulfillment of a personal desire opposes her to Hector's belief that fidelity, self-fulfillment, and self-knowledge are one and the same. In her marriage vows to Hector, in her acknowledgment of his pre-battle speech about their relationship to Astyanax, and again in her restatement of this speech to Pyrrhus, she pledges to be faithful and to respect the past. Her marriage to Hector constitutes a promise to law, a recognition of the conventions that order and give meaning to experience. Measured against the knowledge signified by her promise—against the understanding that binds her to Hector and to the history that he glorifies—Pyrrhus' decision to ignore his promise to wed Hermione is a violation not only of one woman's private life but also of an entire culture. It invalidates the ordering principles through which Andromaque has come to see herself and to project her role into the future. The effects of this rupture are now evident in Andromaque's own intent to distort the meaning of a promise. She will corrupt her promise of marriage to Pyrrhus by refusing to commit the act on which it is stipulated. Andromaque's plan to die negates the performative quality of her stated vows. For if, as modern speech-act theory instructs, to say "I do" is to realize in the utterance the act of marriage, and if the realization of this marriage is an act of union, then Andromaque's promise to Pyrrhus begets a marriage unperformed.[8]

Andromaque's resolution does not simply extend Hector's memory; it does not make of her a being who exists, in Georges Poulet's terms, only to the extent that she represents someone else who has died.[9] "This is what a husband himself ordered me to do" (Voilà ce qu'un époux m'a commandé lui-même [4.1.1098]), Andromaque explains to Céphise after her visit to Hector's tomb. Hector, however, does not dominate this scene. Instead it is Andromaque who controls the decision-making process: "This is my love's innocent stratagem"

[8] See J. L. Austin, *How to Do Things with Words*, ed. J. O. Ormson and Marina Sbisà (Cambridge: Harvard University Press, 1975); and Shoshana Felman, *Le scandale du corps parlant: Don Juan avec Austin ou La séduction en deux langues* (Paris: Seuil, 1980), chap. 2.
[9] Poulet, 152.

FR Paper ideas - Paper 1

Andromasue

characters

Pyrrhus   - traits
oreste   - role
                 - relationships
Andromaque   - what he/she
Hermione   represents to the
                   author

                 - why are their
                   actions like they
                   are

                 - does the author
                   want you to
                   love
                   hate

                 large 2 character.

Racine
opposition blw order/disorder
system/accident
connected to R. eg. of visual space

Andromaque

- w/o Heroine's sacrifice there would be no loss, no tragedy

- A's unique position w/in society that imposes her loss

- Highly competent figure whose role is to open up the process of signification

- Image of A. as Queen ends her struggle vs. Pyrrhus. Signals A's role and the elimination of the threat vs. Astyanax

- fraud/manipulation to protect Astyanax

- Rebuffing Pyrrhus, A. blunts the weapon of the Trojan identity.

- She wins w/out sacrificing her country, her child, or herself.

P— This I say to you: you must either prist. or rules — [Act 3, sc 7) — A. resistance is driving him crazy

- Andro. accepts death w/ neutrality

(Voilà de mon amour l'innocent stratagème [4.1.1097]). What influences the outcome of events is not the real hero, now dead, but the Hector invoked by Andromaque and performed in the drama through her intervention. And this Hector, as he stands for a promise to respect tradition, is a sign collapsed by Andromaque's "stratagem." Although it brings her closer to Hector, suicide denies the unity of the play's model as exemplified by the hero. Andromaque intends to commit an act that will secure Astyanax's survival, but he will survive without the continuity of Hector's promise.

Racine's heroine invalidates Hector's trust that his heritage will pass through her to Astyanax ("he will find me again in you"). Andromaque determines a course of action whose most dramatic consequence will be that Astyanax will not "find" her at all. Suicide removes her from representation; her death takes her out of the history that Hector would have model a life for his son. Despite all that Pyrrhus knows and has promised to share with Astyanax, there is much that he cannot know, memories that cannot survive Andromaque's death.

Beyond the fact of death and physical absence, however, Racine creates a startling ellipsis. The very terms of Andromaque's resolution suggest a departure from the models presented to her, the divergent models of history made by two men who, however opposed in their understanding, would similarly appropriate her identity to their own. By imposing an inviolable space between the roles of beloved husband and loving father, Andromaque's death would undercut Pyrrhus' efforts to provide for Astyanax. The loves that combine so easily in Hector are forever distinguished by Andromaque's refusal to remain with Pyrrhus. At variance, too, is her solution from Hector's worldview. Andromaque distinguishes herself from the heroic ideal rooted in a single line of power that descends, generation after generation, from father (to mother) to son. Hector's faith is a faith in the ability of Troy to sustain itself by systematically transferring power from one hero to the next, that is, through the continuous order of identical heroes separated only by time and their place in history. Andromaque, however, is faced with circumstances that deny the coherence of this vision. Of necessity, but fully conscious of her choice, she establishes for herself an identity that makes her more than a protector of the male right to succession.[10] Experience has changed Andromaque, and

---

[10] Although he argues that Andromaque's suicide is a failure of one kind of representation, namely, that of the past as model ("she sacrifices herself when this Past

she acts here to protect the past without being a slave to it. She refuses the role of captive as it implies her subjection both to Pyrrhus and to a Trojan history that resists the separate identities of hero, son, and self. Uttering a promise (to Pyrrhus) that she means to corrupt in order to respect a promise (to Hector) which can no longer offer the unity and coherence it was intended to convey, Andromaque reserves for herself a space outside all convention. Returning to the hero as she gives over the son, Andromaque models a new possibility for ordering knowledge.

Indeed, it is Andromaque's ability to distinguish her experience from the models offered by both Pyrrhus and Hector that allows one to speak of her as a catalyst within representation. The traditional order modeled by the play might well, as Céphise argues in the lines quoted earlier, justify Andromaque's marriage to Pyrrhus, since this would not only spare her but also grant Hector the greatest victory under the circumstances. Nothing in the play suggests that the appropriate behavior for Andromaque would be to sacrifice either her son or herself. Refusing to be one with Pyrrhus, and separating herself from the line of reasoning defended by Hector, she exposes the purely conventional wisdom that each man offers in the guise of truth. Andromaque's rejection of their respective points of view is all the more dramatic because Racine makes of it an absent center. She is the point to which all eyes are drawn—drawn as it were through rational space. But this center gives way before the knowing gaze of those whose look she has captured.

Racine's theater duplicates the perspective of painting discovered in the Renaissance. The Renaissance marked the break from the medieval bi-dimensional space. The new concept of rational spatiality is dominated by what one critic terms "perspectivist representation" (*la représentation perspectiviste*).[11] In this "monocular" perspective the point of view is reduced to a single vanishing point, thereby opening a three-dimensional space that includes the spectator. In his analysis of Velázquez's *Las meninas* Foucault, as we have seen, delineates a space outside representation that is shared by the artist, the king, and the

---

escapes her''), Roland Barthes describes the positive effects of her sacrifice in similar terms. Andromaque's proposed suicide is the break with established models that signals the passage from death and Hector to life and Astyanax: "She agrees to separate herself from a part of Hector (Astyanax), to amputate her function as loving guardian [*gardienne amoureuse*]; she agrees to an incomplete fidelity" (*Sur Racine* [Paris: Seuil, 1963], 76, 77).

[11] Jean-Joseph Goux, *Les iconoclastes* (Paris: Seuil, 1978), 131.

spectator. Similarly, French classical theater sustained a monocular vision that was specifically monarchic. For if the spectators were not always accustomed literally to viewing the characters onstage from the same vantage point enjoyed by the king, whose perspective duplicated that of the playwright, they readily perceived the centralized authority of France's monarchy mirrored in the drama. I emphasize here not the actual model of court theater but rather this model as metaphor for the rigorous unity of the monarchy which served as context or historic referent for the plays written during the classical period. The court theater organized the total performance space (stage and scenery together with the auditorium and spectators) around an axis that extended from a vanishing point beyond the back wall of the stage to the king's seat, situated at the center of the auditorium, which afforded the ideal perspective. It was not necessary, however, to occupy the king's place in the auditorium to appreciate how the events onstage represented the salutary effects of the very rational order symbolized in contemporary society by the absolutist court of Louis XIV.[12] Andromaque figures at the center of this rational space. She fights for Hector against Pyrrhus, for continuity against discontinuity, for a concentrated and hierarchical power against one man's artificial claim to share in it. Unlike Velázquez's painting, however, Racine's *Andromaque* does not include the mirror through which the privileged viewer sees himself, since Hector, who mirrors back the image of the monarch, is ultimately supplanted by Andromaque. As we have seen, she does more than extend the tradition represented by the hero. By first removing herself from representation at a critical juncture and then creating an identity for herself in what is elided in her proposal to Pyrrhus, Andromaque represents a gap in the drama that breaks the symmetry of the single authoritative perspective.

What occurs in *Andromaque* between acts 3 and 4 is all the more significant because it happens offstage, outside the enclosed and or-

[12] *Andromaque* was first performed in the queen's apartment and subsequently at the Hôtel de Bourgogne. The practice that I detail here, while not intended to deny important differences between court and commercial theaters regarding staging and perspective, is meant to establish the general principle underlying both types of performances. I am indebted to Roger Herzel for information about the history of the theater during this period. For a discussion of the influence of Italian perspective on French classical theater, see Jean-Marie Apostolidès, *Le prince sacrifié: Théâtre et politique au temps de Louis XIV* (Paris: Minuit, 1985), 32–37. For more on the relation of classical theater and the question of legitimation, see Timothy Murray, *Theatrical Legitimation: Allegories of Genius in Seventeenth-Century England and France* (New York: Oxford University Press, 1987), chap. 7.

dered space of representation. Andromaque stands on the other side of representation, outside the traditions that order her life as the wife of a Trojan hero, and within a new history. We are aware that the construction of the tragedy depends on its being seen from a single viewpoint. But we are so far telescoped into the space of representation that we leave it. We enter not the irrational space of *non-sens*, but a space that signifies precisely because it is not confined to the pre-existing epistemological frame.

Andromaque's performance as it extends from act 3 to act 4 constitutes the vanishing point for the parallel lines of displaced loves that the play draws from Oreste through Hector: Oreste loves Hermione, who loves Pyrrhus, who loves Andromaque, who loves Hector, who is dead.[13] If we consider this celebrated formula to suggest (like the distribution of images within the space of a painting) the placement of characters onstage, we discover how the drama's multiple love triangles come together in Andromaque's performance. Oreste's claim to Hermione, like her claim to Pyrrhus, like Andromaque's claim to Hector, all depend on a promise. The position of each of these characters is similarly defended by asserting the authority of the contract that binds the couple. Hector promises to love Andromaque, who eventually promises the same to Pyrrhus, who had promised the same to Hermione, who, in the wake of Pyrrhus' rejection, promises the same to Oreste. Reversing the order of the characters in the initial prescription obtains the following scenario: Hector obligates Andromaque (to him); Andromaque obligates Pyrrhus (to Hector's son); Pyrrhus obligates Hermione (to forget him); Hermione obligates Oreste (to kill Pyrrhus). Far less catchy, if similarly interdependent in composition, this formulation hints at the larger issues exposed by Andromaque's rise to power. For this retrospective view suggests how, in Hector's absence, Andromaque emerges to dominate Pyrrhus, who is dominated by Hermione, whose love is forever frustrated by Oreste. Looked at in reverse, the structures of mediation suggest the importance of Racine's female characters in initiating the actions of consequence: Hermione provokes the murder of Pyrrhus which brings about resolution; Andromaque venerates Troy in Epire.

My inversion of the original formula is not an arbitrary critical exercise. Highlighting the roles of the two female characters as they distort a perspective centered on the model of male desire, this re-

---

[13] Charles Mauron, *L'inconscient dans l'oeuvre et la vie de Racine* (Paris: Corti, 1969), 52.

verse perspective pinpoints the pivotal moment in the play as belonging to Andromaque.[14] The retrospective view of events leads us back to Andromaque's decision to save both her husband's honor and her son's life by a marriage whose only consummation will be her suicide. In contrast to Hermione, who will succumb to hysteria, Andromaque will avoid further tragedy by inventing a role for herself that projects her beyond all predictable circumstances, beyond all knowledge patterned by the drama's permutations of the triangular composition. In the end, meaning depends not on a single substitution of one lover for another. Andromaque, in a second move, is exchanged for either lover.[15]

Modeling an Absence

But, one is certain to object, Andromaque never carries out the promise to kill herself which she makes offstage. Racine spares his heroine a tragic end to her distinguished fight. I do not mean to speculate that the magnitude of Andromaque's response in these scenes justifies her rise to power in act 5. Racine may indeed have projected a heroine so competent as to merit protection from the ultimate sacrifice of her life. The point, however, is not to create a rationale for the drama but to recognize how Racine establishes Andromaque's handling of the critical situation with Pyrrhus in act 3 as a model for the play's close.

[14] It is possible to read into this formulation of male desire the Girardian notion of a male rivalry, namely, that a man is drawn to a woman not for herself but because she belongs to another man. See René Girard, *Mensonge romantique et vérité romanesque* (Paris: Grasset, 1961). Pyrrhus may well be attracted to Andromaque because she is associated with his rival, Hector. But even the simpler view which holds that he is transfixed by her because she is now his captive reinforces the same notion that the woman is an object of exchange in an economy controlled by men.

[15] Leo Bersani observes that there is no "new mode of desire" in Andromaque's behavior; the same psychic structures plot her "obsessive attachment to Hector's memory" (*A Future for Astyanax: Character and Desire in Literature* [Boston: Little Brown, 1976], 49). The consequence of her obsession, however, is that she uses this desire to her best advantage to free herself from the male model which has formed her. The psychological patterns would encourage us to conclude with Bersani that neither Pyrrhus nor Andromaque represents the possibility of a future of difference (Bersani places Astyanax in the role of potential harbinger of change [49]). The play's epistemology has radically shifted, however, toward a difference that is not entirely Other. Deciding to wed Pyrrhus in order to remain faithful to Hector, Andromaque in the end represents a viable alternative to the Trojan identity. She can no longer be explained simply by all that Troy would code as the Same.

The parallels emerge not from a consideration of particular events but from the framing of representation. Andromaque's coming to power in Epire is an event prepared no more by her decision than by Oreste's intent to avenge Hermione against Pyrrhus. The Greeks kill Pyrrhus, thereby denying him as well as Oreste, Hermione, and Andromaque the opportunity to perpetrate on the altar the all-important act of self-determination. Our knowledge of the circumstances that appear to motivate the play's resolution thus proves useless in explaining the actual events that close the play. Pyrrhus' revolt has failed; he is unable to distance himself from the Greek authority. Andromaque accedes to the throne with her son's life secure and her husband's memory intact. Yet her power is the result of a historic contingency; she rules as a consequence of Pyrrhus' murder and not her own efforts. Oreste, though he would regain Hermione's love by assassinating Pyrrhus, suffers first the humiliation of not having issued the fatal blow then the agony of Hermione's disavowal of her call for vengeance (5.3). The models for action that the play sets in place thus provide no basis for predicting or securing the outcome of events.[16] Rather than project the absolute security of knowledge gained through repetition, predictability, and continuity, Racine posits doubt at the center of the model that he sets in place. In Pylade's cautionary remarks to his friend Oreste this doubt is signaled by the possibility (*"peut-être"*) which draws to a close the history of Andromaque's relation to Pyrrhus:

> We must go, sir. Let us leave this palace,
> Or else resign ourselves to never leaving.
> Our Greeks, for the moment, are defending the palace gates:
> The people have assembled and are pursuing us with all their strength.
> Here everything is subject to Andromaque's orders;
> They treat her as queen, and us as enemies.
> Andromaque herself, to Pyrrhus so rebellious,
> Pays him all the honors of a faithful widow,
> Commanding that his death be avenged; and *possibly* against us
> Wants to avenge Troy again and her first husband.

> Il faut partir, seigneur. Sortons de ce palais,
> Ou bien résolvons-nous de n'en sortir jamais.

[16] For an excellent account of the substitutions that pattern the play, see R. Kuhn.

Nos Grecs, pour un moment, en défendent la porte:
Tout le peuple assemblé nous poursuit à main-forte.
Aux ordres d'Andromaque ici tout est soumis;
Ils la traitent en reine, et nous comme ennemis.
Andromaque elle-même, à Pyrrhus si rebelle,
Lui rend tous les devoirs d'une veuve fidèle,
Commande qu'on le venge; et *peut-être* sur nous
Veut venger Troie encore et son premier époux.

(5.5.1583–92; my emphasis)

Pylade's account appears to depict a return to order. Strengthened by the death of Troy's enemy which necessitated no sacrifice on her part, the widow of the beleaguered nation even contemplates a final vengeance. Despite what history tells us was the Epirians' limited assistance, the Trojan force depicted here is sufficient to frighten the Greeks into contemplating a fast retreat. The play's action, however, remains incomplete. Racine's heroine is suspended between two acts: that which would have allowed her to determine her own destiny and that which "possibly" would have her seek vengeance for the Greek crimes against Troy.

At no point is such inconclusiveness more pronounced than in the image of Andromaque performing as a widow funeral rites for Pyrrhus—rites that were denied Hector.[17] The paradox of this scene is manifest with equal poignancy whether viewed with an eye to the captor or with an eye to the beloved. Andromaque's final tribute to Pyrrhus' memory is anomalous, inconsistent with the paradigms that have been used to depict her role thus far. Her respectful observance of burial rites cannot be said simply to accord Pyrrhus posthumously the mediating role that he sought in marriage. Certainly the idea of a final resolution is implicit in the fact that the play here draws to an end; the reference to Andromaque's commemoration of her second husband's death occurs in the aftermath of crisis. Pyrrhus, however, does not take over for Hector. The doubling of widowhood and burial provides no obvious context for the three characters. Pyrrhus' death negates the terms of his revolt, for Andromaque's ritual observances separate out a formal tribute from love. Pyrrhus had fought against the tradition that tied him to the past. Andromaque's cere-

---

[17] "Must I forget Hector deprived of a burial, / And dragged without honor around our walls?" (Dois-je oublier Hector privé de funérailles, / Et traîné sans honneur autour de nos murailles? [3.8.993–94]).

mony now assimilates his struggle for revolution to the tradition that crushed it. Her show of respect for Pyrrhus, moreover, fails to grant Hector, posthumously and by proxy, his rightful place in history. If, in her attention to Pyrrhus, Andromaque perhaps satisfies the very personal need to mourn which she had been denied, it is a mourning detached from any real object. Hector, Troy, the past, and Pyrrhus are all part of her pain. The hero Hector cannot be vindicated by honors accorded to the son of his murderer, a Greek who would in turn allow for the murder of the Trojan progeny. Andromaque's power at this moment in the play thus does not so much connect to Pyrrhus and Hector as it expresses the heroine's personal vindication. Her response exceeds the expectations of the two men whose presence constrained her, whose roles determined her own. Andromaque represents an identity independent of the Other; hers is a self-image constituted outside both the continuous relations modeled by the Trojan hero and the discontinuous relations modeled by Pyrrhus, who asserts his power by loving the enemy. Indeed, the only model for Racine's final depiction of the heroine is the scene cut off from acts 3 and 4 in which she plays out an authentic and unrepresentable desire.

In act 5 Racine offers the same offstage drama. This time, however, Andromaque's silence is even more deafening, for she never returns onstage to speak for herself. The heroine's removal from the action is not dictated by the unities or by questions of proprieties (*bienséances*). We know that Racine's original draft of this scene engaged Andromaque center stage in a heated dialogue with Hermione. In the definitive version Andromaque stands outside the physical space of the stage as outside the rational space through which we view and judge events. Thus here, as before, Racine has Andromaque serve as the vanishing point of representation. She is the center space of maximum knowledge which eludes the understanding modeled by the text's insistence on return and re-presentation of the already known.

Hermione's irrational disclaimers to Oreste before her suicide (5.1) and Oreste's incredulous reaction to the situation in which her actions have placed him (5.4) encourage us to see in Andromaque's performance of funeral rites the victory of law over the threatening power of revolution. But several factors argue against this interpretation. The final reference to Andromaque's honoring Pyrrhus is troubling precisely because it places her at the center of a model for knowledge that cannot account fully for her actions. Her command poised between two nonactions, her performance of ritual an ambiguous expression of fidelity, Andromaque eludes our efforts to categorize her. The heroine's presence behind the scenes cannot be assimilated to a Trojan perspective, to a history of identical heroes. Our view of her in this scene is presented from the vantage point of the Greeks, a sign that the monocentric perspective is breaking down. As it moves across the theater to the stage, our gaze uncovers no certainty in the final resolution of the drama's love triangles.

In the play's last moments, Racine presents Oreste, who hallucinates that Pyrrhus and Hermione are still alive, as a model of irrationality (5.5.1629–44). Andromaque, however, signifies in the absence of an adequate model for knowledge. Paradoxically, her freedom from her captor is depicted as a moment of mourning. Watching the events onstage, we note the passing of Hector and Pyrrhus and we recognize the destabilization of the rationalist perspective. For this model is intended to protect against violence, to eliminate the threat to society posed when identities and power are confused. Andromaque's rise to power cannot be explained by the play's opposition of Greek and Trojan, same and different; this disorder constitutes the drama's ultimate tragedy. Assimilating her call for vengeance against Pyrrhus' killers to the history of violent acts through which men become heroes, the play's model can account for her commanding presence only obliquely: Andromaque the mediator of male history, keeper of the law that subjects her identity to that of the men who desire her. The symmetry of the play's actions inadequately conveys the final order in Epire. For order is merely a convention that events of chance and misguided plans lay bare. It is Andromaque who represents this greater knowledge to us from her place outside the space framed by representation.

Bérénice's Oriental Law: The Emperor's New Clothes

In *Bérénice* Racine stages an impassioned encounter between Rome and the Orient. We are moved by a tragedy defined through a double loss, played out, as it were, on two different world stages. Desire exceeds the power of Rome to provide pleasure. Yet the opulence and excesses of the Orient, the same luxurious existence that satisfies the senses, blocks the path to power. If the official history of Rome's banishment of the Orient from its shores wins out over the private love story of Titus and Bérénice, it is the love story that grips the audience. Racine himself seems excessively moved by the story of the lovers' parting:

> In fact, we have nothing more touching, in all the poets, than the sep-aration of Aeneas and Dido in Virgil. . . . It is true that I have not pushed Bérénice to the point of killing herself, like Dido, because Bérénice, not having here with Titus the last engagements that Dido had with Aeneas, is not obliged, like Dido, to renounce her life. This aside, the last good-bye that she says to Titus, and the effort that she makes to separate from him, is not the least tragic moment of the play; and I daresay that it renews well enough in the spectators' hearts the emotion that the rest was able to excite there.

> En effet, nous n'avons rien de plus touchant, dans tous les poètes, que la séparation d'Enée et de Didon, dans Virgile. . . . Il est vrai que je n'ai point poussé Bérénice jusqu'à se tuer, comme Didon, parce que Bérénice n'ayant pas ici avec Titus les derniers engagements que Didon avait avec Enée, elle n'est pas obligée, comme elle, de renoncer à la vie. A cela près, le dernier adieu qu'elle dit à Titus, et l'effort qu'elle se fait pour s'en séparer, n'est pas le moins tragique de la pièce; et j'ose dire qu'il renouvelle assez bien dans le coeur des spectateurs l'émotion que le reste y avait pu exciter.[18]

Racine here defends his choice not to kill off his heroine, arguing that she need not take her life because her relations with Titus are less obligating than those of the mythological couple. I quote this passage not to rehearse Racine's defense of a tragedy that occurs in the absence of death but to suggest how, by keeping Bérénice alive, the playwright intensifies the ambivalences of his play—ambivalences that he ostensibly eradicates with her departure from Rome. Rather than separate out a space that literally exceeds the boundaries of rep-resentation, as in Andromaque's offstage performance, Racine here assigns even more weight to the problem of indifferentiation (mean-ings not explained through the text's model) by situating Bérénice onstage as she painfully takes her leave of Titus. I am suggesting that this spatial configuration sustains the love story even as the drama performs the lovers' sacrifice. More specifically, although the sacrifice

---

[18] Jean Racine, *Bérénice*, in *Oeuvres complètes*, Préface 165. All subsequent quotations from *Bérénice* are cited in the text.

of Bérénice completes the history of Titus' accession to the throne, it opens this history to another perspective: it traces a knowledge framed from the other side, the side that the text would close off in bringing the Roman history to an end.

Titus and Bérénice love each other and leave each other: "I love him, I flee him; Titus loves me, he leaves me" (Je l'aime, je le fuis; Titus m'aime, il me quitte [5.7.1500]). But are the historical and lovers' discourses so easily severed? Can the Orient be used and expended by Rome? "Farewell," Bérénice says, "For the last time, farewell, sir" (Adieu...Pour la dernière fois, adieu, seigneur [5.7.1502, 1506]). The performative quality of this act is clear. Like its obverse, "I do," the uttered "farewell" realizes the couple's separation. Bérénice turns away and, after Antiochus' final "Hélas" (Alas [1506]), the curtain comes down; but these acts merely support the rupture that has already occurred by her bidding Titus good-bye. Like Andromaque's projected "I do," however, Bérénice's "farewell" does more than perform the designated act. It is Bérénice who closes the play; she assigns representation its final contour. Bérénice speaks and Titus is reduced to silence. She speaks the end of history, the end of their story as it is subtended by Rome's official history. But Bérénice survives this end, proof that the space between the two world stages—the space between the Roman and the Oriental engagements—is never entirely breached. Replicated in the stage directions which call for the action to take place "in a chamber between Titus' apartment and that of Bérénice" (dans un cabinet qui est entre l'appartement de Titus et celui de Bérénice), this space which fills the stage but which partitions off West from East is the mediating space through which all the meanings of the play eventually pass, and where they inevitably remain associated in the mind of the spectator who contemplates Bérénice as she leaves Rome to return to Palestine. The play does oppose reason to passion; duty to pleasure; the real to the imaginary; the death of the father to the life and love of the son. In the end, however, the space of representation does more to associate and exchange these terms—to invalidate their classification according to a West-East polarization—than it does to negate the East by naming it Other.

Viewed in historic terms, Rome consolidates its power by strategically isolating and then eliminating its foreign opposition: "Among the Romans marriage allows only for a Roman woman; / Rome hates all kings and Bérénice is queen" (L'hymen chez les Romains n'admet qu'une Romaine; / Rome hait tous les rois, et Bérénice est reine

[1.5.295–96]). Rome thus exercises on the *theatrum mundi* a law that, by proscribing marriage to foreigners and by denigrating all royalty, reflects the epistemology that grounds Racine's play. The text isolates opposites and then, through an act of exclusion, valorizes Rome's power to identify and negate, to name and reject. I submit, however, that this discourse is not a monolith, an inviolable model for assigning meaning. Certainly, by banishing Bérénice, Rome acts to exclude her difference and to sanction itself as a model of the Same. Still, the model that Racine erects to expose how Rome assigns identities is more properly described as a process than as a structure, a fluid *ordering* of discourse more than an *order* of discourse. For in this play Racine can be said to extend the metaphor of the vanishing point of representation to that of a veil. More precisely, this veil signifies a false backing to the mirror into which Titus looks to see his reflection and into which the audience stares to uncover the truth about Rome. All perspectives into the play flow through this veil; it diffuses Titus' gaze as well as that of the king in Racine's audience, who would see his own absolute power affirmed by what transpires onstage.[19] Significantly, there is another light source that penetrates the scene of self-reflection, traversing the veil from the far side of representation.

I have chosen the concept of the veil for its theatrical connotations of disguise; for its role in defining the Orient as an exotic elsewhere, a stage on which to act out Rome's own repressed desire; and for its effectiveness in describing the process through which the text, by doubling the scene of representation, exposes to the audience, both internal and external, the hidden law of its own functioning. In naming Titus emperor, Rome actually takes its final brilliance (*éclat*) from the Orient which it believes to have put well out of sight. The Roman mirror is the operative model in this play, the medium through which the image of self-representation is linked to an imperialistic ideal. The Oriental veil, however, not only reinforces the alienation implicit in the concept of the mirror image as fiction, a representation of the subject distinct from the subject himself, but also doubles the effects of alienation by dividing the space of the performance into a near and a far side. The notion of light passing through the Oriental veil in this way serves to recontextualize Rome. Showing in effect that the mirror image can be viewed from opposite perspectives, it further

---

[19] The history of Louis XIV's own separation from Marie Mancini in order to meet the demands of the state for a politically astute marriage with the Infanta of Spain is often cited as a possible model for Racine's play.

exposes the difference between subject and object, viewer and viewed, to be but another fiction.[20] Indeed, Bérénice, too, performs in the subject position: as Titus contemplates his own image, he discovers Bérénice, his alter ego, looking back at him. This Other is not simply his own inverted reflection in the present, an image of the pain that Titus shares with Bérénice. Bérénice originates another gaze which defines not only what Titus is with regard to her but also what, as emperor, he is to become. It is this difference, which the Roman model/mirror would negate in denying Bérénice's status as privileged subject, that the tragedy can be shown to perform.

The drama's antimonarchical sentiments, xenophobia, and anti-Semitism are but avatars of a unique law that denies all difference. It is a law, moreover, that captures the centralized power of the French monarchy under Louis XIV and Colbert's efforts to make Paris the new Rome, the *Imperium Francorum,* source of a political power based on the state's regulation of justice, linguistic style, and cultural production.[21] The choice between love and duty imposed on Titus suggests the influence of a stable, inflexible model for knowledge, a paradigm of the One, the Same. Yet Racine's play also produces as part of its ordering an Orient, an Other, that captivates by its difference. This Other, if it is coded as negative by Rome, is no less essential to the process through which Rome comes to identify and to idealize itself.

Taking as an example Titus' narrative of his experiences with Bérénice in the Orient (2.2), we see that the act of exclusion through which the subject affirms his superiority is not so easily distinguished from the act of inclusion which subjects him to the Other. The narrative is structured as a double representation of Titus' transgressions. The Orient figures in these lines as an obsession, as an ineluctable desire to exceed the limits of the law. Significantly, however, the Orient is not represented by Titus as an absence, a forgetting. His transgressive behavior has not been erased, a sign that he has not

---

[20] Referring to Titus' designation of Bérénice as his everything—"I find everything in her" (Je trouve tout en elle [2.2.544])—Mitchell Greenberg observes: "Each for the other is the world. . . . The possibility of distinguishing either the 'subject' or the 'object' of their vision is difficult and tendentious at best. Because each is for the other a *tout,* the world in all its inclusive appropriations, we can never be sure where to situate the protagonists in relation to each other" (*Canonical States, Canonical Stages: Oedipus, Othering, and Seventeenth-Century Drama* [Minneapolis: University of Minnesota Press, 1994], 150).

[21] Orest Ranum, *Paris in the Age of Absolutism: An Essay* (New York: John Wiley, 1968), 261.

internalized Rome's censuring mechanism. Rather, fully aware of what separates him from his duty to Rome, Titus admits to his confidant Paulin the extent of his passion for Bérénice:

> I did more. Before your eyes I have nothing secret:
> For her a hundred times I thanked the gods
> For having chosen my father in the heart of Idumée,
> For having put under his control the Orient and the army,
> And, stirring up the other people as well,
> For having restored a bleeding Rome to his peaceful hands.
> I even wished for my father's place;
> I, Paulin, who, a hundred times, if a less severe destiny
> Had wanted to extend his life's ties,
> Would have given my days to prolong his:
> All that (how a lover knows poorly what he desires!)
> In the hope of elevating Bérénice to rule the empire,
> Of one day recognizing her love and her faith,
> And of seeing at her feet all the world with me.

> J'ai fait plus. Je n'ai rien de secret à tes yeux:
> J'ai pour elle cent fois rendu grâces aux dieux
> D'avoir choisi mon père au fond de l'Idumée,
> D'avoir rangé sous lui l'Orient et l'armée,
> Et, soulevant encor le reste des humains,
> Remis Rome sanglante en ses paisibles mains.
> J'ai même souhaité la place de mon père;
> Moi, Paulin, qui, cent fois, si le sort moins sévère
> Eût voulu de sa vie étendre les liens,
> Aurais donné mes jours pour prolonger les siens:
> Tout cela (qu'un amant sait mal ce qu'il désire!)
> Dans l'espoir d'élever Bérénice à l'empire,
> De reconnaître un jour son amour et sa foi,
> Et de voir à ses pieds tout le monde avec moi.

$$(2.2.425-38)$$

Whether Racine alludes here to Titus' inclinations, as reported by Suetonius, to have himself crowned king in the Orient, or whether he is simply expressing the son's desire to become emperor in the place of his father, it is striking that in this passage memory includes a fantasy linked to parricide. The wish for the father's death is the manifest and not the repressed content: "I even wished for my father's place." Titus is conscious of having had the fantasy of substituting himself for his father, Vespasien, in order to satisfy his own desire; he is aware of wanting to eliminate the father and to assume for himself the paternal authority, the father's law, in order to remain with Bérénice. The wish to become the father so as to render impotent the father's interdictions is as manifest to Titus as is his confessed desire to receive the state's sanction of his love for Bérénice. His wish is to share the throne with her, to "elevate" her so that she might "rule the empire" with him. He resists a law expressly linked with death, with loss, with denial. Law is now built around a void, the absence of the father. In this void "a lover knows poorly what he desires"; he knows both the horror of what should be repressed and the fear of what this exposed wish might still conceal. Freed up by the release of the normally repressed content, this undifferentiated space allows for the structuring of other meanings. Such meanings are found in the still-present maternal, the female presence in the Oedipal triangle that is veiled by Bérénice as she transfixes all who contemplate her.[22] More specifically, the invisible portion of this recollected fantasy, its latent content, relates to the idolatrous image of Rome bowing before Bérénice. Titus' discourse here is inverted upon itself in representing how the father's law would authorize his love rather than prohibit it in this adoration of Bérénice by Rome: "And of seeing at her feet all the world with me."

Although this scene is not, technically speaking, an example of the particular kind of displacement that Freud calls a screen memory (*Deckerinnerung*), the notion of covering up or veiling one painful memory with an innocent one is relevant to understanding the full significance of the image of Rome at Bérénice's feet.[23] The mnemonic

---

[22] With reference to the Oedipus myth and Freud's celebrated analysis of the enemy brothers, Greenberg elaborates the explicitly Oedipal dynamic which similarly positions Bérénice in the maternal role as "originary object" of the son's affections (*Canonical States*, xvii–xxxix; 157–59). My own reason for citing the mother's role, as it will become clear, is to stress how the imaginary does not give way to a symbolic order distinct from it. I allude here to the rudiments of the Lacanian system without seeking to apply rigorously Lacan's theory of the function of language and the symbolic order. It is important for my purposes to note only that the Roman law, this symbolic order which gives closure to the play through Bérénice's expulsion, is inseparable from the image, by which I mean both the imaginary ideal and the image of the Orient, on which the empire's *spectacle d'Etat* is based.

[23] Freud formulated the concept of the screen memory in observing people (including himself) who retained the emotionally insignificant elements of an experience while avoiding its emotionally charged elements. A screen memory is characterized by its unusual and exceptional clarity and by the apparent insignificance of its content. The

experience of projecting an innocent memory onto the highly charged memory trace informs Racine's text to the extent that it exposes a tension between two scenes. At this moment of the drama it is the need to send Bérénice back to the Orient so as to please the Roman Senate—that is, the inverse of the memory content—that is being acted out onstage. In his fantasy Titus prostrates himself before Bérénice in a gesture of adoration. Yet this gesture is likewise that of submission before the woman who subjugates him—she who, albeit his subject, in the end comes to dominate him. In other words, what is veiled here is not, as one would expect, the son's wish to replace his father, this most primitive and destructive of desires. Instead, Titus expresses the more "civilized" fear, one consistent with Vespasien's own concerns about the needs of the state, of subjecting himself, and with him the authority of Rome, to the Orient. Titus fears not just the father's interdict, which would prohibit him from neglecting his duty; he fears not just the law that would deny him the Orient's pleasure. What Titus fears is desire itself as it is constituted through the Other. This Other/Orient looms before Titus as he moves to recognize the Roman law that empowers him by forcing his separation from Bérénice. By its re-presentation, or doubling of one scene with another, by this very *mise en abîme* that is the entire screen memory here, the text conceives of the separation in terms of a layering of histories. The effect is to deny the integrity of the Roman model which would name Titus emperor.

The dead father is replaced by the estranged lover, whose loss is figured center stage. Repressed with Titus' thoughts of Bérénice's departure is not his wish to be with her—to possess her and to be empowered through her. The latent content of the memory refers instead to Titus' fear of recognizing his own abjection in her, of recognizing himself in her image. Through this mediating image he understands that he comes to power as a creature of the state, sacrificing the passion that she has allowed him to know for the numbing truth

---

analysis of these memories leads to childhood events as to fantasies. Freud claimed that the screen memory, as the symptom, is produced from a compromise between repressed elements and defenses. The predominant mechanism for the screen memory is displacement, the act of transferring onto an "innocent" memory the charged content from another period of the analysand's life. There are thus no innocent memories; rather, one memory is neutralized through another, which acts as the screening mechanism. See Sigmund Freud, "Screen Memories," in *The Complete Psychological Works of Sigmund Freud,* ed. and trans. James Strachey, 24 vols. (London: Hogarth Press and the Institute of Psycho-Analysis, 1953–74), 3:303–22.

of a rule ordered through the mortal splitting of his duty from his desire. The image, this specter of death and of the splitting of the subject, will penetrate and haunt the Senate with Titus' entry after the play's last farewell is spoken. Titus is framed in the mirror of representation that figures him at the feet of Bérénice, as dependent on her as an infant is in the arms of its mother.[24]

Significantly, the specular economy of the mirror stage is represented not as a provisional stage, a prelude to entry in the symbolic. Rather than a phase to be entered and then exited, the imaginary functions as an inextricable part of the law that determines Titus' identity as emperor. Titus eventually conforms to Roman law, but the question of his identity as an active subject, as a subject who knows himself independently of Bérénice, is clearly compromised. Titus is never severed entirely from the image, from the Other in which he sees his own alienation. For the mirror stage is represented as the very stage on which the state drama—the exercise of law through which all differences are isolated and negated—is performed. The Roman model for ordering meanings is a public theater. Here the concept of mirrors, mimesis, and reflection finally gives way to an effect of veils. The Roman model affords the drama its eventual closure with Bérénice's evacuation from the scene of representation. But it is the Oriental as Other that exposes how this model operates as a theater of disguise, a state spectacle. Thus, if the infantilizing image of Titus comes into play, it is an effect of the Orient's projection back onto the scene of his desire; Titus is shown to be dependent on the Other/ mother in whose image he is reflected. The Orient recodes the mirror image so that it becomes not a virtual reality, a simulacrum of the real, but instead the actual performance of Rome's masking of knowledge. That is, the Orient exposes the arbitrary process through which Rome represents itself as the sole arbiter of knowledge.

To appreciate how the Orient redirects, or in effect reorders, the information processed through the Roman model, we need to note first that the specular play of the Orient, the role of the Orient in establishing the drama's imaginary register, is by no means limited to the image that occurs in Titus' representation of the couple's history. The characters all make reference to the fact that emotions are experienced as a visual fascination for the Other. Pleasure is the expe-

---

[24] My reading is thus opposed to that of Roland Barthes, who sees the radical separation of the tragic and the political and the "progressive void [*vide progressif*] of the Orient" (*Sur Racine*, 88).

rience of being captured by the image, the reciprocal play of reflections that join subject to object, the viewer with the one viewed:

Bérénice:
He no longer had for me this unquenchable ardor
When he spent the days adoring the sight of me.

Il n'avait plus pour moi cette ardeur assidue
Lorsqu'il passait les jours attaché sur ma vue.

(1.4.155–56)

Antiochus:
Titus, to my regret, came, saw you, and pleased you.
. . . .
Farewell. I am going, my heart too full of your image,
To await, while loving you, death as my share.

Titus, pour mon malheur, vint, vous vit, et vous plut.
Adieu. Je vais, le coeur trop plein de votre image,
Attendre, en vous aimant, la mort pour mon partage.

(1.4.194, 279–80)

Titus:
I loved her, she loved me. . . .
For five whole years I have seen her each day,
And still believe that I see her for the first time.

Je l'aimai, je lui plus. . . .
Depuis cinq ans entiers chaque jour je la vois,
Et crois toujours la voir pour la première fois.

(2.2.531–47)

Both rivals—Antiochus, the Oriental king, and Titus, the Roman emperor-designate—portray Bérénice as a transfixing image. On either side of the cultural divide a viewing subject is attached to this same image; in the East as in the West we find a subject who is sundered by Bérénice's absence. Representation therefore functions more as filter than as frame. That is, the inviolable barrier that Rome would erect to protect its identity from a foreign influence is veiled with a discourse that is none other than the Other subject's discourse.

What happens when this image speaks, when it assumes its role as subject? Bérénice, appropriately communicating via her veils, shows all the signs of melancholia:

Phénice:

Do not doubt it, Madam, he will come.
But do you want to appear in this extreme disorder?
Compose yourself, Madam, and find yourself again.
Let me rearrange these detached veils,
And this disheveled hair hiding your eyes.
Allow me to repair the damage wrought by your tears.

Bérénice:

Leave it, leave it, Phénice, he will see his work.
Well, what, alas, do these vain ornaments mean to me,
If my faith, if my tears, if my moans . . .
But what am I saying? my tears! if the certainty of my loss,
If my imminent death itself does not bring him back,
Tell me, what will your superfluous attentions produce,
And all this feeble splendor that no longer touches him?

Phénice:

N'en doutez point, madame, il va venir.
Mais voulez-vous paraître en ce désordre extrême?
Remettez-vous, madame, et rentrez en vous-même.
Laissez-moi relever ces voiles détachés,
Et ces cheveux épars dont vos yeux sont cachés.
Souffrez que de vos pleurs je répare l'outrage.

Bérénice:

Laisse, laisse, Phénice; il verra son ouvrage.
Eh, que m'importe, hélas! de ces vains ornements,
Si ma foi, si mes pleurs, si mes gémissements . . .
Mais que dis-je? mes pleurs! si ma perte certaine,
Si ma mort toute prête enfin ne le ramène,
Dis-moi, que produiront tes secours superflus,
Et tout ce faible éclat qui ne le touche plus?

(4.2.966–78)

Prey to a despair that renders her almost indifferent, Bérénice nevertheless does not diminish her importance in soliciting Titus' pity.

Separating her from all that she represents for Rome, Bérénice's performance here will ultimately elevate her above her condition as abject queen, persona non grata.[25] In this mournful dialogue with her confidante, Bérénice separates herself from what she terms her "vain ornaments." Refusing to wear her veils, she in effect distances herself from all supplements that condemn her in the eyes of the Roman Senate to being queen, Oriental, inessential, the outcast whose role is simply that of an object to be discarded once the real work of statecraft has begun.

The veils recall by their inessential status the Orient as perceived by the Romans: a world whose riches lie passive before Western domination; an exotic and decadent land whose unfamiliar customs stir the Western imagination; an unreality in which obligations—to the past which ties Titus to Vespasien; to the present needs of the state— all slip away. Now a disheveled Bérénice calls into question not only her own power to be recognized in Rome, but also the power of Rome to know itself without the mediation of the Orient, this Other that Rome believes will contaminate the empire. The Bérénice who lets herself be seen here—the Bérénice who exposes her unveiled body, a body in disarray—seeks Titus' pity but also forces his recognition. In spite of a dispassionate refusal to claim any interest in her appearance, Bérénice reveals herself to be both involved, engaged, and engaging in this scene. Her somber tone prevents us from seeing in the removal of the veils an attempt to deny her royalty, to effect a seduction of compromise by appearing to become less than Oriental, as she will later propose to be less than an empress: "I do not speak to you about a happy marriage" (Je ne vous parle point d'un heureux hyménée [4.5.1127]). Rather, by their absence the veils force Titus to "see his work," to contemplate the woman whom he has brought to Rome, and whom he is now preparing to send back. Bérénice in this scene exercises the only power available to her in Rome, that of projecting before Titus an image which, in refusing the hero all possibility of abstraction, all identification with the sublime, denies the transcendency of his power. Here the creature Bérénice prepares to meet unadorned the eye of her creator as he contemplates her without the royal accoutrements which have in part attracted him to her. She

---

[25] On abjection, see Julia Kristeva, *Pouvoirs de l'horreur: Essai sur l'abjection* (Paris: Seuil, 1980). For an application of Kristeva's study to *Bérénice*, see Marie-Florine Bruneau, *Racine: Le jansénisme et la modernité* (Paris: Corti, 1986), chap. 7.

refuses him the sign of her power—as enchantress but also as queen of a great nation—that he would have her reinvest in him.[26] Thus, if earlier Bérénice reflected back onto Titus the fantasy of his desire, she now resets the stage by essentializing herself. Abandoning her veils, she forces Titus to confront his own abjection in Rome.

It is to the latter image that Titus remains attached as he ascends the world's stage.[27] Even as he steps back from his beloved Bérénice, he cannot successfully differentiate himself from her:

> Ah, prince! Swear to her that always too faithful,
> In agony in my court, and more exiled than she,
> Taking even to my grave the name of her lover,
> My rule will be only a long banishment.

> Ah, prince! jurez-lui que, toujours trop fidèle,
> Gémissant dans ma cour, et plus exilé qu'elle,
> Portant jusqu'au tombeau le nom de son amant,
> Mon règne ne sera qu'un long bannissement.

(3.1.751–54)

Titus situates the center of power far from Rome, in the Orient. To be banished, however, is to be banished from a particular place, from an identifiable person, from a discernible model. In this profound expression of his alienation—from the Palestine that gave free rein to his desire; from Bérénice, whom he loves and whom he is about to lose; from the identity that he had fashioned for himself—Titus internalizes the lack that has pushed him toward Bérénice and that now defines him. A *res publica*, he has become this Other: "Dear Paulin, I had to renounce myself" (Il fallait, cher Paulin, renoncer à moi-même [2.2.464]). Titus prepares to perform as emperor, burying deep inside himself the authentic voice of his desire. His reign makes

---

[26] In her reading of *Bérénice* Michèle Longino has explored how the attraction of the Orient grounds a concept of exoticism which France uses to develop its own national identity ("The Staging of Exoticism in Seventeenth-Century France," unpublished manuscript).

[27] It is Titus who introduces the metaphor of the theater into the text. Distrusting the insincere and flattering remarks of the court, he charges his confidant, Paulin, to tell him the undisguised truth of his situation: "I do not take as a judge an idolatrous court, / Paulin; I propose for myself a more noble theater" (Je ne prends point pour juge une cour idolâtre, / Paulin: je me propose un plus noble théâtre [2.2.355–56]).

him, with Bérénice, a victim of the state apparatus that, to borrow Foucault's expression, "searches him, pulls him apart [*le désarticule*], and recomposes him."[28] Titus' repression is all the more painful because it ushers in the hero's greatest opportunity to influence the course of history: "Master of the universe, I rule its fortune; / I can make kings; I can depose them; / However, I cannot dispose of my heart" (Maître de l'univers, je règle sa fortune; / Je puis faire les rois, je puis les déposer; / Cependant de mon coeur je ne puis disposer [3.1.721–23]).

In a scene that parallels the one in which Bérénice, depressed, awaits Titus, the hero expresses a melancholy just as intense if less controlled. But whereas she forces him to confront her, he is traumatized into near-hysteria in a scene reminiscent of Hermione's behavior following Pyrrhus' death. Unable to account for himself, Titus speaks, bewildered, of his own impotence: "I have just pierced a heart that I adore, that loves me, / And why pierce it? Who orders it? I do!" (Je viens percer un coeur que j'adore, qui m'aime. / Et pourquoi le percer? qui l'ordonne? moi-même! [4.4.999–1000]). The opposition between the masculine Rome and the feminine Orient is undercut here by the text's doubling of her scene with his.

In this vacillating and indeterminate state of affairs/affair of state, Titus cannot act alone. Before being able to pronounce the words "We must separate" (Il faut nous séparer [4.5.1061]), he asks Bérénice to mediate their love, as fully conscious of the power that he accords her as of his own desire not to assume the obligation that weighs upon him: "Madam, do not crush an unhappy prince.... / Summon up instead this heart, which, so many times, / Made me recognize the voice of my duty" (N'accablez point, madame, un prince malheureux.... / Rappelez bien plutôt ce coeur qui, tant de fois, / M'a fait de mon devoir reconnaître la voix [4.5.1045–50]). But what does "mediate" mean in this context? Claiming that she earlier served as his inspiration, Titus requests that Bérénice now assume responsibility for the pain for which he alone is responsible; he masks the truth of a choice that is incumbent upon him. Moreover, if by mediation one means the passage to a definitive end, to a resolution of some sort, one is disappointed. Titus cannot conceive of his imperial power except in terms that subject him to the state's authority. He becomes the agent, the actor, who in delivering prescribed

---

[28] Michel Foucault, *Surveiller et punir: Naissance de la prison* (Paris: Gallimard, 1975), 139.

speeches before the Senate becomes Rome's sacrificial victim just as Bérénice is his. Respecting the law against marriage to a foreign monarch, the law established to correct the excesses of the past, Titus exercises power only as a servant of the state, object of a discourse which, in an epistemological configuration that could not be more blurred, tragically deprives him of his identity in naming him emperor: "I feel that without you I would no longer know how to live, / That my heart is ready to leave me; / But it is no longer a question of living but of ruling" (Je sens bien que sans vous je ne saurais plus vivre, / Que mon coeur de moi-même est prêt à s'éloigner; / Mais il ne s'agit plus de vivre, il faut régner [4.5.1100-02]). This profound testimony to the alienation of the ruling subject allows the audience to recognize the compelling presence of the woman whose mediation ultimately reverses the drama's perspective. One no longer sees the Orient situated beyond the empire's borders. The image of the Other perceived to be outside instead imposes itself as an outside within Titus' heart as well as in the heart, or center, of the Roman Senate. Thus, the alienated subject, the abject, is no longer elsewhere but in Rome, product of Rome's own representation of itself.

Titus claims to have been irresistibly drawn to Bérénice in order to find himself: "I came toward you without knowing my intentions / My love carried me; and I came perhaps / To find myself and to recognize myself" (Je suis venu vers vous sans savoir mon dessein: / Mon amour m'entraînait; et je venais peut-être / Pour me chercher moi-même et pour me reconnaître [5.6.1382–84]). Explaining the magnetism that initially caused him to bond with Bérénice as his need to use her to satisfy his own desire to know himself, Titus admits to his passivity and dependence. Later foisting the responsibility of their relationship onto her, Titus once again asks Bérénice to "recognize" him, to put him on the right course to do his duty. But what he comes to recognize is how this final act through which he assumes his political responsibilities merely echoes the earlier pain of a lost self.

Bérénice does inform Titus of his duty; she eventually comes to make the decision for him: "I will live, I will follow your absolute orders. / Farewell, Sir, rule: I will see you no more" (Je vivrai, je suivrai vos ordres absolus. / Adieu, seigneur, régnez: je ne vous verrai plus [5.7.1493–94]). That is, Bérénice makes valid the pain of their separation by allowing Titus to know himself as emperor. Validation, however, occurs for him at the price of having her serve as mirror of his own alienation. This reflection survives Bérénice's departure; it survives to be played out within the Roman Senate by an emperor whose new imperial clothes fail to mask the image of Bérénice to which he will remain exposed long after her ship sails for Palestine.

Rome can no longer conceive of itself as origin, as self-sufficient. Yet Rome after Bérénice is no longer Rome, a solidly hierarchical and homogeneous state. Rome has been contaminated by the Orient, whose difference reflects back to it the image of a court/theater, a state/spectacle, representation of a lost original. Rome cannot conceive of itself without the Orient, and in this doubling of the subject position one discovers the truth of an order of things which exceeds that imposed by Roman law.

In leaving the stage at the end to return to Palestine, Bérénice escapes Rome's power to identify her as pure theater, as a representation of Titus' desire. She leaves Titus' Other scene for the scene of her own history, to assume her place within an Oriental discourse that ascribes to her an original identity which is a simulacrum of nothing in the West. This, at least, is how Titus' Oriental fantasy concludes. For the Orient exists in this play only as figured within Roman discourse, as a product of the Roman configuration of history.[29] Titus' experience depends on the existence of the unifying Other, this imaginary that he invents and conserves to compensate his own lack. We have seen, however, that from the point of view of knowledge produced through representation, there is value assigned to Bérénice's role in this process. Bérénice figures permanently within representation to the extent that she makes us see how the image, as represented by the veil and the theater of disguise, is the final knowledge produced by the text. Through her performance we see how Racine posits an Other that is not implicitly negated, for it is expelled but not expunged.[30]

[29] I am alluding here to Edward W. Said's notion that the Orient exists only as a fiction created by the West (*Orientalism* [New York: Vintage, 1979]). Although this view has much to say about how knowledge is modeled within the Roman frame, it would preclude our knowing Bérénice as an independent subject, which is an identity I claim for her. In an interesting critique, Ali Behdad dismisses what he calls the coherence of Said's Orientalism, which functions as a closed system to the extent that it generalizes about what "all" Europeans perceive. In its categoric refusal to recognize the Orient except as it is produced in accordance with the hegemonic discourse of the West, Said's Orientalism, Behdad argues, is just the other side of prejudice, the other side of the same essentialist discourse (*Belated Travelers: Orientalism in the Age of Colonial Dissolution* [Durham: Duke University Press, 1994], 11). See also Aijaz Ahmad, *In Theory: Classes, Nations, Literatures* (London: Verso, 1992). I return to Said's theory in my discussion of *Zaïde* in Chapter 4.

[30] It should be clear that I am not attempting to refute the well-established idea that

To recognize Bérénice in this fashion is not necessarily equivalent to recognizing the rights of a Jewish Palestine, although the importance of this Other cannot escape the notice of the audience engaged by the drama's politics. It is more a question of determining whether, in defining Bérénice negatively as the image responsible for the subject's split identity, Racine does not exceed the capacity of Rome to speak the truth.

The history depicted onstage, the chronology of lived events, testifies to Bérénice's existence as victim of Roman law. It does so, however, by placing her at the locus of meaning, where the model ordering society is applied and tested. Bérénice does not cancel the identities set in place by Roman law. Rather, framed within this law, her role allows the unprecedented to signify. The text posits Bérénice at the cusp of that which, emerging from behind the model for knowledge, behind the Roman law, places this order of things *en abîme*. She is named abject by Rome, but in leaving Rome she marks the limits of the knowledge it formulates; she identifies the constraints of the order that conceives her as Other. Situated outside Roman authority, she suggests what is lacking in this order. The Roman model put in place by the text as a monolithic frame is thus exceeded in some way by Bérénice, for she makes us understand that this model, which would arbitrarily exclude her from signification, has in fact created her as its liminal sign.

Bérénice represents what is but what nevertheless escapes the formal symmetry of a drama that ensures the conciliatory presence of Titus before the Senate. She thus extends our view beyond the boundaries of Roman experience; she pushes our knowledge outside the limits of the exclusionary law that condemns her. By her presence and by her dignity, Bérénice in leaving the stage marks the passage between sanction and interdiction, known and unknown, as between power and the knowledge that representation models an identity that knows nothing of the something that always surpasses it, the Other that is always subject to itself.

---

the exclusion of the Other is vital to the process of legitimation. Certainly Bérénice's return to the Orient is the act of exclusion that allows Rome to consolidate its power. Rather, I am suggesting that the status of the power legitimized by the play needs to be reevaluated in light of the primacy it accords to the imaginary register. It is not enough to say that Rome legitimates its authority by expelling Bérénice; Roman authority cannot be adequately explained without her, that is, without reference to her status as Rome's mirrored Other.

In *Andromaque* and *Bérénice* Racine details how the political apparatus is affected by two heroines who submit to society's law without
succumbing to it entirely. Andromaque inscribes herself within the
discourse of the state; she affirms the primary or regulatory function
of Troy as it models the powers of Racine's own prince and patron,
Louis XIV. Andromaque's efforts to assume a place as subject within
this discourse suggest, however, something more than the capacity to
acknowledge differences between two kinds of power, two traditions,
and two actions as dramatized by the radical division of the space of
representation into Trojan and Greek camps. Andromaque effectively
reworks the play's binary logic to suggest a more expansive, triadic
structuring of knowledge. As informed by the series of love triangles
which the play configures and then reconfigures, the triadic discourse
is more open to change, more fluid and uncertain, than is the idealized model of a unique Trojan identity which extends itself unchan-
ged from the past into the present and future. So, too, through
Bérénice's function as a marginalized presence outside Rome do we
discover the openness of a system that, though it would deny all difference, in the end represents a new knowledge. Within the narrowly
defined limits of the exclusionary principle through which Bérénice's
difference is established, representation determines, elegiacally, both
the tragedy of Rome's final separation from the Orient and the tragedy of Bérénice's haunting presence long after this separation is complete.

Chapter Three

∿

The Play Is the Thing:
The Inscrutable Subjects of Molière,
Descartes, and La Rochefoucauld

In a calculated effort to dramatize the epistemic practice as it evolves in the classical period, I turn now to the comedy of Molière's *Amphitryon*, using it to stage a presentation of La Rochefoucauld's maxims. Meaning in these texts is very much a product of performance. In Chapter 2 knowledge was shown to be grounded in an ability to contextualize. It now assumes the added dimension of a strategy for mastering the world in which illusion serves as more than a theatrical conceit. In representation where the play is the thing, the sleight of hand which I shall call the feint is the act through which the author places a mask on the very model he constructs to restrict the flow of meanings. It is the sign behind the sign ordered in his text.

Molière's theater does not simply provide a metaphor for understanding La Rochefoucauld's more realistic, if no less playful, depiction of society and the subject's efforts to affirm his identity within the human comedy.[1] On Molière's stage, where gods mirror the

---

[1] La Rochefoucauld introduces this metaphor: "Pride, as if tired of its artifices and its different metamorphoses, after having played all by itself all the characters of the human comedy, shows itself with a natural face, and reveals itself as arrogance; such that, properly speaking, arrogance is the overt sign and the declaration of pride" (L'orgueil, comme lassé de ses artifices et de ses différentes métamorphoses, après avoir joué tout seul tous les personnages de la comédie humaine, se montre avec un visage naturel, et se découvre par la fierté; de sorte qu'à proprement parler la fierté est l'éclat et la déclaration de l'orgueil). François, Duc de La Rochefoucauld, *Maximes et réflexions diverses*, ed. Jacques Truchet (Paris: Garnier-Flammarion, 1977), max. sup. 6. All subsequent quotations from La Rochefoucauld are cited in the text. For more on the human comedy, see Philip E. Lewis, *La Rochefoucauld: The Art of Abstraction* (Ithaca: Cor-

forms and actions of mortals, resemblance is invalidated as a criterion for knowledge. By introducing Jupiter as Amphitryon's perfect
double, along with Mercure as a carbon copy of the hero's valet, Sosie, the play frustrates, delegitimizes, and otherwise occults the
knowledge process. La Rochefoucauld is not untrue to the spirit of
Molière's comedy, however, when he makes clear that if resemblance
is unmasked as deficient, the difference produced through such debunking still bears signs of the comedy of error. "The only good
copies are those which make us see how ridiculous the poor originals
are" (Les seules bonnes copies sont celles qui nous font voir le ridicule des méchants originaux [max. 133]). All copies, La Rochefoucauld asserts, falsify the original.[2] By extension, and with palpable
irony, the moralist posits that any appreciation of a good copy requires that we measure its faithfulness to what is corrupt in the original. Resemblances thus do not simply give way to enlightened
differences, to pure (untainted and therefore authentic, identifiable)
subjects. Whether conceived in terms of a moral that condemns the
modeling of inappropriate behavior—the imitation of vice—or in
terms of resemblances that foster an individual's alienation, this
maxim informs us that no final knowledge is solidified by isolating
the original, since this subject is marked by a natural corruption.
Elsewhere La Rochefoucauld indicates more explicitly that the negative behavior manifest by man is the effect of both his moral de-
pravity and his self-delusion, his seeing himself as Other. For the
subject is always conceived as a representation (copy) of itself:
"Nothing so much prevents us from being natural as the desire to
seem so" (Rien n'empêche tant d'être naturel que l'envie de le paraître [max. 431]).

There is no final corrective value to be gained by assuming that the
differences which emerge with the collapse of resemblances themselves provide a clear order of things. What grounds the formation of
knowledge is the mask, the feint that celebrates the artful confusion
of identities. In Molière's play, as in La Rochefoucauld's *Maximes*,
knowledge is based no more on a science of resemblance than on a
science of difference; it is not the product of a fixed classification
scheme. Rather both works elucidate the process through which representation celebrates its own power to impose meaning by defying

nell University Press, 1977), 108 and Tzvetan Todorov, "La comédie humaine selon La
Rochefoucauld," *Poétique* 53 (February 1983): 37–47.
    [2] See réfl. 3 and 7.

the rigors of the subject/object classification, which is the ostensible model for knowledge. Face to face with the disguised Mercure, Sosie exposes the fallacy of this model:

> He is right. Without being Sosie,
> One cannot know all that he says;
> And, in the shock with which my soul is overcome,
> I am beginning, in turn, to believe him a little.

> Il a raison. A moins d'être Sosie,
> On ne peut pas savoir tout ce qu'il dit;
> Et, dans l'étonnement dont mon âme est saisie,
> Je commence, à mon tour, à le croire un petit.[3]

The same confusion of identities is underscored by the moralist:

> One is sometimes as different from oneself as from others.

> On est quelquefois aussi différent de soi-même que des autres.
>
> (max. 135)

Behind the epistemological stage on which Molière and La Rochefoucauld both perform, we detect the imposing shadow of another famous player in the classical epistemological drama. No less a figure than Descartes can be said to inform their writing. What penetrates the texts under study is not the presence of the Descartes who is suspicious of resemblances, although it is arguably the case that the subjects created by both the playwright and the moralist would encounter far less tension if they were to take more seriously the philosopher's dictum that "we must at least note that there are no images which can in all ways resemble the objects that they represent; because otherwise there would be no difference between the object and its image" (Il faut au moins que nous remarquions qu'il n'y a aucunes images qui doivent en tout ressembler aux objets qu'elles représentent: car autrement il n'y aurait point de distinction entre l'objet et son image).[4] If Descartes's science comes into play here, it is only as

---

[3] Molière, *Amphitryon*, in *Oeuvres complètes*, ed. Pierre-Aimé Touchard (Paris: Seuil, 1962), 1.2.468–71. All subsequent quotations from *Amphitryon* are cited in the text.

[4] René Descartes, *La dioptrique*, in *Descartes: Oeuvres et lettres*, ed. André Bridoux (Paris: Gallimard, 1953), 204; my trans.

a by-product of the larger representation that establishes the hero as a personage in his own right.[5]

The Descartes who informs this chapter is the figure exposed by Jean-Luc Nancy to be hidden behind the method. This persona is first introduced as the invisible author of the *Préambules:*

> The actors, called onstage, in order not to show the redness of their faces, put on masks. Like them, as I climb onto this theater of the world where, until now, I have only been a spectator, I go forward wearing a mask (*larvatus prodeo*).

> Les comédiens, appelés sur la scène, pour ne pas laisser voir la rougeur sur leur front, mettent un masque. Comme eux, au moment de monter sur ce théâtre du monde où, jusqu'ici, je n'ai été que spectateur, je m'avance masqué (*larvatus prodeo*).[6]

Descartes's statement figuratively translates his assumption of a pseudonym for the publication of his work. Nancy further suggests, however, that this passage likewise seems literally to perform the Ovidian maxim that Descartes cites elsewhere: *"Bene vixit, bene qui latuit"* (He who has hidden himself well has lived well).[7] What Descartes masks is the importance of his own role as originator of representation, as the creator of meaning. Transforming his *"larvatus prodeo"* [I go forward wearing a mask] into *"larvatus pro Deo"* (I am masked in order to take the place of the supreme author, God), Nancy plays with the text to unveil what it has concealed. He argues that, despite appearances, meaning does not originate in the scientific method itself. Rather, the knowledge that grounds the text is shaped by the representation in which it is conceived, namely, the autobiographical

---

[5] Many scholars, among them Lionel Gossman, Suzanne Relyea, and Max Vernet, have stressed the influence of Cartesian science on Molière's play. See Lionel Gossman, *Men and Masks: A Study of Molière* (Baltimore: Johns Hopkins University Press, 1963); Suzanne Relyea, *Signs, Systems, and Meanings: A Contemporary Semiotic Reading of Four Molière Plays* (Middletown, Conn.: Wesleyan University Press, 1976); and Max Vernet, *Molière: Côté jardin, côté cour* (Paris: Nizet, 1991). My purpose here is to highlight the autobiographical persona of the *Discours de la méthode* in order to emphasize the notion of a performing subject that overrides the boundaries set by the text. I reserve a discussion of aspects of the method for Chapter 5.

[6] René Descartes, *Préambules,* in *Oeuvres philosophiques,* ed. Ferdinand Alquié, vol. 1 (Paris: Garnier Frères, 1963–73), 45; cited in Jean-Luc Nancy, *Ego sum* (Paris: Flammarion, 1979), 64.

[7] Nancy, 64.

narrative, the fable that frames the *Discours de la méthode*. The efficacy of the method notwithstanding, its truth value is a function of Descartes's exposition, his authorship/authorization of the method in his text: "Here 'representation' denotes not the copy—second, imitated, and, consequently, more or less artificial—but the presentation itself, the presentation of the thing itself."[8]

To say that meaning originates in representation is to acknowledge that in the *Discours* Descartes posits himself as unique model, incapable of being imitated by others. John Lyons argues that although Descartes offers himself as an exemplar of the new science which he proposes—though he would inspire imitation in order to validate his method—he fears a loss of control over his invention: "As author, Descartes wants to set forth what he himself has done as an example and yet withhold part of the example, preventing others from imitating the entirety of what he has done."[9] In the opposing claims of originality and imitability, in the proffering and withholding of examples, we detect the complex movement of the autobiographical "I" across the text.

On the one hand, the *Discours* offers a certain pretense of self-effacement. Descartes asserts that it is up to others to judge the veracity of what he presents:

> My present aim, then, is not to teach the method which everyone must follow in order to direct his reason correctly, but only to reveal how I have tried to direct my own. One who presumes to give precepts must think himself more skilful than those to whom he gives them; and if he makes the slightest mistake, he may be blamed. But I am presenting this work only as a history or, if you prefer, a fable in which, among certain examples worthy of imitation, you will perhaps also find many others

[8] Ibid., 66. It could be objected that Nancy's interpretation, because it in some sense removes itself from the history of science in the classical period, is an inappropriate vehicle for my study, which focuses squarely on knowledge formation in the seventeenth century. Although he does not engage in discussions of the scientific method, the role of mathematics, and other issues preoccupying the scientific community in the classical period, Nancy does suggest by his total immersion in textuality—in representation as representation—the very complexity of signification that I mean to underscore throughout this book by emphasizing the mirroring of literature and the literary (narrative, rhetorical, unclassifiable) aspects of science.

[9] John D. Lyons, *Exemplum: The Rhetoric of Example in Early Modern France and Italy* (Princeton: Princeton University Press, 1989), 156. See also Dalia Judovitz, *Subjectivity and Representation in Descartes: The Origins of Modernity* (Cambridge: Cambridge University Press, 1988).

that it would be right not to follow; and so I hope it will be useful for some without being harmful to any, and that everyone will be grateful to me for my frankness.

Ainsi mon dessein n'est pas d'enseigner ici la méthode que chacun doit suivre pour bien conduire sa raison, mais seulement de faire voir en quelle sorte j'ai tâché de conduire la mienne. Ceux qui se mêlent de donner des préceptes se doivent estimer plus habiles que ceux auxquels ils les donnent, et s'ils manquent à la moindre chose, il en sont blâmables. Mais ne proposant cet écrit que comme une histoire, ou, si vous l'aimez mieux, que comme une fable, en laquelle, parmi quelques exemples qu'on peut imiter, on en trouvera peut-être aussi plusieurs autres qu'on aura raison de ne pas suivre, j'espère qu'il sera utile à quelquesuns, sans être nuisible à personne, et que tous me sauront gré de ma franchise. (112/127)[10]

On the other hand, Descartes undercuts the exemplary quality of his narrative by making this autobiographical "I" of the *Discours* an inimitable model of the truth:

As for the benefit that others might gain from the communication of my thoughts, this could not be so very great. For I have not yet taken them sufficiently far: I need to add many things to them before applying them in practice. And I think I can say without vanity that if anyone is capable of making these additions it must be myself rather than someone else— not that there may not be many minds in the world incomparably better than mine, but because no one can conceive something so well, and make it his own, when he learns it from someone else as when he discovers it himself.

Pour l'utilité que les autres recevraient de la communication de mes pensées, elle ne pourrait aussi être fort grande; d'autant que je ne les ai point encore conduites si loin qu'il ne soit besoin d'y ajouter beaucoup de choses avant que de les appliquer à l'usage. Et je pense pouvoir dire sans vanité que s'il y a quelqu'un qui en soit capable, ce doit être plutôt moi qu'aucun autre: non pas qu'il ne puisse y avoir au monde plusieurs esprits incomparablement meilleurs que le mien; mais pour ce qu'on ne

---

[10] Lyons quotes this passage in *Exemplum*, 159.

saurait si bien concevoir une chose et la rendre sienne, lorsqu'on l'apprend de quelque autre, que lorsqu'on l'invente soi-même. (146/173)

Rhetorically, Descartes posits the very plausible argument that he is best suited for guiding the public's interpretation of his discovery. Viewed in this context, the verbs *to invent* (*inventer*) and *to conceive* (*concevoir*) suggest, moreover, that meaning is a function of representation. These verbs indicate that the truth about the world is achieved through the specific relations between things that are invented or conceived as signs in language. More specifically, the reference is to the relations between things that Descartes specifies in his research as recorded here.[11] If, however, the science of this ordering and measuring is a product of method, it is also true, in another register, that the validity of the method is in turn apparent in the representation that orders it, that is, in the autobiographical narrative which in Descartes's text is no mere decoration. Instead, this fiction (invention, conception, feint) is an intrinsic part of the performance of the meaning the philosopher constructs. To recognize the feint of the *Discours*, then, is to note that more than method as content—method as a self-contained entity that can be detached from representation and imitated, applied by others—accounts for the text's veracity. Descartes offers the method as a model within a representation whose model, paradoxically, is the inimitability of its own example. This is not to say that Descartes himself, as autobiographical narrator, is not in turn a subject within language—that his representation of his method situates him as the originator of meaning in the absolute sense of creating ex nihilo. The point is rather that Descartes's representation of his belief in the rationality of discourse and his efforts to determine the subject is colored by his need, in all plausibility well founded, to assert his function as master of his text so as to preclude the reader's deviation from the path to knowledge that he prescribes.

In the reading of Molière and La Rochefoucauld that follows, I argue that the maxim of the mask—"*Bene vixit, bene qui latuit*"—is a literal interpretation of epistemic praxis. The point is not simply to

---

[11] Timothy Reiss elaborates how *concevoir* contributes to the evolution of the Cartesian formulation of a discourse that represents the natural world analytically, as signs in language. See Timothy J. Reiss, "The 'Concevoir' Motif in Descartes," in *La cohérence intérieure: Etudes sur la littérature française du XVIIe siècle, offertes à J. D. Hubert*, ed. Jacqueline Van Baelen and David Lee Rubin (Paris: Jean-Michel Place, 1977), 203–22.

see Molière and La Rochefoucauld behind their respective texts. Nor is it just a question of being able to perceive a meaning only once it is adorned, like an ornament, in an otherwise nondescript text. Rather, to know the mask is to know that meaning originates in representation, which sets in place a classification scheme only to obscure it. The mask accounts for the performance of the subject in and around the grid, or taxonomic model, that the text establishes in an effort to fix identities. The subject of Molière's and La Rochefoucauld's texts exposes the system governing representation; it shows how representation is ordered. But in calling attention to the model in this way, the text propels the subject into a signifying space that eludes the model's capacity to identify it. Like Descartes's "I," both the subject conceived in Molière's play of doubles and La Rochefoucauld's subject, who is always prey to meanings that double back on themselves, outperform the system in which they are conceived. This ability to elude the model, to resist the text's efforts to specify its difference, is the secret of the subject's disguise.

Staging Identities: *Amphitryon*

In an excellent reading of *Amphitryon* based on the semiotic systems elaborated by the *Logique de Port-Royal*, Suzanne Relyea calls attention to the text's establishment of specific contexts for meaning and their eventual confusion. The notion of a blurring of categories, what Relyea terms the "alienation of context," remains essential to my reading. I mean, though, to shift the focus away from the personalized discourses of individual characters and the originality of identities which Relyea analyzes and look more closely at the issue of classification as it unites the various elements in the play into a unified whole.[12] Against this model I situate the ambivalences which the play offers in the guise of knowledge, in the form of a final revelation.[13]

---

[12] Relyea, 109.

[13] For more on the treatment of masks and invention in Molière's theater, see especially Gérard Defaux, *Molière, ou les métamorphoses du comique: De la comédie morale au triomphe de la folie* (Lexington, Ky.: French Forum, 1980; 2d ed. Paris: Klincksieck, 1992); Georges Forestier, *L'esthétique de l'identité dans le théâtre français (1550–1680): Le déguisement et ses avatars* (Geneva: Droz, 1988); Gossman; Marcel Gutwirth, *Molière ou l'invention comique: La métamorphose des thèmes et la création des types* (Paris: Minard, 1966); and Judd D. Hubert, *Molière and the Comedy of Intellect* (Berkeley: University of California Press, 1962).

In *Amphitryon* knowledge is a function of the characters' ability to identify themselves and others. From the vantage point of the gods, who deliberately manipulate and confound identities, the potential to expand the possibilities for knowing is a source of pleasure:

> When one has the happiness of appearing in a high rank,
> All that one does is always beautiful and good;
> And, following what one may be,
> Things change their names.

> Lorsque dans un haut rang on a l'heur de paraître,
> Tout ce qu'on fait est toujours bel et bon;
> Et, suivant ce qu'on peut être,
> Les choses changent de nom.

> (Prologue, 128–31)

Despite this enthusiastic declaration of the gods' empowering capacity to change identities and thus subvert the epistemological landscape, the experiment that the gods perform on the mortals fails utterly to please. Mercure successfully assumes the form of Sosie, Amphitryon's valet, in order to facilitate Jupiter's designs on the hero's wife, Alcmène. Jupiter, in the guise of Amphitryon, succeeds in ravishing Alcmène as she awaits her husband's return from battle. Yet in the end neither the mortals nor the gods are satisfied. Their dissatisfaction correlates directly with the naming process. The order established through such arbitrary exercises of power is always vulnerable to new disguises, new attacks on its integrity/authenticity. Epistemological instability is apparent in the feint which persists even after the gods depart, having seemingly restored the human world to its proper order. Indeed, we learn that the gods have not originated but instead mirrored the feint that conditions relations in the mortal realm.

To recognize the Other as the self is to lose one's identity. The pain of this particular ontological lesson is registered onstage through the blows that Sosie receives from Mercure, which suppress him physically in order to impress upon him the need to suppress his representation of himself as Sosie. These blows impress on Amphitryon's valet the fact that what is being demanded is that he learn to "renounce himself" (renoncer à [lui]-même [1.2.400]). Along with his name and his appearance, Sosie must abandon his very being to another. Yet he thinks, *donc* he has trouble accepting the notion of his eventual disappearance in the wake of Mercure's transformation:

I could not deny, in face of the proofs being shown to me
That you [Mercure] are not Sosie, and I give my voice in assent to this.
But, if you are he, tell me who you want me to be.
Because it is still necessary that I be something.

Je ne saurais nier, aux preuves qu'on m'expose,
Que tu [Mercure] ne sois Sosie, et j'y donne ma voix.
Mais, si tu l'es, dis-moi qui tu veux que je sois.
Car encor faut-il bien que je sois quelque chose.

                                        (1.2.509–12)

Mercure plays on the tensions already inscribed in the opening scene, where Sosie dialogues with an imagined Alcmène (represented by his lantern), rehearsing the message Amphitryon has told him to deliver to her. The scene, a celebrated *mise en abîme* of theatrical practice, also rehearses the differences between master and valet, history and its re-presentation, as between the subject empowered through representation (the active cultivation of a stage role) and the real being. Confronted by his divine double as he performs this role, Sosie loses the mastery he has realized as an actor/agent. He is "disempowered before an image of himself which he does not originate, does not understand . . . and which concretely puts him in a position of inferiority."[14]

Resemblances here obscure knowledge; they disturb the world as the characters know it by depriving them of the narcissistic confirmation they expect to find in a mirror image. One of the more interesting aspects of the play, however, is how it precludes our deducing meaning from the obverse relation: to recognize the Other as Other is still not to know. If the resemblance succeeds in diminishing my identity, it does little to clarify yours: "What will you get from taking away my name?" asks Sosie, "And can you, even if you were a demon, make it so / That I not be myself, that I not be Sosie?" (Que te reviendra-t-il de m'enlever mon nom? / Et peux-tu faire enfin, quand tu serais démon, / Que je ne sois pas moi, que je ne sois Sosie? [1.2.413–15]). Sosie cannot imagine the state of his nonbeing; therefore he cannot conceive of another who would be he.

---

[14] Abby Elizabeth Zanger, "Classical Anxiety: Performance, Perfection, and the Issue of Identity," in *L'âge du théâtre en France/The Age of Theater in France*, ed. David Trott and Nicole Boursier (Edmonton: Academic Printing and Publishing, 1988), 333.

This frustration is not restricted to the servant class. To know Jupiter disguised as Amphitryon is still not to know Jupiter in an unequivocal fashion. Not, that is, if one is Alcmène, who in making love to the disguised god believes that by expressing her devotion and affection she is validating the mortal hero. Assuming Amphitryon's appearance, Jupiter exists in Alcmène's mind only as Amphitryon. She frustrates the god by refusing to separate passion from duty, her role as lover from that of wife. She denies Jupiter the recognition he needs in order to feel loved and validated in turn:

Jupiter:

Hate, detest the husband,
I consent to this, and I abandon him to you;
But, Alcmène, rescue the lover from this anger
That such an offense gives you;
Do not throw onto him the effects of such rage;
Separate him a bit from the guilty party;
And, in order finally to be fair,
Do not punish him for what he has not done.

Alcmène:

Ah! All of these subtleties
Have but frivolous excuses,
And for irritated minds
Such words are only annoyances.
You take this ridiculous detour in vain.
I make no distinctions in my offender;
Everything in him becomes the object of my anger,
And, in its just violence,
The lover and the husband are confused,

. . .

Both are criminals; both have offended me,
And both are despicable to me.

Jupiter:

Haïssez, détestez l'époux,
J'y consens, et vous l'abandonne;
Mais, Alcmène, sauvez l'amant de ce courroux

Qu'une telle offense vous donne,
N'en jetez pas sur lui l'effet,
Démêlez-le un peu du coupable;
Et, pour être enfin équitable,
Ne le punissez point de ce qu'il n'a pas fait.

Alcmène:
Ah! toutes ces subtilités
N'ont que des excuses frivoles,
Et pour les esprits irrités
Ce sont des contre-temps que de telles paroles.
Ce détour ridicule est en vain pris par vous.
Je ne distingue rien en celui qui m'offense,
Tout y devient l'objet de mon courroux;
Et, dans sa juste violence,
Sont confondus et l'amant et l'époux,

. . .

Tous deux sont criminels, tous deux m'ont offensée,
Et tous deux me sont odieux.

(2.6.1319–40)

The gods do not merely double the mortals in appearance; they spy on and otherwise intrude in the mortals' lives. At one level the intrusion is easy to trace because it involves the events of the drama as they unfold, that is, adultery as a part of the characters' enacted history. Yet knowing how the lovemaking between Jupiter and Alcmène is in turn perceived by the characters and the audience is a far more intricate, or, in her words, *subtle* process. Is it seduction or is it rape? Is the wife's behavior an act of infidelity or fidelity? Is the play a comedy or a tragedy? The answers to these questions are all over-determined.

Mercure is openly antagonistic to Sosie in the scene quoted earlier. His hostility indicates that the gods' intervention is not a neutral act, one that can eventually be righted by their removing their masks and revealing the truth of their imposture. Sosie's perception of the gods' arrogance would survive the exposure of their true identities. Arguably, Jupiter displays no real belligerence toward Alcmène in his efforts to win her over, since he wants not to violate her so much as to be loved by her. But is this love on his part or simply the demand that Alcmène satisfy him not only sexually but psychologically as well? The fact that he is motivated out of jealousy at the newlyweds' ardor,[15] that he violates not only Alcmène and her honor but also Amphitryon and his glory, and that he upsets the whole order of things through which the mortals secure their identities underscores the sinister quality of Jupiter's transgressions. The play does in the end compensate the mortal figures by bestowing on their history the gift of a divine context in which to re-present the behavior that has caused their pain. Jupiter exposes himself as the author of the chaos that has ruled their lives. In true dramatic fashion this divine context produces its own effect in the form of a stunning conclusion: Jupiter announces that Alcmène is carrying his son, the god Hercules. This final moment offers no harmony, however, no definitive knowledge. The god's tendering of Hercules is connected to the ambivalent exchange of identities that marks the play from the outset. The gift functions as a failed mediator; it is the object of exchange that does not facilitate relations between parties but is itself transformed by these events.[16]

First appearing in the form of the diamond cluster that Amphitryon instructs Sosie to give to Alcmène, the gift from the general to his wife is a war trophy, replete with the symbolism of conquest. Yet once it is usurped by the gods, the diamond cluster becomes an accessory to their performance, a tool for their seduction. Preempting Sosie's presentation of the diamonds to Alcmène, Jupiter effectively transforms the gift into a humiliating sign of the hero's lost honor and the god's own prowess. These machinations reduce Alcmène to a possession of the gods. Anne Ubersfeld notes, moreover, that they identify Amphitryon as a figure dispossessed of all that he has and knows: "His wife (an other has taken her), his glory (an other celebrates his victory), his name, his physical appearance, and to complete his attachment to others, *recognition*, the primary element of his identity; the depersonalization is complete; an other has taken his place."[17]

---

[15] Mercure explains the triangular origin of Jupiter's desire: "Marriage joined them only a few days ago; / And the young warmth of their tender loves / Has made Jupiter in this fine artifice / Think to take recourse" (L'hymen ne les a joints que depuis quelques jours; / Et la jeune chaleur de leurs tendres amours / A fait que Jupiter à ce bel artifice / S'est avisé d'avoir recours [Prologue, 67–70]).

[16] For more on the theory of the obligations implicit in the gift exchange, see Marcel Mauss, *Essai sur le don: Forme et raison de l'échange dans les sociétés archaïques* (Paris: Alcan, 1925). Although Mauss's theories have not gone unchallenged, his text remains an essential reference for explaining the function of gift giving.

[17] Anne Ubersfeld, "Le double dans l'*Amphitryon* de Molière," in *Dramaturgies: Langages dramatiques; mélanges pour Jacques Scherer*, ed. Jacqueline de Jomaron (Paris: Nizet, 1986), 238.

As a sign of possession, the gift bestowed by Jupiter mirrors Amphitryon's gift. Even in the relations governing husband and wife, the gift
obligates the receiver not only to be beholden to the giver but to recognize and validate him as well. That is, the receipt of the gift obligates
Alcmène to project back to Amphitryon the idealized image in which
he chooses to recognize himself. Amphitryon is thus deflated—physically, one suspects, as well as morally—by Alcmène's failure to uphold
her end of the gift exchange: "What! home so soon?" (Quoi! de retour
si tôt? [2.2.857]). Her lackluster reception of the real gift, the man
himself in all his glory, is a reversal of the intended relation whereby
she submits to his need to be adored. Amphitryon replies:

> Certainly, on this day this is how
> To give poor proof of your ardor;
> And this "What? home so soon?"
> On such occasions is scarcely the language
> Of a heart really inflamed with love.

> Certes, c'est en ce jour
> Me donner de vos feux un mauvais témoignage;
> Et ce "Quoi! si tôt de retour?"
> En ces occasions n'est guère le langage
> D'un coeur bien enflammé d'amour.
>
> (2.2.857–61)

In the larger context represented by the gods, however, this male-
female economy, which mirrors that of master and servant, is transformed. Not Amphitryon but Alcmène is the purveyor of meaning and
power here. For in her refusal to see in Jupiter anything but her
husband, she frustrates the god. Alcmène, albeit through a naive dis-
belief, a certain incredulity, exposes the instability of the god's rule;
she reveals him as imposing an order of things that is no more precise
for being Other, for being his. Referring to the "evidence" of the
locked box from which the diamond cluster has been removed by the
gods, Max Vernet suggests that the question of virtue, the sanctity of
the marital bed, is likewise ambiguous:

Fidelity and infidelity are indistinguishable; closure does not block the
transfer. The diamond cluster knots nothing at all—the inside is empty;
what needs to be understood is that it is always empty, that what is enclosed is always moving, that fidelity is always a sort of infidelity, if we

persist in representing it as a superposition, of a copresence in one and the same place. This is likewise valid for the presence to oneself [*la présence à soi*]: in this play everyone is double.[18]

There is no containment within categories. Instead, the entire classification system is itself exposed as a sort of Pandora's box, a grid from which meanings escape despite the best efforts of the mortals to contain them. Hercules, son of a divine father and a mortal mother, is the final sign of such indifferentiation, a sign that Molière bestows as his play draws to a close.[19] Hercules, moreover, ensures the sustained divine presence among the mortals after Jupiter and Mercure have withdrawn. The mortal realm is conceived in vitro, as a microcosm of the world of the gods which it continues to mirror even as Jupiter draws a final line of separation between them. Hercules' impending birth thus represents a new obligation for the mortals to recognize themselves in their divine counterparts.

One might object that pregnancy forces the "truth" on Alcmène, a truth that releases both her and her husband from their ordeal. Ambiguities nonetheless persist because the question of history, of having made love, is distinct from that of infidelity. The latter is the product of representation, interpretation. The audience is left with the impression that Alcmène is indeed faithful in all that concerns her intent, and, more important, in all matters of her self-knowledge, as well as in our identification of her. Significantly, her presence is virtually eclipsed from the time of her "infidelity" to the end of the play, when Jupiter reveals his scam. Secluded offstage, Alcmène is protected in the audience's mind from this recontextualization; she remains within the frame of her own representation. This power is not merely passive, since her behavior has determined Jupiter's final admission to Amphitryon of defeat:

> And it is I, in this adventure,
> Who, even though I am a god, must be the jealous one.
> Alcmène is entirely yours, whatever care one takes;
> And for your love it must be a most sweet object
> To see that, to please her, there is no other way

---

[18] Vernet, 98.
[19] Granting the last word to Sosie, the most disempowered member of mortal society, Molière reinforces the notion that the order of things has been permanently disrupted by the gods.

Than to appear to be her husband;
That Jupiter, clothed in his immortal glory,
By himself could not triumph over her faith;
And that what he received from her
Was given by her ardent heart only to you.

Et c'est moi, dans cette aventure,
Qui, tout dieu que je suis, dois être le jaloux.
Alcmène est toute à toi, quelque soin qu'on emploie;
Et ce doit à tes feux être un objet bien doux
De voir que, pour lui plaire, il n'est point d'autre voie
Que de paraître son époux;
Que Jupiter, orné de sa gloire immortelle,
Par lui-même n'a pu triompher de sa foi;
Et que ce qu'il a reçu d'elle
N'a, par son coeur ardent, été donné qu'à toi.

(3.10.1903–12)

Sexual potency, and with it a god's ability to perform an act of love-making that produces a divine progeny, is inferior to the human act that names the "object." It would be a misrepresentation to say that Alcmène possesses the ultimate power, since she is prey to Jupiter's manipulations and acts in ignorance of his deceit. But the impact of her refusal to acknowledge an Other who is not Amphitryon is no less striking because she is duped. Jupiter seems anything but godlike in exposing his lack; he must become an Other in order to be recognized as himself. There is nothing omnipotent in this impotence.[20]

Jupiter's performance has not, however, failed to inform our view of how knowledge is ordered. He has effectively mirrored the elusive and illusory truth that grounds the mortals' mastery of the world as expressed through their leader, Amphitryon. Without Jupiter's intervention Amphitryon would be the hero returning home to bask in the light of victory. Yet in Amphitryon's response to the events set into motion by the god, we see not just an unwitting cuckold but a man who is not restored to reason after Jupiter's revelation. As Lionel Gossman persuasively argues, Amphitryon's deficiency is merely confirmed, not created, by Jupiter's role. Amphitryon argues through

---

[20] Gossman, 25–30, and Ubersfeld argue for the inferior position of the god who would be mortal.

will and might rather than empirical evidence or rational demonstration:

> It is only in the hypothetical realm of fantasy that there is any doubt as to whether Amphitryon is really Amphitryon. At the same time this hypothetical doubt reveals the weakness of Amphitryon's position. His rightness about himself—or about anything—can never be more than an *accident*, for what he holds to be true is simply willful and undemonstrated belief. He cannot and will not answer the challenge of reason, he cannot demonstrate the validity of his beliefs, and there is consequently *no reason* to believe that his opinions are true.[21]

But they are true. He, not Jupiter, is Amphitryon. And in the very viciousness of the process through which this fact is affirmed, we discover knowledge in the text's feint. Reason is unreasoned, and the unreasoned beliefs are in turn confirmed by the events of the play.

Thus, Sosie is not altogether naive in his assessment: "The real Amphitryon / Is the Amphitryon where one dines" (Le véritable Amphitryon / Est l'Amphitryon où l'on dîne [3.5.1703–04]). By substituting the home ("where") for the proprietor (Amphitryon), that is, by inverting the content or payoff of his relation with his master and the container/provider of his wages, Sosie suggests that the proof is in the pudding, literally and figuratively. He is clearly interested in the real, the food in his stomach. But any Amphitryon would do—the master who bluffs his way to mastery or the impostor god who would do the same. In the figurative sense of my expression, the proof is in the doing, in the enactment that determines the subject's perceptions. Identity is a product of representation perceived as the power to perform and through performance to transform—food into sustenance of life, self into Other, god into man, fidelity into infidelity, history into a re-presentation that is something more than an exact copy. This final knowledge reflects the power of the gift that, in the economy of the epistemological relations explored by the play, is always transformative, always incomplete. Knowledge is not a stable relation so much as a skill, an ability to make one's way through the grid that the play erects to fix identities. The subject conceived within this model remains essentially unknowable, or, as La Rochefoucauld's maxims similarly demonstrate, knowable only as representation.

---

[21] Gossman, 6.

La Rochefoucauld: The Feint as a Strategy for Social Mastery

La Rochefoucauld evidences much the same trompe l'oeil effect noted in Descartes's hidden presentation of his method. The philosopher's "I" is above all else a performing subject, an entity that comes into being as a result of a "play on method" or subversion of the grid of identities established by the text. For the most part, of course, there is no identifiable subject in La Rochefoucauld's work comparable to the autobiographical "I" of the *Discours*. Except in those cases where gender is an issue, the subject of the *Maximes* is most frequently an indeterminate "one" (*on*) or "we" (*nous*). If we feel La Rochefoucauld's presence, it is because his aphorisms are so carefully crafted. The intricate linguistic and syntactical devices that La Rochefoucauld employs to abstract an idea of a subject possessed, as it were, by amour propre provoke the reader to puzzle out a meaning.[22] Caught in the web that the text spins as it subverts the expected associations between terms, the reader is always, inevitably, aware of the commanding presence of the author behind the text. For the possibility of deciphering the enigma posed by the text depends on the reader's faith that the author does in fact have a meaning, or meanings, in mind.[23]

The maxim is often no more than a single sentence. Yet it functions as a mirror unto itself, often splitting the text into two distinct spheres of perception: that of the viewer and that of the subject viewed. "We are so accustomed to disguising ourselves to others," La Rochefoucauld observes, "that we end up disguising ourselves to ourselves" (Nous sommes si accoutumés à nous déguiser aux autres qu'enfin nous nous déguisons à nous-mêmes [max. 119]). Does this "we," which becomes aligned with the "others," exclude the elliptical "I" of the writer? Or is the moralist implicated as much by the precision

---

[22] I shall use the English *amour propre* to refer to the range of experiences that La Rochefoucauld represents through this term in French, although in translating specific maxims I shall also use "self-love" and "self-interest."

[23] There is no lack of critical discussion on the formal properties of the maxim. Particularly useful is Jonathan Culler's attention to the function of paradox in this connection: "A paradox presents two terms which ordinarily are in a clear semantic relationship to one another (either opposition: *vices/vertus, folie/sagesse, amour/haine* [vices/virtues, folly/wisdom, love/hate]; or equivalence: *chasteté/chaste, louer/louange, reconnaissance/reconnaissant* [chastity/chaste; to praise/praise, gratitude/grateful]), but it presents them in a logical structure which denies that relationship and asserts the converse" ("Paradox and the Language of Morals in La Rochefoucauld," *Modern Language Review* 68 [January 1973]: 29). Culler further observes: "We must provisionally accept the paradox as true if we are to come to understand it" (28). See also Lewis, 154–67.

of language that inverts the subject and object positions? Can he be exempt from this text that in its reciprocity allows for no exceptions? Serge Doubrovsky argues that the moralist's absence from his text is anything but innocent, for he must work to conceal the fact that what he condemns in others is his own failing: "Aphoristic writing is a permanent manifestation of the *superiority* of the writer with regard to the reader, who puts into play and into use, by a supreme irony, the fault that is denounced as the other's primary vice. Nonetheless, to avoid seeing his reflection in the mirror that he holds up to others, the writer must pay the price: *anonymity*."[24]

In one instance La Rochefoucauld does offer a self-portrait. The "Portrait de M. D. R. fait par lui-même" enables us to situate the moralist as a direct inheritor of the Cartesian feint. Like the philosopher, La Rochefoucauld arrives at a notion of an inimitable subject whose "gift" is not its capacity to facilitate the reader's understanding of his method, his art of representation. Rather this gift corresponds with the philosopher's performance, his essential role as purveyor of knowledge, a role that precludes imitation. For the moralist the notion of the gift translates as the knowledge about himself that he would impress on his reader. Here it is the science of modeling a knowledge submerged in the text that offers itself directly as the author's own gift of himself. Like the gift in Molière's play, however, the model that La Rochefoucauld offers is transformed. The self-portrait asserts that representation corrupts the more imposing figure who stands behind it: La Rochefoucauld is better than he is portrayed to be. Yet it is representation that allows us to abstract an idea of this more imposing figure. In an instability reminiscent of *Amphitryon*, where the gods' gift is to reflect back to the mortals the illusion of their own truths, the final gift of the moralist's text is the unresolved mediation between imitable (representable) and inimitable (unrepresentable)—between what is named in representation and what, despite his claims to be absent, La Rochefoucauld succeeds in sketching without naming.

The moralist seeks affirmation in a representation that measures the relation between his physical and moral traits. Representational

---

[24] Serge Doubrovsky, "Vingt propositions sur l'amour-propre: De Lacan à La Rochefoucauld," in *Parcours critique* (Paris: Galilée, 1980), 226. For more on the self-effacement of the author, see Roland Barthes, "La Rochefoucauld: Réflexions ou sentences et maximes," in *Le degré zéro de l'écriture suivi de Nouveaux essais critiques* (Paris: Seuil, 1972), 69–88; and Lewis, chap. 2.

accuracy, however, is overshadowed by La Rochefoucauld's expressed regret that society will never know him for what he is:

> I have something melancholy and proud in my appearance; this makes most people believe that I am scornful, although I am not at all. . . . I am very reserved with those whom I do not know, and I am not extremely open even with most of those whom I do know. I am well aware that this is a fault, and I will neglect nothing to rid myself of it; but since a certain somber look that I have in my face contributes to making me seem even more reserved than I am, and since it is not in our power to release ourselves from a mean look that comes from the natural disposition of our features, I think that after having corrected myself on the inside, some undesirable signs will nonetheless always remain on the outside.

> J'ai quelque chose de chagrin et de fier dans la mine; cela fait croire à la plupart des gens que je suis méprisant quoique je ne le sois point du tout. . . . Je suis fort resserré avec ceux que je ne connais pas, et je ne suis pas même extrêmement ouvert avec la plupart de ceux que je connais. C'est un défaut, je le sais bien, et je ne négligerai rien pour m'en corriger; mais comme un certain air sombre que j'ai dans le visage contribue à me faire paraître encore plus réservé que je ne le suis, et qu'il n'est pas en notre pouvoir de nous défaire d'un méchant air qui nous vient de la disposition naturelle des traits, je pense qu'après m'être corrigé au dedans, il ne laissera pas de me demeurer toujours de mauvaises marques au dehors. (165–66)

The moralist endeavors to achieve a certain objectivity through his depiction of negative and positive attributes. The negative traits, in particular, ensure his credibility as a narrator, and thus substantiate the particular view of himself that he wishes to communicate. Yet the moralist's professed willingness to correct deficiencies in his character is equivocal. His appearance, he mournfully asserts, will continue to belie his inner being. The oppositions established by the text—positive/negative, authentic/inauthentic, interior/exterior—resist synthesis; they offer no cohesive model for generating a knowable subject. La Rochefoucauld means to persuade his reader to look past appearances to a truth about himself. The dialectical energy of his portrait, however, moves the reader beyond the fullness of the image reflected in the mirror and the certainty of knowing. Indeed, against the moralist's assertion that others do not know him as he knows himself, we must posit the limits of his self-knowledge.

La Rochefoucauld's narrow introspection is reflected in the depiction of his principled, generous, and self-sacrificing nature:

> I am fond of my friends, and I am fond of them in such a way as not to hesitate an instant to sacrifice my interests to theirs; I am accommodating toward them; I suffer their bad moods patiently and I excuse easily everything that results from them; but I am not very demonstrative, and in their absence I experience no great concerns.

> J'aime mes amis, et je les aime d'une façon que je ne balancerais pas un moment à sacrifier mes intérêts aux leurs; j'ai de la condescendance pour eux, je souffre patiemment leurs mauvaises humeurs et j'en excuse facilement toutes choses; seulement je ne leur fais pas beaucoup de caresses, et je n'ai pas non plus de grandes inquiétudes en leur absence. (168)

Affirming that his nondemonstrative character betrays the sincerity of his emotions and his solicitude toward friends, La Rochefoucauld asks the reader to authenticate a subject obscured by even a faithful representation. Although he does not carry on when a friend is absent, his reserve should not, he insists, be confused with indifference. Yet we cannot but be struck by a most significant omission in La Rochefoucauld's reflections. The moralist fails to apply to himself the category of amour propre which he invokes to judge others: "Self-love is the greatest of all flatterers" (L'amour-propre est le plus grand de tous les flatteurs [max. 2]). Such gaps in representation inform a subject that is more complex, a subject that elides the model designed to frame it in representation.

If it surpasses the appearance of things in the world, the self of this portrait is nonetheless other than the autobiographical "I" would recognize. The question becomes: Is this "other" more or less a subject? Both Descartes and La Rochefoucauld see the potential for misstatement and misconstrued judgment about themselves. Anxious about posterity, they seek protection away from the rigorous categorization of science that would, in labeling them, make them subjects to be copied and thereby degraded. Each establishes, as I have observed, an elliptical persona. Moreover, each in his own way calls attention to a subject uniquely dependent on the act of representation. In the body of the *Maximes* this subject, represented in the various posturings of amour propre, is neither fully knowing (self-aware) nor knowable (accessible through analysis). While this subject so egregiously elided in the self-portrait comes to occupy a prominent role in the maxims, it performs there largely unharnessed by the epistemological framework that the moralist employs to expose and to judge it. Significantly, though many diverse aspects of La Rochefoucauld's human comedy can be said to reflect the influence of this subject, nothing allows us to condemn amour propre any more than reason—the ability to isolate such behavior and to order it into a system—which amour propre is held to corrupt.

La Rochefoucauld makes no secret of his contempt for the belief that reason can elucidate the world: "The mind is always deceived by the heart" (L'esprit est toujours la dupe du coeur [max. 102]); "Chance corrects us of many faults that reason could not correct" (La fortune nous corrige de plusieurs défauts que la raison ne saurait corriger [max. 154]). He expresses even less hope in man's ability to reason effectively. There is no incentive, the moralist asserts, for looking beyond illusions to the truth about ourselves: "Fortunate people rarely correct themselves; they believe that they are always right when good luck supports their bad conduct" (Les gens heureux ne se corrigent guère; ils croient toujours avoir raison quand la fortune soutient leur mauvaise conduite [max. 227]). Nothing in these lines is reminiscent of the confident assertion with which Descartes opens the *Discours*: "Good sense is the best-distributed thing in the world" (Le bon sens est la chose du monde la mieux partagée [111/126]). Yet it would be wrong to conclude on the basis of such maxims that the moralist and the philosopher are writing at cross-purposes.

If he doubts the efficacy of reason, disparaging the claim of science to improve man's lot by systematically increasing his knowledge, La Rochefoucauld is himself anything but an inspired writer of unstructured and inexact observations about the world. The achievement of his maxims, namely, their ability to pierce through misconceptions and to lay bare the delusions that the *honnête homme* cultivates in the guise of truth, depends on the establishment of a vast taxonomy. Insisting on the intellectual rigor of the *Maximes*, Louis Van Delft draws attention to La Rochefoucauld's meticulous and detailed classification system:

> In a manner that is sometimes somewhat rigid, he distinguishes almost everywhere categories and the norms that correspond to them. Old age, for example, constitutes a clearly defined and precisely circumscribed "state." This very precisely determined category has its conventions, its rules, its own "character." The moralist's approach, here and elsewhere,

consists of asking whether a certain behavior conforms to the norms or is instead incongruous. If a discrepancy exists, this should be exposed, indeed denounced. What is most astonishing in this way of proceeding is the attention paid to detail: everything is classified, ordered, distinguished, codified. There is no allowance for the least vacillation. . . . Deviance has the value of ridicule; a discrepancy is not very different from an indiscretion. The world must be described, inventoried, ordered, and regulated, no doubt because it must be conquered by knowledge, but also because it falls to certain people to conquer it in another way: order begins with them, the *"grands"* and the *"premiers"* of the state. One names in order to know better, yet one can command well only when one has a solid understanding of the terrain.[25]

Van Delft's insistence on categories, inventories, orders, and rules shows the underlying logic of La Rochefoucauld's representation to be a system of identification whose precision resembles that of the philosopher. The moralist's comprehensive taxonomy for human activity encompasses all forms of behavior including the deviant. The same logic that allows the classification of such exceptional comportment can be applied to the *Maximes*'s own underlying epistemology. To recognize that something does not fit into an established paradigm—to perceive its incongruity—is not to condemn it to either a provisional or a permanent vacillation. Rather than simply being dismissed as unknowable, suspended from meaning, this unusual or abrasive thing is perceived to be "excluded" or "denounced" and is thus known (positively) as a negative. In this sense the labels excluded and denounced become viable categories for knowledge. If one were to exhaust all possibilities for knowledge, even the improbable or the dubious would serve as categories for ordering information. In the most radical yet reassuring form of classification, therefore, the unknown becomes an identifiable category for knowledge within the moralist's extensive epistemological network.

Van Delft's analysis brings to light a classification system of considerable breadth. Indeed, were we to consider the enumeration of items in the editor's index of principal themes in the *Maximes*, we might well conclude that, although La Rochefoucauld's work is vast, there exists in it a finite number of categories for understanding man. That is, the list of themes is theoretically expandable to an eventual point

[25] Louis Van Delft, *Le moraliste classique: Essai de définition et de typologie* (Geneva: Droz, 1982), 164.

of completion. The initial problem, however, is not knowledge as ordered sequentially, or horizontally, in this manner but rather the vertical extension of individual paradigms. A given class of behavior may well include both positive and negative attributes. Paul Bénichou observes, for example, that the same motivation for glory is not universally condemned by the moralist:

> When he writes, "The clemency of princes is often only a political means for gaining the people's affection" (La clémence des princes n'est souvent qu'une politique pour gagner l'affection des peuples), he denounces a motive for action that is unquestionably selfish. A clement prince, if he wants his conduct to be admired, can only deny the reality, conscious or unconscious, of the motive that La Rochefoucauld assigns to him. But, in other cases, the person in question could accept the moralist's psychological explanation without believing himself to be morally diminished by it. When La Rochefoucauld calls magnanimity "pride's good sense, and the most noble path to praise" (le bon sens de l'orgueil, et la voie la plus noble pour recevoir des louanges), he defines a conduct whose moral appreciation remains subject to controversy and which could continue to pass for greatness.[26]

Michael Moriarty echoes this emphasis in observing that La Rochefoucauld's taxonomy of tastes (*goûts*) is perhaps more accurately described as a "pathology." The moralist defines two kinds of taste, one corresponding with the appetites and the other with learned behavior: "the taste that attracts us to things, and the taste that teaches us to know and discern their qualities by having us stick to the rules" (le goût qui nous porte vers les choses, et le goût qui nous en fait connaître et discerner les qualités, en s'attachant aux règles).[27] Yet, according to Moriarty, La Rochefoucauld "mixes the two senses more or less indiscriminately":

> La Rochefoucauld's formulation of the distinction between two senses of *goût* is . . . far from transparent. First of all, it does not seem to cover his own use of the word, the complexity of which belies the trimness of the definitions. Secondly, by the very rigidity of the distinction between cor-

---

[26] Paul Bénichou, *L'écrivain et ses travaux* (Paris: Corti, 1967), 6. Bénichou cites maxims 15 and 285.

[27] Michael Moriarty, *Taste and Ideology in Seventeenth-Century France* (Cambridge: Cambridge University Press, 1988), 130. Moriarty cites La Rochefoucauld, réfl. 10.

rect knowledge of the object and blind inclination towards it, it excludes rational argument about tastes, for reason, by definition, must be on one side of the argument only.[28]

In La Rochefoucauld's work it is perhaps pride's good sense that comes to compensate for the Cartesian good sense. In this chapter, however, I show that it does not do so without reflecting the problems inherent in the ordering of knowledge in the classical period.

To read up and down a given category in the *Maximes*—to recognize the various forms within a given paradigm of knowledge such as age, love, wisdom—is to recognize that man escapes definition. "The intention of never deceiving," La Rochefoucauld contends, "makes us vulnerable to being frequently deceived" (L'intention de ne jamais tromper nous expose à être souvent trompés [max. 118]). Although it refers to men's social interactions, this maxim can be used to underscore the problematics of representation. Paradoxically, the more one enumerates, the more elusive meaning becomes. We are deceived by the very classification system intended to preclude error and confusion. Vertically, at least, the possibility of substitution is endless. Hence knowledge, as critics have observed, is destined to remain fragmentary and uncertain.

Knowledge, then, is ascribable not to a vertical integration of similar forms within a paradigm but rather to a lateral expansion or dispersion of signs. But where in this expansion do we find the subject? Van Delft rightfully equates intellectual mastery with a certain political mastery. In the passage cited earlier he asserts that the moralist shows those who have a better control of information—those, we might say, who make better use of language's capacity to analyze the world—to enjoy an increased authority. Yet breadth of perception does not ensure depth of penetration. The subject's self-awareness is scarcely enhanced by his awareness of the world: "But this thick obscurity, which hides it [self-interest] from itself, does not prevent it from seeing perfectly what lies outside it, in which respect it is like our eyes, which discover everything and are blind only to themselves" (Mais cette obscurité épaisse, qui le [amour-propre] cache à lui-même, n'empêche pas qu'il ne voie parfaitement ce qui est hors de lui, en quoi il est semblable à nos yeux, qui découvrent tout, et sont aveugles seulement pour eux-mêmes [max. sup. 1]). The subject of the *Maximes* surfaces

---

[28] Moriarty, 132.

from the text's classification system only to be resubmerged by it. This movement does not, however, preclude the establishment of meaning. The subject communicates with us even though it eludes the taxonomy constructed by La Rochefoucauld to identify and contain it.

The subject performs what might be called, in an anachronistic adaptation of contemporary business terminology, a series of lateral moves. Like the executive who must abandon hope of reaching the top of the corporate ladder in exchange for relief at having avoided termination and having secured a new role at the same rank and level of competence, the subject of La Rochefoucauld's maxims does not accede to the truth: he does not rise, as it were, to the top of the signifying chain. Indeed, the competence of the subject in the maxims as I define it relates specifically to the renunciation of an absolute knowledge.

Jean Starobinski has argued that the failure of the maxims to provide a clear knowledge is the result of a significant inversion: "the *deficiency of being* [*le défaut d'être*] in each of us is signaled indirectly but faithfully by the *failure of appearing* [*l'échec du paraître*]."[29] In this parodic reversal of the dictum which holds that the more one penetrates behind appearances, the more one perceives the truth, Starobinski affirms how in the maxims appearances instead become a measure of knowledge. For it is in the act of displaying one's masks that the meaning is constructed. Working his way deeper and deeper into the psyche of man, La Rochefoucauld touches bottom without ever falling into the abyss of ignorance and depression. For to know this limit is to know how to manage it, how to compensate for the shallowness of perception by accentuating all that can still be produced and made to signify. The choice, after all, is life itself:

> For he who has shown the nothingness of man, worldy [*mondaine*] life cannot continue except as a concern for finding a form for it, it being well understood that this form could only be arbitrary and gratuitous, bearing no relation to a despair to which it brings no remedy. But this is, if you will, a false solution: a diversion in the Pascalian sense, but a diversion fully conscious of its futility. The disabused man returns to the game not to forget his condition but because once the impostures are unmasked, this is the only thing that can still be done in the worldly order. An entire world of vanity (and which knows itself to be vain) will

[29] Jean Starobinski, "La Rochefoucauld et les morales substitutives," *NRF* 163–64 (July-August 1966): 34.

be constructed with vain words (that know themselves to be vain); but for us this is the narrow zone that remains habitable.[30]

The "love of the game" described by Starobinski amounts to a deliberate strategy to transform the imperfections of a compromised *savoir* (knowledge) into the perfections of a *savoir-faire*.[31] Thus, mastery can be said to reflect less the subject's ability to consolidate information than his oblique position relative to the behaviors classified by the moralist. For it is in this oblique relation to the categories established by the text to explain the world that the otherwise constrained subject emerges as a player on the world's stage, an active agent in the formulation of meaning as it has come to be inseparable from the feint of performance.

Playing the Text

La Rochefoucauld claims that any established view can be challenged and any opinion set in opposition if the desire *to know*—to make or establish knowledge—is motivated by the desire *to be known*:

> It is most often out of pride rather than for lack of intelligence that we oppose the most accepted opinions with such stubborn resistance: we find the first places taken for the right course of action, and we do not want anything to do with the last ones.

> C'est plus souvent par orgueil que par défaut de lumières qu'on s'oppose avec tant d'opiniâtreté aux opinions les plus suivies: on trouve les premières places prises dans le bon parti, et on ne veut point des dernières. (max. 234)

The acquisition of knowledge within society is portrayed as a game of intellectual sparring. No one wants to be the last soldier killed in the war. And no one, La Rochefoucauld posits, wants to be the last to follow a trend. It is better to buck the received idea, however well grounded, in order to found a new one. The moralist probably did not have the example of Descartes in mind when he composed this maxim, yet in the *Discours* the philosopher testifies that he committed

---

[30] Ibid., 212.
[31] My thanks to Julia Simon and my graduate class for helping to define this concept.

himself to rejecting the example of his predecessors in order to surpass them. After a lengthy discussion of what he has learned, Descartes
concludes: "I was, then, unable to choose anyone whose opinions
struck me as preferable to those of all others, and I found myself as
it were forced to become my own guide" (Je ne pouvais choisir personne dont les opinions me semblassent devoir être préférées à celles
des autres, et je me trouvai comme contraint d'entreprendre moi-
même de me conduire [119/136]). Is there vanity in this constraint?
La Rochefoucauld might have us believe so.

In the maxim the *honnête homme*'s bid for recognition leads to no
understanding more profound than that of social play. By subordi-
nating the quest for knowledge to the expression of amour propre
and the satisfaction of the ego, La Rochefoucauld accentuates the
player rather than the game played. But in order to play this game
well, the player must demonstrate sufficient skill. And La Rochefoucauld, whose own opposition of forms within the maxim reveals a
subtle appreciation of the rules of the game, implies that there are
no limits to the intellectual capacities of the ego intent on satisfying
itself. Science has found its sparring partner in the moralist's literary
wit. In the maxim just cited obstinacy and resistance substitute for
acumen and intellectual penetration as the text inverts back on itself.
Although *opiniâtreté* (stubbornness) and *opinions* share the same ety-
mological root, there is no symmetry suggested by the recurrence of
semantic forms. If one can oppose opinions, it is because there is no
more truth to what is stubbornly affirmed than to what is, even more
stubbornly, denied. Knowledge, therefore, is always uncertain—and
never finite, never beyond the influence of one who would attempt a
new order.

Whereas La Rochefoucauld consciously attends to the practices of
the aristocracy, to their predilections and tastes, his maxims force us
to see beyond conventional limits, "the most accepted opinions." He
understands that if one is to know things well, "they must be known
in detail" (Il en faut savoir le détail). La Rochefoucauld nevertheless
teaches us that the epistemic burgeoning—the confidence in science
and discovery, the positive faith in an ability to invent and conceive
that Descartes's representation of his method brings to light—characterizes a potential of the age distinct from its actual mastery: "And
since there is an almost infinite number of details, our understanding
is always superficial and imperfect" (Et comme [le détail] est presque
infini, nos connaissances sont toujours superficielles et imparfaites
[max. 106]). Any assessment of the epistemological functioning of

the maxims must therefore weigh evidence of the proliferation and dispersion of meanings against those elements that resist dispersion. Indeed, we need to confront a fundamental inconsistency. While La Rochefoucauld advances knowledge by systematically suspending or deferring meaning, he denies that knowledge is ever secure, ever complete. The point, he insists, is never without its counterpoint.

La Rochefoucauld's text deflates itself by systematically undermining the identities that it establishes. Roland Barthes has rapturously depicted the movement through which the moralist sounds the vacant depths of human knowledge:

> There is in this *profound* edifice a vertigo of nothingness; descending from one level to the next—from heroism to ambition, from ambition to jealousy—one can never reach the full depth of man; one can never assign him a final definition that would be irreducible. When the ultimate passion has been designated, this passion itself fades away; it can be only laziness, inertia, nothingness. The maxim is an infinite route of deception; man is no longer but a skeleton of passions; this skeleton itself is perhaps but the fantasy of nothing: *man is not certain.* This vertigo of the unreal is perhaps the price to be paid for all the efforts at demystification, so that to the greatest lucidity there often corresponds the greatest unreality.[32]

Barthes helps us to see that against the perfection of science and the analytical method there must be measured the weight of an epistemological collapse. Similarly, Philip Lewis has convincingly demonstrated that in the *Maximes* "abstract truth imposes itself . . . in the ongoing process that parcels and restates it as a composite of truths."[33] The fragments, however, fail to offer a final synthesis, a finite and adequate knowledge. The result, Lewis maintains, is a critical process best characterized as debunking: "Since maxim after maxim works to unsettle 'realities' perceived at all levels of human experience, when the *Maximes* are viewed as a collection they seem to demonstrate almost endlessly that one debunking merely lays bare another notion to be reduced, that critical analysis can subvert any reality, even basic phenomena discovered deep within the self."[34] Lewis's idea of the fragmentation of La Rochefoucauld's maxims implies

---

[32] Barthes, "La Rochefoucauld," 84–85.
[33] Lewis, 186.
[34] Ibid., 108.

a deconstruction, or decentering of meaning.[35] That is, the maxim's richness corresponds not only with a concentration or reduction of words but also with wordplay such that no fixed locus of knowledge is discernible.[36]

One notes nonetheless that the epistemological breakdown in this work cannot be equated with the moralist's failure to benefit from the logic of classical discourse, particularly as it implies, to adopt Foucault's expression, the display (*étalement*) of elements.[37] La Rochefoucauld's claim for amour propre appears to put it beyond the reach of science—"Its transformations exceed those of metamorphoses, and its refinements those of chemistry" (Ses transformations passent celles des métamorphoses, et ses raffinements ceux de la chimie)—as well as beyond representation: "Its suppleness cannot be represented" (Ses souplesses ne se peuvent représenter). Yet in this maxim La Rochefoucauld does represent his subject at length, culminating with an intricate metaphor:

Here is the portrait of self-love, of which all of life is but one great and long agitation; the sea is its perceptible image, and self-love finds in the to and fro of its continual waves a faithful expression of the turbulent succession of its own thoughts and its eternal movements.

Voilà la peinture de l'amour-propre, dont toute la vie n'est qu'une grande et longue agitation; la mer en est une image sensible, et l'amour-

[35] Louise K. Horowitz also concludes: "The *Maximes* totally defy critical discourse as we know it; their fragmented structure is at variance with a continuous, organized flow of words" (*Love and Language: A Study of the Classical French Moralist Writers* [Columbus: Ohio State University Press, 1977], 29).

[36] There is an important difference here from the Cartesian protocol that takes a complex whole and divides it into its constituent parts. For here there is no working back to a primary intuition, no center that is secure. Amour propre forms the *Maximes*'s thematic core. And to the degree that it suggests, like Descartes's cogito, the self's representation of itself, amour propre constitutes the *Maximes*'s formal model for ordering together many of the fragments. As such, however, amour propre is polymorphous, and, from the point of view of the reader who seeks to know the depths of human existence, perverse. For it systematically resists the reader's attempts to achieve a synthesis, a full and unchanging knowledge of the subject.

[37] Foucault depicts the classical episteme as an order based on the infinite substitution of signs: "When the *Logique de Port-Royal* states that a sign can be inherent in what it designates or separate from it, it is demonstrating that the sign, in the Classical age, is charged no longer with the task of keeping the world close to itself and inherent in its own forms, but, on the contrary, with that of spreading it out [*étaler*], of juxtaposing it over an indefinitely open surface, and of taking up from that point the endless deployment of the substitutes in which we conceive of it" (61/75).

propre trouve dans le flux et le reflux de ses vagues continuelles une fidèle expression de la succession turbulente de ses pensées, et de ses éternels mouvements. (max. sup. 1)

Drawing a parallel between amour propre and the sea, the moralist establishes then subverts a logic for understanding: his text instills and denies a comparison. Similarity is projected as a function of movement and time, whereas dissimilarity relates to the imagistic and spatial capacity of mimetic representation. The metaphor legitimizes duration while dismissing the specific act of imitation as inadequate and incapable of producing certain knowledge. The result is a meaning that, although we are unable to perceive it directly, cannot be ignored. There is no evidence here of a paradigm that asserts the fixity of the observable world. Instead, we are confronted with a constant evolution of thoughts which, like the sea, suggest the irreversible process of time and metamorphosis as synonymous with the discovery of meaning. In other words, the belief that representation can produce no knowledge is denied by the act of representation, the flow of signs, which becomes the truth value of the text.

Thus, it would be inaccurate to claim that no knowledge is exposed by La Rochefoucauld's application of science. Barthes's "unreal" does not imply that the uncertainty produced through the collapse of the text's paradigms correlates with error, with a deficient model. Rather, the maxims establish identities without restricting meaning through the act of naming; this is the feint of La Rochefoucauld's representation. The subject born in this discourse grows at a pace that outstrips our ability to identify him. As in Molière's play, the categories constructed by the text do not suffice to protect the subject from reinventing itself before our eyes. Amour propre, like all other behavior reflected in the *Maximes*, does not therefore emerge from the moralist's discourse as an identifiable quality if by identifiable one means static. Amour propre does, however, represent the state of the subject affirmed and preserved in language. The maxim systematically overrides itself, casting off the subject just as it verges on being named. Yet, to borrow a concept from Bénichou, this subject is as "irrefutable as it is undemonstrable."[38]

Emerging from the maxims' carefully measured oppositions, how-

---

[38] Bénichou refers to the status La Rochefoucauld assigns to generosity: "By virtue of evidence that is as impossible to refute as it is to demonstrate, he condemns generosity to exist only as an idea" (7).

ever, are the mirrored signs of a world that looks outward for an Other knowledge, only to discover in this otherness the truth of its own self. "There are different kinds of curiosity," La Rochefoucauld observes: "that of [self-]interest, which causes us to desire to learn what can be useful to us; and that of pride, which comes from the desire to know what others do not know" (Il y a diverses sortes de curiosité: l'une d'intérêt, qui nous porte à désirer d'apprendre ce qui nous peut être utile, et l'autre d'orgueil, qui vient du désir de savoir ce que les autres ignorent [max. 173]). The moralist's neat classification of two kinds of intellectual activity belies the meaning that the maxim holds up to us. There is but one dominant passion/impulse: the desire to satisfy one's desire to use the Other (knowledge/person) to one's best advantage. The difference is all tautology, the same desire to know how to satisfy desire.

To survive in society one must learn to adapt, and it is this process that is reflected by La Rochefoucauld. The maxims react against the expansion of information that threatens to leave man behind, distancing his desire in a flow of meanings that substitute for it: "There is only one kind of love, but there are a thousand different copies of it" (Il n'y a que d'une sorte d'amour, mais il y en a mille différentes copies [max. 74]). Insisting on the principle of amour propre, the moralist affirms that each of the self's perceptible forms is capable of undergoing metamorphosis. But these diverse masks for the self acting in its own interest merely confirm the need to survive intact, to discover oneself in all that one is capable of representing. There is a real knowledge in this feint: "He who lives without madness is not as wise as he thinks" (Qui vit sans folie n'est pas si sage qu'il croit [max. 209]).

Among the lessons to be extracted from the *Maximes* is that if people were to act on the knowledge of amour propre, they would be incapable of engaging in relations, for to do so would be to acknowledge their partners' deception as well as their own. It is the fiction of generosity, the ability to engage oneself in service to some person or activity not directly beneficial to the self, that encourages and maintains relations between individuals. Knowledge in this context refers to the speech, pose, honesty—the appearances—that allow the *honnête homme* to secure his position within society. Indeed, what we frequently discover in La Rochefoucauld's text is that the feeling of efficacy produced when one agrees to play by society's rules is a knowledge unto itself.

Lewis observes that the *Maximes* do not enable us to extract logically one meaning from another in a continuous interpretative gesture:

> By virtue of its discontinuous form and its cognitive force, the work of La Rochefoucauld puts up strong resistance to a reductive reading, to a reordering of its components; it challenges us to read it as an ensemble of statements, all of which are valid simultaneously. What these statements, in their plurality, leave to be worked out is not a single synthetic or conclusive statement, but the context of their validity.[39]

In Lewis's formulation this context is part social—La Rochefoucauld attempts to study "the limits of human potential and to delineate the sphere of assessable action"—and part a function of language.[40] His tone betraying an attitude of "how to make the best of a bad situation," Lewis concludes that the moralist, in his meticulously devised wordplay, represents the maximum control that one can exercise over language. But this control, Lewis goes on to argue, is in turn qualified by the fact that language is the medium that identifies and thus restricts the subject.[41] The problem is that the subject is caught between the constraints of social reality, on the one hand, and, on the other, those of language, which surpasses the moralist's ability to assess and to guide the subject in history. This subject is to some degree always alienated, always at a distance from knowledge. Thus, Lewis concludes that any meaning that might develop in the maxims is no more than an indication of the potential "for a certain movement or opening within [these poles], for a margin of adjustment, for a strategic skewing of combinations."[42]

Lewis's negative emphasis may seem misplaced, if only because the alternative to reformulating one's position within language is a melancholic submission to its alienation, a certain death of the desire to know. Love, Doubrovsky observes in a style worthy of La Rochefoucauld, "can no more perceive itself loving than the eye can see itself seeing, except by an act of reflection, mirror or maxims."[43] Similarly, one cannot have a perspective on language, access to knowledge, since

---

[39] Lewis, 142.
[40] Ibid., 143.
[41] Ibid., 187.
[42] Ibid., 185.
[43] Doubrovsky, "Vingt propositions," 207.

one is always *in* language. Not even Descartes could hope to bridge this gap. What he does accomplish is the constitution of a new discourse within language. This scientific discourse empowers man to the degree that he frees himself from the concept of a preexistent knowledge. Science shifts the balance of power over to man as inventor, maker of signs. More than an inventory of signs, the philosopher's text offers an inventory of how he conceptualizes an order for these signs. In the split between the world of things and their representation, the text functions as a mirror that lets us see the philosopher as he views the world. With this perspective, moreover, Descartes contributes a new knowledge to the culture of his age. He does so without ever betraying our notion that his text is one of many that together constitute a founding cultural discourse out of which he can never step. The larger bounds of representation, which Lewis so judiciously analyzes, are perhaps more a part of the modern episteme than the classical order of things. For even the *Maximes*, which decry the pretensions of science, paradoxically exemplify the spirit of the new science in their constant testing and retesting of the validity of identities.

To account for the dynamic energy through which one identity is systematically reappropriated by another—that is, to account for the *Maximes*'s very fertile exploration of all that might be—we need to recontextualize an order within the broad limits of the context set in place by Lewis. In other words, La Rochefoucauld's work needs to be examined from his point of entry into language, which is the same origin assumed for Descartes and all other authors studied in this book. La Rochefoucauld posits science, or logical discourse, there where Lewis emphasizes the global functioning of language. And instead of the real sociohistory of the *honnête homme* whom the moralist contemplates as he writes, the text generates his own model of a faceless, nameless subject with whom he, the absent author, interacts by having this subject interact with science. We find, then, in place of the language in which all subjects are formed, the specific discourse—a subset of this language—modeled through the moralist's effort to flesh out an elaborate account of the *honnête homme*'s world. Likewise, there is no single, real person behind the text's multiple descriptions of amour propre but rather a generic being, a subject formed by and inscribed in this discourse.

The context (re)defined by these new parameters, which fit comfortably within the boundaries delineated by Lewis, is that of representation that denies the validity of resemblances and differences—the whole taxonomy that science would elaborate—precisely because these categories are static. If it is accurate to insist on the fragment as the essential component of La Rochefoucauld's representation, therefore, it is not a reference to the part of an unattainable whole. Rather, in a more positive light, "fragment" refers to the discontinuity of parts that flow within the text and continue to multiply there. These discrete parts are discernible as they are reformed, take on new shapes, reconstitute themselves in a representation that is, as a result, ever more complex in its structuring. As readers we do know more and more, even though the ultimate goal of a complete knowledge eludes us.

Behind the text that fixes identities only to reconceive them, there is evidence of the mind of the moralist very much intent on outpacing the reader who would know him well enough to imitate him. Like Descartes, and like Jupiter, La Rochefoucauld, moreover, knows how to "sugar-coat the pill" (*dorer la pilule*).[44] The unpleasantness of his message as it refers to the limits of truth, duly noted by Lewis, is more than compensated for by the successful performance through which the moralist makes his mark within the science that would classify him, a writer of maxims, as a nonplayer. Science, in the end, cannot exempt the fiction writer. For science, too, offers itself as a written text, a representation that is subject to the same constraints of language explored by La Rochefoucauld. In the sparring between those who defend the cause of reason and those who repudiate it, the final results are a victory for the one who can show the other's limits. And here, in its ability to elude the categories erected to shape knowledge, the subject masters best who masters last, offstage, producing nonetheless: gods, philosopher, and moralist.

[44] *Amphitryon* 3.10.1913.

Chapter Four

The Refracted Gaze:
Zaïde and *La Princesse de Clèves*

Chapter 3 showed how the feint, in a fundamental reconfiguration of the space of representation, subverts the boundaries established by the text to fix identities. Madame de Lafayette's novel *Zaïde* takes up this question once again, but only, it would appear, to expose and expel the feint from the scene of representation once and for all. All undifferentiated and ambiguous elements having been filtered out, representation in its most overt formulation is shown here to model a new, concentrated knowledge. One notion that is not filtered out, however, is that appearances deceive—even those that pertain to representation's modeling of its own inner workings.

Zaïde marks an important departure from the works studied in the previous chapter. The model ordering Lafayette's text not only is deficient in the sense of inadequate to the task of classifying all that occurs but also is itself a fiction. We have seen that the model embedded in La Rochefoucauld's maxims is insufficient because the meanings multiplied by the text ultimately exceed the capacity of its taxonomy to name them. That is, the taxonomy proposed by La Rochefoucauld coheres as far as it goes, but it cannot go nearly far enough to keep pace with the meanings that the text generates. In Lafayette's novel the problem is even more insidious, for the model of representation is representation itself. This model is placed *en abîme*, yet the paradoxical effect of such mirrorings is a conflation and not an affirmation of the mirrored content. Although the model ordering *Zaïde* does not fail to account for the many disparate events of the narrated history, it can be seen to occult the truth that it uncovers.

The novel's feint corresponds not with a meaning situated outside the model so much as with the fallacy of the model that represents knowledge by concealing what it knows, by suppressing what it has identified.

Zaïde once again presents the self as Other. This time, however, the Other is recuperated by the self; the model functions to deny the Other's difference and to name it the Same. Nevertheless, as I shall explore in this chapter, the novel exposes the reader to the alterity that lies beneath the surface of representation. *La Princesse de Clèves* takes this conundrum one step further, denying the capacity of representation to provide an order of things. That is, the novel obscures the principle of mimesis as a device for knowing the real. Yet this apparent collapse of the representational model does not imply a failure to structure meaning. What is prepared in Lafayette's earlier novel and then celebrated in her later one is precisely how the subversion of mimetic relations is responsible for opening up the text to new possibilities for signification. Lafayette's grid of knowledge in *La Princesse de Clèves* is therefore best appreciated not through a determination of similarities and differences, although such relations can be delineated. Rather, her text can be said to offer a more challenging experiment with method to the extent that it endeavors to posit an original for which no model exists.

Zaïde: The Other Self's Other Side

With the following passage from *Zaïde,* Lafayette brings her reader into the world of the Oriental women's baths,[1] an exclusive space reserved for the pleasures of the privileged, the opulent, the magnificent:

> The baths are magnificent palaces; the women go there three or four times a week; they take pleasure in showing off their magnificence by having an infinite number of slaves walk before and after them, carrying all the things that they need. Entry to these houses is forbidden to men on penalty of death; and there is no power that could save them if they were to be found inside.

[1] In my discussion of *Zaïde* I use the designations Oriental, Moorish, Islamic, and Arab interchangeably to refer to characters from the Near East.

Les bains sont des palais magnifiques; les femmes y vont trois ou quatre
fois la semaine; elles prennent plaisir à faire paraître leur magnificence,
en faisant marcher devant et après elles un nombre infini d'esclaves qui
portent toutes les choses qui leur sont nécessaires. L'entrée de ces mai-
sons est défendue aux hommes sur peine de la vie, et il n'y a point de
puissance qui pût les sauver, s'ils y étaient trouvés.[2]

The palaces described here represent a world of indulgences and se-
crets, that of the unique trust created when the normally veiled body
exposes itself completely to others similarly exposed. Prince Alamir,
rival to the novel's Spanish hero, is described as he penetrates this
space. The reader's gaze follows him as he violates the law separating
the sexes; it registers the movement through which he transgresses
the barriers protecting the women. During the night the Islamic
prince steals into the room that will be occupied the following day by
the woman whose charms now occupy his thoughts, the object of his
next seduction. Yet this seduction of bodies and of space is likewise
one of cultural difference. For Lafayette's reader is carried by Alamir
away from Western customs and into different mores, different excesses. And the breach of law committed by this prince, a violation of
mysteries and of sanctions, suggests in its mirroring of the reader's
own perverse pleasure a radical impingement on the privilege that
the novel accords to the Other. My reading of the novel locates the
text's model in the Orient as it doubles and recontexualizes the West.

Lafayette cultivates, or flatters the intentions of, a reader who is the
Islamic prince's witness and, paradoxically, his collaborator. Like Alamir, the reader crosses over and takes for himself or herself that which
is reserved for the Other: the Oriental's woman is the European's
Orient. Just as Alamir embarks on another conquest (eventually pur-
suing not Zoromade, as he intends, but Elsibery, who, while her
mother bathes, by chance enters the room where he is hidden), so
Lafayette's reader is poised to assimilate the entire scene of exotic
delights into French experience. That is, her public commits a similar
violation of difference by incorporating the Orient into its own grid
of knowledge, its own model for knowing the world.

Lafayette's depiction of the Orient, however, provides no real trans-
port, no escape route to the exotic. Instead, Lafayette posits the Ori-

---

[2] Marie-Madeleine Pioche de La Vergne, Comtesse de Lafayette, *Zaïde*, in *Romans et
nouvelles*, ed. Alain Niderst (Paris: Bordas, 1990), 191. All subsequent references to *Zaïde*
are cited in the text.

ent as the mediating agent through which the hero, Consalve, like her own contemporary reader, engages in an act of self-discovery that is a dramatic and potentially violent history of reappropriation. It is not sufficient to say that the knowledge gained here is that of the resemblance between self and Other, that of the subject who discovers his own identity in the image of his rival. What my reading intends to uncover is how the final knowledge modeled by Lafayette's text is the process through which this mirroring of self and Other ultimately collapses the identities it sets in place.

In recent years the notion of the Orient as a distant and enticing "elsewhere" has been challenged. Critics, notably Edward Said, have argued that Orientalism is a Western invention. The fictional Orient conceived by the West is informed by the West's own values and prejudices. It differs dramatically from the actual Orient, in which Orientals are subjects and not simply the objects of discourse; in the real Orient Orientals do not play Other to the West's Same. "At most," Said observes with regard to prior attempts to represent the Near East, "the 'real' Orient provoked a writer to his vision; it very rarely guided it."[3] Separate from and opposed to the Occident, therefore, is not the idea of the Orient produced by Orientals themselves but the Occidental Orient, the Other perceived through the codes of the West.

By this logic we understand that the contemporary reader of *Zaïde* was likely to respond to parallels between France under Louis XIV and the medieval Spain of the novel. Spain in the year 850 or 900, the period when the Christians regained territory from the Moors, effectively mirrors the upheavals of the Fronde years as well as the revival of the crusading zeal during the latter half of the seventeenth century. Moreover, if we consider just the sentence with which *Zaïde* draws to a close—"Afterwards the only thoughts were of the wedding preparations, which were made with all the gallantry of the Moors and all the decorum of Spain" (On ne songea ensuite qu'aux préparatifs des noces, qui se firent avec toute la galanterie des Maures et toute la politesse d'Espagne [247–48])—we see that the novel's depiction of the Orient, like its depiction of the court of Castille, is grounded in a spectacular world of celebration which covers, or cloaks in rich images, a political intrigue all too familiar to Lafayette's contemporaries. Gallantry (*galanterie*) is, of course, the word that the novelist would adopt to describe the spurious engagements of the court

[3] Edward W. Said, *Orientalism* (New York: Vintage, 1979), 22. Critics have disputed some of Said's claims. See above, Chapter 2, note 29.

of Henri II in *La Princesse de Clèves*. Image, however, is the operative term. The French court represented in these novels mirrors the court of Louis XIV, where, as Louis Marin has analyzed, power correlates with the monarch who "is absolute only in the official portrait that his subjects draw of him."[4] Marin insists that power is centered on the king's persona, as distinct from his person, the man of flesh and blood:

> What, then, is a king? He is a king's portrait, and that alone makes him king, and besides that he is also a man. To which it is appropriate to add that the "portrait effect," the effect of representation, *makes the king*, in the sense that everyone believes that the king and the man are one, or that the king's portrait is only the king's image. No one knows that, on the contrary, the king is only his image, and that behind or beyond the portrait there is no king, but a man. No one knows this secret, and the king less than everyone else perhaps.[5]

Elaborating the specular nature of courtly power rooted in representation, Marin defines the alienation of the subject who knows himself only as Other. Thus, if it is true, as Said makes clear, that the European cannot know the Oriental, it is likewise true that the European cannot know himself. *Zaïde* can be said to take shape in the epistemological gap, the unknowing, which is exposed when we pair Marin's theory with Said's. For the novel explores precisely how, in fabricating an Orient that replicates the West, Europe fails to fix its own self-knowledge.

As John Lyons has demonstrated, the alienation of the subject is dramatically represented in *Zaïde* by a formal portrait of the Spanish hero in Oriental dress, an image that negates as it resembles.[6] But Lafayette's depiction of the Orient actually implies for her contemporaries a dual feint: that of the false Other who is (really) the self, and that of the false integration produced when this Other is (not

---

[4] Louis Marin, *Portrait of the King*, trans. Martha Houle (Minneapolis: University of Minnesota Press, 1988), 237 (*Le portrait du roi* [Paris: Minuit, 1981], 290). In all subsequent references, the first page number refers to the translation; the second refers to *Portrait du roi*.

[5] Marin, *Portrait*, 218/267.

[6] John D. Lyons, "Speaking in Pictures, Speaking of Pictures: Problems of Representation in the Seventeenth Century," in *Mimesis: From Mirror to Method, Augustine to Descartes*, ed. John D. Lyons and Stephen G. Nichols, Jr. (Hanover, N.H.: University Press of New England, 1982), 166–87.

really) suppressed. Though seeming to hold up a mirror to the Orient, *Zaïde* reflects back to the French an idealized image of French society's own *doxa*; the end of the novel in particular reflects the values of love, marriage, and religion that Lafayette's contemporaries maintained against the deficiencies of lived experience. We must therefore first consider how the novel organizes events into a history that defends the French position. To understand fully the possibilities for knowledge modeled by the text, however, we must look beneath the text's surface harmony and the assimilation of the Orient into the European perspective. Much of the present study is dedicated to examining the text's reciprocal mirroring: the Orient as both reflecting and reflected in the eyes of the Occident.

There is no equivalent here to Bérénice, no subject who assigns a positive value to difference by fixing from the outside—from the Orient—the limits of a knowledge system based on resemblances. Unlike Racine's play, *Zaïde* situates a unique subject on both the near (seeing) and the far (seen) side of representation. Because the European gaze and that of the Oriental are in important respects made to be identical, the space of representation in Lafayette's novel remains undifferentiated, resistant to the eye/I that seeks to affirm identities. That is, by locating the same image both in Europe and in the Orient, the novel in effect obstructs the viewer's (the Spanish hero's and the reader's) gaze; it denies the locus of power that depends on the subject's clear and uninterrupted perspective of the object. The lost privilege of the viewing subject, the self that sees and writes the world in an attempt to control it, can once again be explained by the movement from the imaginary, or pictorial, to the symbolic order of language. As in *Bérénice* this movement is all the more significant because it remains incomplete, leaving both the characters and the reader in the "wound" of the text, the space of mourning and alienation that is the mirror image. Yet here it is the comedic end, and not the tragic resolution, that signifies how representation empowers the subject at the cost of knowing that his power is a fiction, an identity that can be collapsed and reconstrued as the Other it would deny.

In *Zaïde* Lafayette presents two fathers, two falls from grace. The one, a Spanish count, has been exiled by the king as a consequence of a bungled military exploit. The other, a prominent Moorish prince, has abandoned his wife and child and, not insignificantly, his adoptive Christianity to return to his native Islam. In the end, however, the enemy fathers are united as fathers-in-law by the baroque mirrorings of a narrative that brings the bride and groom to marriage through

a string of resemblances connected to an Oriental portrait. The Spanish father had this handsome portrait made "by an excellent painter
who had traveled all over the world and to whom African dress had
appeared so beautiful that he used it in all of his portraits" (par un
excellent peintre qui avait voyagé par tout le monde et à qui les ha-
billements d'Afrique avaient paru si beaux, qu'il les donnait à tous ses
portraits [244]). Certainly the reader is intended to discover a final
redemption for these fathers in the knowledge, provided in the novel's last pages, that the Oriental prince whom the Moorish father
thought would be an appropriate husband for his daughter is none
other than the Spanish father's son, who is figured in the portrait
dressed as an Oriental. Throughout the novel Lafayette has exposed
her reader to the Oriental difference. In the end, however, this difference conveniently slips away.

All of the major events of the novel, which Lafayette unequivocally
labels a "Spanish story" (*histoire espagnole*), confirm this Euro-
centeredness. Consalve, the Spanish hero, falls hopelessly in love with
Zaïde, whose stunning beauty reflects her exotic origins. Although she
appears to be Oriental, her true identity is mixed. She speaks no Spanish when Consalve first encounters her; nor does she speak Arabic, a
language in which he is also fluent. It is important, given the ending,
to note that the reader's initial encounter with the novel's principal
female character is with a supposedly Moorish woman near death
from a shipwreck, then with a Moorish woman already somewhat de-
Orientalized by the information that she speaks no Arabic, and again
by the knowledge that she speaks Greek, the language that grounds
the Western tradition. The reader's perspective is thus telescoped
here in much the same way as in the scene of Alamir's penetration
of the women's baths. The reader/voyeur's gaze is similarly titillated
by the act of appropriation, here experienced as the compression of
the image of the Other into a less foreboding, less remote vision. The
reader eventually learns that Zaïde is in fact only half Islamic. Her
father, Zuléma, a descendant of the Caliph Osman, married the Christian daughter of a Cypriote prince (172). The eventual marriage of
Consalve and Zaïde is, more literally than anachronistically, ordered
by what we now, after Lacan, term the subject's accession to language.
Each lover learns the other's language as a prelude to their eventual
union. Moreover, as Lyons has observed in connection with the love
triangles that pattern the action, it is significant that there is no real
rival for the hero—no real Other. Rather, in a perfect consummation
of the self-reflexive model through which the text narrates and re-

narrates stories from different points of view, Consalve discovers a rival in himself.[7] Although Alamir, the Islamic rival, loves Zaïde, she has been promised to the man in the portrait, believed to be the Prince de Fez. The real mediator is thus not the Oriental (who shares a complex idty as Alamir, the Prince de Fez believed to be a Moor, and the European-linked Prince de Fez discovered to be Consalve's first cousin)[8] but the Orient, the medium through which the hero re-Orients, or redirects, his knowledge away from the Other and toward himself.

The plenitude of the story's resolution is ensured by the Islamic father's public reconversion to Christianity. Zuléma explicitly renounces his earlier incrimination against the Christians, made after his marriage and initial conversion, when he rediscovered Africa's "corruption": "I returned to Africa; the pleasures and corrupt ways engaged me in my religion more than ever before, and gave me a new aversion to the Christians" (Je m'en retournai en Afrique; les délices et la corruption des moeurs me rengagèrent plus que jamais dans ma religion, et me donnèrent une nouvelle aversion pour les chrétiens [245]). The fallen are saved. The Orientals who figure among the novel's principal characters have all either died or converted to Christianity. Zaïde is given in marriage as a Christian to the man behind the portrait, whose Islamic identity has been discovered to be mere ornamentation. Or so it seems.

The full European vision that draws the action to a close confirms that to read *Zaïde* is not to leave the known for the chiaroscuro of a mysterious foreign land. The novel inscribes this Other within the purview of the European experience so as to justify the political and religious integrity of this model. Entering the novel, Lafayette's readers step far enough into a romanticized contemplation of the real world beyond France's shores to conquer it and make it their own. The voyage, however, is not without costs. For ultimately the reader who discovers a final harmony in the marriage of the Spanish hero announced in the novel's last page remains precariously tied to a portrait, to a strange (foreign) image of the Spanish hero in the enemy's clothes. Tantalizing the reader with realistic depictions of an

---

[7] John D. Lyons, "The Dead Center: Desire and Mediation in Lafayette's *Zayde*," *Esprit Créateur* (Summer 1983): 58–69; see also his *Exemplum: The Rhetoric of Example in Early Modern France and Italy* (Princeton: Princeton University Press, 1989), 200–217.

[8] The Prince de Fez (thought by Zaïde's father to be depicted in the portrait) is the son of Consalve's aunt, his father's sister (247).

exotic land, then filtering this foreignness into the familiar French perspective, and finally contorting even this perspective so that what is seen is always the subject framed in representation—the painted subject, his image captured in the mirror that deceptively exposes what he would repress—Lafayette's representation denies the authority of the subject to know himself and his world independently of the Other that is both his enemy and his (truth) maker.

In many obvious ways the Spanish encounter with the Moors and the descriptions of Islamic rituals such as the baths, marriage, and royal ceremonies do bring the French reader out of European culture and into the obscurity of an exotic land, stretching the limits of knowledge. Yet what is striking about Lafayette's novel is that the gesture outward is consistently equated with the movement inward through which the hero Consalve penetrates the truth about his own identity. This process, moreover, is perfectly synchronized with the reader's knowledge, for the characters and the reader share the same perspective. Thus, the voyage that removes Consalve from Castille and carries him (directly, through personal experience, and vicariously, through internal narratives) across the Levant and then back into the protective bosom of the Spanish court reproduces the reader's own itinerary.[9] Lafayette's audience travels from the court of Versailles via the novel's cultural geography. The reader, however, returns to the court enriched less by a knowledge of the Oriental world, whose appearance and outward characteristics are displayed in the text, than by the authority of the model of resemblances which brings this world back into the French orbit and thereby consolidates France's own centrist position.

It must be acknowledged, however, that the political process which breaks down and assimilates the other culture is a violent one. The abuses and biases of such repression are not effaced by the many passages in which the Oriental beauty is held in genuine admiration. Islam and the treasures of the Orient are necessary to European power; Europe conceives of these objects only to identify itself, to fix its own prestige. There is perhaps no greater exploitation than that of conjuring, or setting in place, an Other in order to conquer it.

One detail in particular—that of the Oriental clothing worn by

---

[9] Consalve has fled the Spanish court after being deceived by his lover in collusion with his friends. The circularity of the novel is evident in the fact that, during his absence, one of these friends, Don Garcie, honors Consalve's family name by marrying his sister, making her queen of Spain.

Consalve in the portrait—undercuts by its very supplementarity the authority that it assigns through its opulence. The supplement is necessary to identify the subject. In this privileging of the nonessential, this dependence on extraneous ornamentation, Lafayette signals the collapse of the model through which the subject in representation and the reader come to know and to be invested (*investire:* to clothe, surround) with power. In her study of the detail, Naomi Schor has analyzed the traditional associations of ornamentalism with effeminacy and decadence.[10] It would be extreme in Lafayette's case to posit a link between a woman's dress and the Oriental clothing worn by Consalve in the portrait. Other associations, however, link the Orient more explicitly with effeminacy. In the scenes following his clandestine entry into the women's baths, Prince Alamir dons feminine attire to gain access to his lover, thereby risking his authority as a prince to satisfy his passion. I have suggested that the European reader's captivation with the Orient mimics the Oriental prince's seductions of his various women. What underlies these transgressions is the disempowerment implied by the concepts of effeminacy and decadence. By their negativity these terms explain the Spanish hero's disaffection. They further point to the problem masked by the novel's very European (and hence monarchical, patriarchal) resolution. So long as it depends on the ornamental, on the aura of images, European society's mastery of the world is less than certain. Europe stakes its claim to power on appearances that hide the insidious truth of its alienation in the world it would govern.

The cultivation of the Other as an image for the self is illustrated in Consalve's military encounters with the enemy. There occurs a certain courting of the Orientals even in battle, an active promotion, as it were, of the Other, in order to elevate the Spanish hero's own position. Passages in the novel that show the Spanish hero's respect and generosity toward his enemy reflect the same genuine admiration for the Oriental that the painter of the portrait expressed in representing the beauty of Oriental clothing. Yet in both instances the status of the Other is clearly that of an object to be appropriated by the European master, be he artist or military general. In a revealing segment Consalve chastises his own men for failing to respect the dignity of the enemy leader:

---

[10] Naomi Schor, *Reading in Detail: Aesthetics and the Feminine* (New York: Methuen, 1987).

As he was going through the city in order to stave off disorder, he saw
a man who was defending himself alone and with admirable valor against
several others and who, in withdrawing, was trying to reach a castle that
had not yet been taken over. Those who were attacking this man were
pressing him so strongly that they would have pierced him with many
blows had Consalve not thrown himself in the middle of them and com-
manded them to withdraw. He made them see the shame of what they
were about to do; they apologized, telling him that the man they were
attacking was Prince Zuléma, who had just killed an infinite number of
their men and who wanted to enter the castle. This name was too famous
on account of this prince's greatness and his authority in the Moors'
army for Consalve not to recognize it. He went toward the prince, and
this valiant man, seeing that he could no longer defend himself, handed
over his sword with such nobility and courage that Consalve knew that
he deserved the great reputation that he had attained. Consalve gave
him over to the officers who were following him, and went toward the
castle in order to call upon those inside to give themselves up. He promised to spare the lives of those who were inside.

Comme il allait lui-même par la ville pour prévenir le désordre, il vit un
homme qui se défendait seul contre plusieurs autres avec une valeur
admirable et qui, en se retirant, tâchait de gagner un château qui ne
s'était pas encore rendu. Ceux qui attaquaient cet homme, le pressaient
si vivement qu'ils l'allaient percer de plusieurs coups, si Consalve ne se
fût jeté au milieu d'eux, et ne leur eût commandé de se retirer. Il leur
fit honte de l'action qu'ils voulaient faire, ils s'en excusèrent en lui disant
que celui qu'ils attaquaient était le prince Zuléma, qui venait de tuer un
nombre infini des leurs et qui voulait se jeter dans le château. Ce nom
était trop célèbre par la grandeur de ce prince et par le commandement
général qu'il avait dans les armées des Maures, pour n'être pas connu
de Consalve. Il s'avança vers lui, et ce vaillant homme, voyant bien qu'il
ne pouvait plus se défendre, rendit son épée avec un air si noble et si
hardi que Consalve ne douta point qu'il ne fût digne de la grande ré-
putation qu'il avait acquise. Il le donna en garde à des officiers qui le
suivaient et marcha vers ce château pour le sommer de se rendre. Il
promit la vie à ceux qui étaient dedans. (149–50)

One might well argue that generosity such as Consalve's is all too
easily exhibited since his victory has been assured. Despite earlier references to the barbarism of the Moors, however, this passage refuses
to condone the "eye for an eye" retribution sought by the Spanish

officers. True justice, it would appear, depends not on the codes of battle as they imply decency and respect for law (for this code has been flouted by the Moors), but on a higher sense of chivalry that connects, whatever side one defends, to honor and glory. Dignifying the commitment of all valiant soldiers, Consalve acts even as he defeats the enemy to recognize his accomplishments. Consalve's honor is increased not only by the measure of his generosity but also by the value of his foreign "prey." Thus, if the Spanish hero acts in deference to the Oriental, the real tension of the scene depends on a denial of difference. By honoring the enemy's same identity as hero, Consalve ultimately reappropriates for himself what (love, identity) was lost to him. For this enemy is Zuléma, and Consalve's move to defend him eventually leads to Zaïde, who has taken refuge with the other women in the castle to which the soldiers refer.

We must ask ourselves, however, whether the cultivation of the image is complete, that is, whether the glorification of the Other reflects back to the hero an image of himself sufficiently grand, sufficiently empowered, to satisfy him. To do so, I have suggested, the image must be *seen*, but must not be *seen seeing*. The Oriental cannot mirror back to the European an image of his disunity as this term implies either his disembodiment from or his dependence on the image. The fiction has to be sustained as a fiction; the place of the Other's image in history must be suppressed, effaced by the image that it produces in the mind of the subject who views it. There can be no excess, no meaning that emerges from the frame of representation. For any such infidelity with the viewing subject, any imperfect resemblance, serves to remind him that he is only the image he has created for himself. There can, then, be no difference that affirms to the subject that he is other than this Other (image) in which he sees his desire written and satisfied.

Yet Lafayette's history of the Spaniards' encounter with the Moors, predicated as it is on the Oriental image, brings the Europeans beyond the limits they have set for themselves. It takes them outside the model of the perfect self-portrait which they authorize—the image of fidelity to God and to woman—and into the very real (lived) excesses of the Orient which they would suppress. It is significant in this respect that the tensions that mark the history of Consalve and Zaïde are expressed not in terms of beliefs about respective divinities but in terms of the specific customs and practices separating the two cultures. Zuléma's reference to Christianity as the "true religion" (*véritable religion* [247]) expresses the prejudice of the French public,

whose pleasure in reading the novel correlates with having the superiority of its own beliefs confirmed.[11] Nevertheless, discussions of the
Christian God and Muhammad are conspicuously absent. Indeed, the
polemic is not merely religious but sexual; it pertains to the infidelities
of men before a hidden, if not absent, God. The infidel, of course, is
so named by the Europeans because he is unfaithful to the Christian
deity. But the term is also appropriate because the Oriental is a big-
amist, and, by Christian standards, unfaithful to women. The contrast
could not be more striking: the Christians have recourse to a pro-
scriptive law that condemns relations with more than one woman,
while the Moors have laws that instead prescribe such relations. The
Spaniards, however, move in and out of the space they order for themselves. No slouches in the area of infidelities, they also substitute one
woman for the other. But they do so in every instance with the added
psychological stress of deceit, since in their world no law accords a
man more than one woman.[12] Significantly, Consalve's initial decision
to retire from the court and to enter a life of anonymous solitude is
precipitated by an unhappy love affair that results from the multiple
infidelities of his former friends at court. The problems of the hero's
disreputable father, Nugnez Fernando, like the dauphin's tumultuous
relations with his own father, King Léon (conflicts so intense as to
result in Don Garcie's accession to power before his father's death),
point to the breakdown of the law ordering the Spanish court. Lafayette's representation of the Oriental thus merely confirms an unwel-
come truth about the European; it mirrors the disintegration of his
own social fabric and thus undercuts his authority to know himself as
the world's moral and political arbiter.

The Orient, moreover, stands out as visual representation—local
color—in a story constructed primarily through lengthy internal narratives. As the following discussion reveals, the visual quality ascribed
to the Orient functions finally as a lure that collapses the resemblances woven together by the narrative for the benefit of a European

[11] Following the return of Zuléma to Africa, a visit sufficiently protracted to be considered an act of desertion by Zaïde's mother, Zaïde had been raised to mistrust all
Moors. After the approach of a young Moorish prince, her friend Félime remarks: "My
astonishment and that of Zaïde were extreme; we were not accustomed to being ap-
proached so freely, and especially by Arabs, for whom we had been taught to have a
great aversion" (Mon étonnement et celui de Zaïde étaient extrêmes, nous n'étions pas
accoutumées à nous voir aborder avec tant de liberté, et surtout par les Arabes, pour
lesquels on nous avait inspiré une grande aversion [174]).

[12] In many instances the Orientals also deceive, but in other circumstances they,
unlike the Spanish, are able to possess several women without being unfaithful.

audience. The story of one man's desire to possess the infidel, though seeming to correct by its obsessive dedication to a unique love the various transgressions that occurred in Castille, ultimately serves as an allegory for the entire scene of representation and the failure of imitation to order knowledge. *Infidel* (unfaithful) is a term that is overdetermined by Lafayette's history, for it comes to signify not simply religious or sexual deviance but the very aesthetic realized by the text itself.

A portrait that offers a poor or unusual likeness, a narrative that fails to give the truth, and a drama that transforms the world are all unfaithful representations. They fail similarly to imitate the real. The history of such infidelities forms part of the novel's own praxis, the modeling process through which the novel orders knowledge. If the infidelities of the novel's painting, intercalated stories, and theatrical design are more difficult to describe, it is because the standard for their consistency is established and then subverted by the text. Such representational infidelities are perhaps more insidious than sexual and political transgressions because no law, except the law of nature as it is shown throughout the novel to triumph over reason, is invoked to explain them. Chance defeats man's ability to structure a world in which resemblances order past, present, and future into a coherent whole.[13] And with this defeat must be measured the effects of all that Lafayette does to thwart the integrity of the mimetic process—the effects of all that her characters risk in an effort to know and to control their world.

The breakdown of the representational model is clearly manifest in the scene of the painting which mediates the early stages of Consalve's relationship to Zaïde. A shipwreck brings her to the coastal town where he has taken refuge under the assumed name of Théodoric. Later Consalve happens to see a painter at work on a seascape of a storm and shipwreck for Alphonse, the hero's friend and protector in exile. Through Consalve's intervention this painted scene will allow the lovers to communicate in the absence of a common language. The hero asks the painter to incorporate three figures into his work: a young woman in tears bending over a male corpse as another male figure kneels in an effort to "take her away from this dead man" (l'ôter d'auprès de ce mort [98]). It is immediately clear to Zaïde, as it is to the reader, that Consalve has had himself incorporated into

---

[13] For more on the characters' efforts to exert control over their lives, see Lyons, "Dead Center."

the painting as the observer figure. She corrects his re-presentation of the painter's original representation by rubbing out the picture of the dead man. Consalve's initial joy at thinking that the lover whom Zaïde believes he resembles is dead—that is, his joy at the death of his rival—gives way to despair when he reinterprets this sign as an indication that there is a lover, and that the lover is not dead. John Lyons offers a detailed analysis of how this painting models the portrait of the Oriental Consalve to the extent that each indicates the failure of resemblances to name the truth.[14] I will not rehearse the subtleties of Lyons's argument here. Rather, I want to focus briefly on one point that spins off from his.

Lyons has convincingly argued that the image is collapsed in this scene of representation. To persuade Zaïde of his message, Consalve finally resorts to labeling the figures that represent them in the painting. He writes her name above her image and inscribes his own name above the picture of the kneeling man. Lyons indicates that the "figures resemble the two protagonists but do not 'represent' them until the words are inserted into the image."[15] It is worth noting, however, that in the subsequent interpretation of this scene given by Félime, the friend of Zaïde who was rescued in the same shipwreck, there occurs an important elision:

> Then he made her understand, through use of the painting in which he had had painted a beautiful woman who was crying over a dead man, that he was convinced that her severity toward him was the result of her attachment for this man whom she had lost. It caused Zaïde considerable pain to have Théodoric think that she loved another; she hardly doubted his love any longer, and she loved him with a tenderness that she no longer sought to overcome.

> Ensuite il lui fit entendre, par le moyen d'un tableau où il avait fait représenter une belle personne qui pleurait un homme mort, qu'il était persuadé que les rigueurs qu'elle avait pour lui, venaient de l'attachement qu'elle avait pour cet homme qu'elle regrettait. Ce fut une douleur sensible à Zaïde de voir que Théodoric croyait qu'elle en aimât un autre, elle ne doutait quasi plus de son amour, et elle l'aimait avec une tendresse qu'elle n'essayait plus de surmonter. (222-23)

[14] Lyons, "Speaking," 170–75.
[15] Ibid., 175.

Félime's account is striking in that its complementarity—the other view that it provides of the same scene—effectively negates the eventual conclusion drawn by Consalve. Striking, too, is the fact that Félime's supplementary interpretation fails to mention the most basic fact of the history. Zaïde at this time was mourning not her lover but her mother, who died in the shipwreck. If, then, we recognize the inability of the painting to arrive at truth through resemblances, we must accord some of this same inability to the narrative about the painting. Like the names sketched above the figures, the narrative that fills in the account of this scene eclipses the actual history, for it never specifies the truth of Zaïde's emotions during this moment of mourning.

Where the pictorial representations and the language ordered by the character both prove deficient, the theater of the text fills in.[16] For we must distinguish between the diegesis, which successfully integrates the various parts of the characters' histories into a unified whole, and the internal narratives, recited by the characters like so many lengthy dramatic roles, which offer only limited views, particular perspectives of the events that they have lived. Where Lafayette succeeds, therefore, her characters fail, and her reader inevitably falters. The characters cannot extract from the internal representations the truth about themselves.[17] Instead, their history serves to develop the unfaithful (*infidèle*), or nonmimetic, elements as represented in both the painting and Félime's description of it by the masking (and I use this term advisedly) of the mother's story. Indeed, it is through the duplicity of disguise that the two cultures, West and East, are best understood. On the novel's stage, in the world of disguises created by Lafayette through a series of accidental meetings and improbable coincidences, the European confronts the Oriental in a dubious battle for self-dominion. The latter amounts to a curious appropriation of the shipwreck scene—the shipwreck perceived as the representation of representation, the topos for modeling knowledge.

[16] Lafayette's novels have been perceived in terms of their theatricality since their publication. See J.-B. de Valincour, *Lettres à Mme la Marquise . . . sur le sujet de "La Princesse de Clèves,"* ed. Jacques Chupeau et al. (Tours: Université François Rabelais, 1972); Lyons, "Dead Center"; and Mitchell Greenberg, *Subjectivity and Subjugation in Seventeenth-Century Drama and Prose: The Family Romance of French Classicism* (Cambridge: Cambridge University Press, 1992), chap. 7.

[17] Lyons makes this point with regard to *La Princesse de Clèves* (*Exemplum*, 221). I reexamine his position later in this chapter.

Consider the following passage from Pascal's *Trois discours*, from which Louis Marin, in the chapter of *Le portrait du roi* previously cited, takes his title, "L'usurpateur légitime ou le naufragé roi" ("The legitimate usurper or the shipwrecked king"):

> To enter into a true understanding of your condition, consider it in this image. A man is thrown by the storm onto an unknown island, whose inhabitants were at pains to find their king, who had been lost; and, bearing a strong resemblance in body and face to this king, he is taken for him and recognized as such by the entire population. At first he did not know what role to assume; but he finally resolved to yield to his good fortune. He received all the respects offered to him, and allowed himself to be treated as king.

> Pour entrer dans la véritable connaissance de votre condition, considérez-la dans cette image. Un homme est jeté par la tempête dans une île inconnue, dont les habitants étaient en peine de trouver leur roi qui s'était perdu; et ayant beaucoup de ressemblance de corps et de visage avec ce roi, il est pris pour lui et reconnu en cette qualité par tout ce peuple. D'abord il ne savait quel parti prendre; mais il se résolut enfin de se prêter à sa bonne fortune. Il reçut tous les respects qu'on lui voulut rendre et se laissa traiter de roi.[18]

The secret of this scene is, of course, that the man taken to be king, and who comes to know himself as king, is really someone other: "The secret of the absolute monarch, . . . the secret of the all-powerful king, is that he is not so."[19] In Lafayette's novel we have two other versions of this same tale, two different stories of self-empowerment which are nevertheless oddly similar permutations of a unique model for ordering knowledge.

Alamir's transvestism and other elaborate attempts to conceal his identity, and thereby ensure that he is loved for himself and not for his elevated social position, are collapsed by the novel, which has him fall in love with Zaïde, the one woman who causes him to see the unworthiness of his infidelities. The array of costumes thus represents accurately the truth of his inconstancies in love, and suggests that, as with Consalve but for different reasons, his rival has always been him-

---

[18] Blaise Pascal, *Opuscules et lettres*, ed. Louis Lafuma (Paris: Aubier-Montaigne, 1955), 165; quoted in Marin, *Portrait*, 218/267 (trans. modified).

[19] Marin, *Portrait*, 237/289.

self.[20] Alamir is, then, the prince who does not want to be prince, the inverse of the king in Pascal's discourse. Like this king, however, he shares until his death the same fiction, "that of the impossibility of forgetting that he is not what he is."[21]

The Spanish hero's narrative is likewise punctuated with disguises. Concealing his true identity when he leaves the Spanish court, Consalve eventually comes to recognize himself dressed as an Oriental prince. He knows that Zaïde is to marry the man figured in the portrait, the Oriental whom he resembles. But like the "dead lover" that Consalve earlier had the artist insert in the painting, the status of the Other, specified as "African," here resists rather than imparts the desired knowledge. For the Oriental classification does not preclude the painted image from being Consalve's own. The hero's identity is deformed, contorted as it imitates; he comes to resemble the image of himself as Other. Lyons characterizes Consalve as an "ironic anti-Narcissus, compelled to seek the person who resembles him, compelled to project his likeness onto canvas, but at the same time repelled by that 'other self,' whom he would not embrace but destroy."[22] The truth gained in the novel's last pages with the confirmation of Consalve's identity merely affirms, moreover, a certain exteriority, or arbitrariness of meaning, that never meshes completely with his need to ensure not only his desire but also his efforts to reason this desire. We see this need played out repeatedly in his struggles to uncover the cause of Zaïde's displeasure by working logically back from its effects. His attempts to represent the world according to logical principles—not only cause and effect but also the coincidence of appearances and things—all fail.

---

[20] Lyons, "Dead Center," 61.

[21] Marin, *Portrait,* 237/289. On the Oriental side there occurs another instance of cross-dressing that merits attention. Alamir's lover Elsibery is accompanied by her elderly slave Sélémin, who is actually a Christian woman of high birth. Having broken off a good marriage prospect, much against her parents' will, she long ago assumed a male disguise so as to be able to accompany her husband. After his painful desertion and her capture by the Moors, she retained her male identity. Sélémin has become (in appearance) a man in order to avoid becoming an object for a man. In a perfect acceptance of the theme of alienation which the novel develops, she describes her tragedy in terms that mirror the histories of both Alamir and Consalve. For she assumes the identity of the Other as the only means of protecting her integrity, that is, of remaining faithful to herself. Moreover, since this woman who becomes a man is but a slave, the disempowering image of the Orient through associations with effeminacy is still operative.

[22] Lyons, "Speaking," 173–74.

Yet Consalve learns that appearances may dictate new truths, that representation plays an active role in history. Like the king of Pascal's shipwreck, Lafayette's hero is the benefactor of felicitous resemblances. Nevertheless, like the king whom Pascal describes, Consalve defines the "negative of a lost original."[23] This phenomenon occurs not because, like this king, Consalve takes the place rightfully belonging to another but because, with his having become that Other who is the Oriental in the portrait, there is no longer a self—an original—that exists independently of it. The negative of this equation is that what is finally elided from representation is the real history of the hero whose persistently valorous actions and efforts to know the world have failed to provide him with the truth about himself. In the guise of this truth, and against the background of the waves that wash over the dead mother's corpse, the failure of representation to convey knowledge is finally buried under the joyous preparations for a court marriage.

The proposed wedding summons Lafayette's contemporaries back to the pomp of royal ceremony, back from the Orient and into Castille, back again from the Middle Ages and into the spectacular sophistication of Versailles. Her reader would have penetrated the novel's fiction of fulfillment so completely that the possibilities for meaning would appear to be exhausted in the final image of monarchic authority which brings the novel to a close. Submerged by this fiction, the reader would very likely fail to comprehend that France, which in seventeenth-century Europe maintained an unusual and exceptionally advantageous alliance with the Ottomans, was trapped in the image of its own importance. The king's image, the sign of royal privilege under which France assumed its power, was so active a part of history that the reader was probably able to register the positive effects of the couple's impending marriage without noting that the subject, the real subject of history, has slipped from representation, and that the subject of representation who has assumed his place is but "an empty monument."[24] Having proved his fidelity to Zaïde against numerous obstacles, Consalve now experiences the illusory sense that knowledge and desire are in total harmony, the inequities of the past having been corrected by a portrait, an image of the self as Other, and the price of this fictional integration ignored. The secret of his empowerment is that what empowers him is a chance like-

---

[23] Marin, *Portrait,* 219/267.
[24] Ibid., 238/290.

ness to the Other he would negate in order to know himself as Zaïde's lover.

If it mediates a return to origins, the Orient in fact represents a double fiction within representation. The Orientals who survive the vicissitudes of war return to assume their initial identities as Christians, while the Christians rejoice in finding the identity lost to them, in recuperating the past as this means friends, political fortune, and love. This is the fiction of the full Orient, the fiction that serves to mirror back to the European reader a perfected view of himself or herself. Lafayette also structures what might be called a split Orient. By this I mean the way in which representation doubles back upon itself by projecting into the space of representation all that it appeared to exclude. The privileging of the image has created a fissure in the text, and the space that it opens up is not recuperated by the European model. Instead, it is the portrait as it mirrors by its very alienation the mother's shipwrecked absence from representation—as it reflects an image of the self that does not know itself except through this lost Other—which conditions the joy of the novel's final scene.

Neither the groom's father, who never returns to the action, nor the bride's, who mistook the portrait of Consalve for that of the Prince de Fez, nor the seer, who spoke not an oracular message about the couple's marriage but merely a speech corroborating Zuléma's plans, can be said to order the novel. Lyons thus concludes that "the authority figures do not control the likeness they create nor can they control the world through that likeness."[25] In this sense mediation can be said to be ongoing, and the novel's happy ending a last nod to the Orient as the image that ties the West to the fiction of representing itself as source of its own power. Marriage joins Consalve with another Oriental image that is, paradoxically, the source of its own negation. The Oriental Zaïde initially captivates Consalve, and it is with this image that he remains obsessed throughout the novel. If the belated exposure of her Christian upbringing does nothing to diminish his pleasure, it is unlikely that he will ever detach himself completely from the Oriental image that first took his heart. Yet nothing in the European model sanctions this Other, this image without which Consalve and Zaïde cannot know love.

Significantly, the promise that unites Consalve and Zaïde occurs after the Spanish are fully in control. Nevertheless, they summon Zu-

[25] Lyons, "Dead Center," 66.

léma to the court in order to obtain his permission for the marriage. Certainly the return of the Oriental father is a convention necessary for the final details of the history to emerge. But beyond any technical finesse, Lafayette manages here to create a spirit of cooperation which is perhaps the final disguise set in place for her reader's benefit, a veil with which to conceal Louis XIV's politics of self-interest and commercial expansionism with regard to the Ottoman menace.[26]

Exemplary Teaching: *La Princesse de Clèves*

In *La Princesse de Clèves* Lafayette models a series of re-presentations that are exposed as so many displacements of the subject whom they mean to identify and contain. The court of Louis XIV is mirrored in the court of Henri II, whose histories are narrated to the princess as models for her own behavior. The mirrored roles and repeated histories would all be "classic" enough, however, were the mimetic process able to provide absolute continuity. Mademoiselle de Chartres's arrival at court, fraught as it is with the perils of numerous suitors and the pressure to make a politically astute marriage, announces, at least potentially, another chapter in the mercurial history of royal society. But while the princess comes to experience the same conflicts and jealousy as those whose lives are held before her as instructional models, she demonstrates a resoluteness of character, an act of fidelity, that distinguishes her.

The princess's virtue is more than a simple act of marital devotion. In this novel the issue of fidelity in marriage is once again inseparable from the act of fidelity in representation. To discover the truth about herself, the princess must ultimately move to a space away from the court, away from the world as spectacle, and into a reality where her virtue correlates not only with sexual restraint but also with the knowledge that her true identity is not negotiable. The virtue of her position is that it cannot be performed by anyone but herself. In the end she slips out of the frame of representation and into an "inimitable," unmirrored space:

> Madame de Clèves lived in such a way as to give the impression that she would never return. She spent one part of the year in this religious house

---

[26] I thank Cornell Fleischer for information concerning the history of France and the Ottomans.

and the other at home; but in retirement and engaged in more saintly occupations than those of the most austere convents; and her life, which was rather short, left inimitable examples of virtue.

Mme de Clèves vécut d'une sorte qui ne laissa pas d'apparence qu'elle pût jamais revenir. Elle passait une partie de l'année dans cette maison religieuse et l'autre chez elle; mais dans une retraite et dans des occupations plus saintes que celles des couvents les plus austères; et sa vie, qui fut assez courte, laissa des exemples de vertu inimitables.[27]

Representation claims no exhaustive epistemology. The knowledge that the text provides is decidedly vague. We know that the princess dies, but we cannot know whether this death occurs in her home or in the religious retreat. The conflict experienced by the princess while her husband was alive has survived his death, leading her to renounce all society. She acts as if she believes it impossible to achieve authenticity in any context with other people. This we must infer from a narrative that ceases to reveal her thoughts to us. Eliding all dialogue, and in a minimalist narrative depiction, the text leads us away from imitation and toward the princess's inner world, away from discourse to a secret maintained in silence.[28]

Yet everything in the novel first conspires to model a knowledge based on resemblances. Moreover, since knowledge is believed to be consonant with virtue, the mimetic function can be said to ground the pleasures of the soul, if not those of the body. The princess is

[27] Marie-Madeleine Pioche de La Vergne, Comtesse de Lafayette, *La Princesse de Clèves*, ed. Antoine Adam (Paris: Flammarion, 1966), 195. All subsequent quotations from *La Princesse de Clèves* are cited in the text.

[28] Much has been made of the princess's end. A long tradition of scholarship views the heroine's story as a tragedy, and many critics today still perceive the novel in these terms. See especially Serge Doubrovsky, "*La Princesse de Clèves*: Une interprétation existentielle," *Table Ronde* 138 (1959): 36–51; and Jean Rousset, *Forme et signification: Essais sur les structures littéraires de Corneille à Claudel* (Paris: Corti, 1962). Other critics have offered positive interpretations of the novel's resolution. See Jules Brody, "*La Princesse de Clèves* and the Myth of Courtly Love," *University of Toronto Quarterly* 38 (1969): 105–35; Dalia Judovitz, "The Aesthetics of Implausibility: *La Princesse de Clèves*," *MLN* 99 (1984): 1037–56; and Domna Stanton, "The Ideal of 'Repos' in Seventeenth-Century French Literature," *Esprit Créateur* 15 (1975): 79–104. Most celebrated for this radical departure are feminist critics. See Joan DeJean, "Lafayette's Ellipses: The Privileges of Anonymity," *PMLA* 99 (October 1984): 884–902; and Nancy K. Miller, "Emphasis Added: Plots and Plausibilities in Women's Fiction," in *Subject to Change: Reading Feminist Writing* (New York: Columbia University Press, 1988), 25–46.

expected to learn the virtues of fidelity from the vignettes about royal personages recounted to her by those who play a major role in her life: mother, husband, friend, and lover each narrates a piece of court history.[29] The modeling process is not simple, however. Nancy Miller has shown how the princess's behavior is at variance with social norms as expressed in maxims. Similarly, John Lyons has demonstrated how the princess's knowledge is often out of step with examples put forward for her instruction. Lyons argues persuasively that though the novel means to structure knowledge according to the predictability of events, that is, on the certainty that the future will follow the past, this iterative structure does not account for the princess's own story.[30] The recurrent patterning is but a symptom of a more specific failure, namely, the inability of representation to provide knowledge since the truth behind appearances at court is often another appearance. Thus, the novel, reminiscent of La Rochefoucauld, whom many believe to have had a hand in its writing, shows the fallacy of efforts to uncover a more profound truth than that of the feint of court gallantry. Consequently, representation does not so much shape a knowledge of the court as participate directly in the court's celebration of its powers. Ultimately, representation functions less as an analytic device than as an object in and of the court's self-promotion.

Lafayette represents the court as a dynamic spectacle, a theater in which the characters' political aspirations and love interests are played out time and time again:

> Ambition and gallantry were the soul of this court, and occupied men and women equally. There were so many interests and different intrigues, and the ladies played such a role in them, that love was always mixed with politics and politics with love. No one was calm or indifferent; everyone thought about how to advance, please, serve, or harm; no one knew either boredom or idleness, and everyone was always occupied with either pleasures or intrigues.

[29] The novel contains four principal internal narratives, or *mises en abîme*, which designate the princess as the object of moral instruction: Madame de Chartres tells Madame de Clèves about Diane de Poitiers (51–55); Monsieur de Clèves tells Madame de Clèves about Madame de Tournon and Sancerre, renarrating the story told to him by the latter (71–79); Madame la Dauphine tells Madame de Clèves about Anne Boleyn (90–92); and the Vidame de Chartres tells Nemours about his relation to the queen, a story Nemours later recounts to Madame de Clèves (104–20).

[30] See especially Lyons's study of the intercalated stories (*Exemplum*, 217–36).

L'ambition et la galanterie étaient l'âme de cette cour, et occupaient également les hommes et les femmes. Il y avait tant d'intérêts et tant de cabales différentes et les dames y avaient tant de part que l'amour était toujours mêlé aux affaires et les affaires à l'amour. Personne n'était tranquille, ni indifférent; on songeait à s'élever, à plaire, à servir ou à nuire; on ne connaissait ni l'ennui, ni l'oisiveté, et on était toujours occupé des plaisirs ou des intrigues. (38)[31]

Given the instability of the court commerce (*commerce du monde*), any representation that attempts to fix identities can be shown to be ineffective. The text's model, which in reflecting the court's parallel histories implies a knowable and predictable behavior, is at odds with the lives of characters who are indistinguishable from one another, except as they assume their chameleonlike roles in the various intrigues that are said to dominate court life. This passage makes no reference to the pomp of royal protocol—the presence of the king, the magnificence of wedding ceremonies, the pageantry of tournaments—which Lafayette evokes elsewhere to foster the image of the monarchy as absolute power. In its focus on ambition and gallantry, on what subtends the imaginary register of court history, the text here allows us to perceive court spectacle as an elaborate theater of deception. The pomp of these other events is described to highlight their ceremonial importance. But the description here of pleasure and lack of boredom scarcely disguises the baser relation through which all court subjects are transformed into objects of exchange. Substituting one lover or intrigue for another, the members of court society in effect trade not just bodies but one image for a more empowering one, and it for another, and so on. The imaginary is a real aspect of political life, an integral part of the socioeconomic exchange highlighted by Lafayette's description. As Mitchell Greenberg writes, the court functions as a masked ball "where there is no adequately knowable fit of *être* [being] and *paraître* [seeming]."[32]

If we explore further the world of the court's spectacle, we see that

---

[31] Arnold Weinstein argues that the novel "depicts an inexorably public world where individual lives and loves retain little integrity but are rather transformed into official record" (*Fictions of the Self: 1550–1800* [Princeton: Princeton University Press, 1981], 72). Privacy, he observes, is precluded in the novel by the "transformation of intimacy into public spectacle" (73).

[32] Greenberg, *Subjectivity*, 198. With an emphasis on how the visual informs the text, Greenberg offers a detailed examination of court spectacle in terms of its political, economic, and sexual relations.

for representation to order relations *en abîme* so that one reflects the other, it must isolate identities that are simple (an individual is good or bad, faithful or unfaithful). Yet, owing to their role in a series of interlocking events, all significant relations in the novel are complex (the king is both husband and lover; the queen seeks solace in the Vidame de Chartres, who deceives her with other lovers). The novel places the mirror at the center of its text in an attempt to pattern what is unpatternable. At best the knowledge modeled by the text's recurrent forms is a distortion; the effect is that of a round peg that will not fit into a square hole. The fluid and multifaceted history of the sustained exchange of bodies, gossip, portraits, and letters is compressed into a simple tale of likeness, of identical copies: everyone (*on*); no one (*personne*). At worst this mimeticism turns around a void, substituting an ideal—virtue—in place of the real *commerce* that it pretends to imitate.

It is in this context that we come to appreciate the princess's performance, her extraordinary departure from the court. The princess moves away from narrative and the public domain into her own inimitable role. I am here separating out a notion of performance linked to privacy and silence, a nondiscursive event, from both narrative and what, because of its reliance on dialogue, has been called dramatic mimesis. Gérard Genette offers a clear explanation of the difference between these two forms of representation:

> The very notion of showing, like that of imitation or narrative representation (and even more so, because of its naively visual character) is a complete illusion: contrary to dramatic representation, no narrative can "show" [*montrer*] or "imitate" [*imiter*] the history that it recounts. It can only recount the story in a detailed, precise, and "lively" [*vivante*] fashion, and can thereby provide more or less the *illusion of mimesis* which is the only narrative mimesis possible.[33]

Transforming the concept of mimesis, whose roots are Aristotelian, into narrative theory, Genette enables us to see how Lafayette's representation is conflated. What is so striking in *La Princesse de Clèves*, a novel almost entirely dependent on narrative rather than on dramatic technique, on direct rather than indirect discourse, is that the text

[33] Gérard Genette, *Figures III* (Paris: Seuil, 1972), 185.

appears, in contradistinction to the possibilities outlined by Genette, to ascribe a dramatic function—that of showing—to narrative. The novel can be said, however, to reverse its own explicit prescription, to subvert the *showing* for the illusion. That is, in this text, where all appearances seem to give the lie to representation, the narrative, too, can be said not to show, as it intends, but to enact another history that in claiming to show it actually elides.[34]

What is at issue is not Lafayette's narrative, her narrator's text, but representations placed *en abîme* in the diegesis. These include, in addition to the intercalated stories, narrative segments that highlight both verbal and visual renderings of history. The point is to study how these representations confound the mimetic process by obscuring the critical distance that distinguishes narrative (analytic) from dramatic (performative) functions.

Madame de Chartres instructs her daughter in the ways of the court by citing the example of those who have fallen prey to the evils of deceit:

> Most mothers imagine that to keep young people from gallantry it is enough never to speak of it in front of them. Madame de Chartres was of the opposite opinion; she often depicted love to her daughter; she showed her what was agreeable about love in order to persuade her more easily that what she taught her about love's perils was right; she told her about the lack of sincerity shown by men, their deceptions, and their infidelity, the domestic miseries wrought by love affairs; and she made her see, on the other hand, what serenity accompanied the life of an honest woman, and how much virtue gave distinction and elevation to a person who had beauty and noble birth; but she made her see as well how difficult it was to conserve this virtue except by an extreme caution

[34] In dramatic representation (direct discourse), the act of mimesis is the acting out of history; one is drawn into the action as if one were there. In narrative (indirect discourse), however, this distance is never bridged: what *is shown* is distinct from what is. Language, therefore, is always separate from the event. This is not to say, of course, that dramatic representation is a pantomime, that it occurs without language. Rather, dramatic representation is conceived in language as history, as a first-level experience. It is distinct from narrative, in which language reconceives, and thus can be said to add a perspective and to analyze an event that has already occurred. A narrative re-presents the event, reproducing it in language, after the fact. Dramatic representation is also analytic to the degree that it recreates and thus reformulates an experience. Unlike narrative, however, dramatic representation denies the perspectival distance, or critical dimension, through which events are ordered, made knowledge. See Genette, 184.

[mistrust of oneself] and by taking great care to subscribe to that which alone ensures a woman's happiness, which is to love her husband and to be loved by him.

La plupart des mères s'imaginent qu'il suffit de ne parler jamais de galanterie devant les jeunes personnes pour les en éloigner. Mme de Chartres avait une opinion opposée; elle faisait souvent à sa fille des peintures de l'amour; elle lui montrait ce qu'il a d'agréable pour la persuader plus aisément sur ce qu'elle lui en apprenait de dangereux; elle lui contait le peu de sincérité des hommes, leurs tromperies et leur infidélité, les malheurs domestiques où plongent les engagements; et elle lui faisait voir, d'un autre côté, quelle tranquillité suivait la vie d'une honnête femme, et combien la vertu donnait d'éclat et d'élévation à une personne qui avait de la beauté et de la naissance; mais elle lui faisait voir aussi combien il était difficile de conserver cette vertu, que par une extrême défiance de soi-même et par un grand soin de s'attacher à ce qui seul peut faire le bonheur d'une femme, qui est d'aimer son mari et d'en être aimée. (34)

Madame de Chartres distinguishes herself by being unlike other mothers, who censor the court's history to protect their daughters.[35] Ironically, what ultimately guides the princess is the inimitability of Madame de Chartres's own example. We perceive this irony by noting the ways in which the mother's pedagogy means to emphasize the reverse effect, namely, the acquisition of knowledge based on imitation. The text here champions mimetic behavior through an emphasis on "showing," a representation so complete as to merit, anachronistically, the label "realist." Madame de Chartres holds up a mirror to royal society, reflecting not only the positive behavior that all mothers idealize to their daughters but also the negative behavior that occurs at court. Although *faire une peinture* (literally, to make a painting), *montrer* (to show), and *conter* (to tell) all point to the act of demonstration—that is, the displaying of examples to be rejected or imitated—the final expression in this series—*faire voir* (to make [her] see)—carries a different nuance. In an echo of *persuader* (to persuade)

---

[35] Many critics have elaborated the importance of the mother-daughter relation. See especially Marianne Hirsch, "A Mother's Discourse: Incorporation and Repetition in *La Princesse de Clèves*," *Yale French Studies* 62 (1981): 67–87; Peggy Kamuf, *Fictions of Feminine Desire: Disclosures of Heloise* (Lincoln: University of Nebraska Press, 1982), 67–90; and Greenberg, *Subjectivity*, 187–91.

earlier in the sentence, the mother here makes an inference; she pre-
vails on the princess to "see," understand, what cannot be shown in
the history of the court. Madame de Chartres constructs—invents—a
model for virtuous behavior to compensate for the lack any real
model. Indeed, although the novel portrays characters in love, the
dangers as well as the pitfalls of love, and men's insincerity—all models that are specified by the first three "picture" verbs—there is no
example of a woman's virtue as depicted by Madame de Chartres that
figures prominently in the novel.[36]

"Fallen" women include the king's mistress, Diane de Poitiers, as
well as the queen. Catherine de Médicis takes the Vidame de Chartres
as a lover and suffers his infidelities. Madame la Dauphine and Madame de Chartres appear to represent a more certain virtue. Although
the crown princess is implicated in stories about the Duc de Nemours,
her reputation is never tarnished. Yet no reward accompanies her
virtue:

> I have but a mediocre power; I am so hated by the queen and the Du-
> chesse de Valentinois that either they or their followers always oppose
> all the things that I desire.

> J'ai un médiocre pouvoir; je suis si haïe de la reine et de la duchesse de
> Valentinois qu'il est difficile que, par elles ou par ceux qui sont dans
> leur dépendance, elles ne traversent toujours toutes les choses que je
> désire. (42)

The crown princess's expression of alienation is a clear departure
from Madame de Chartres's model of happiness. The mother herself
is a more complex case still, for she is described in the passage just
quoted as a woman "whose goodness, virtue, and merit were exceptional" (dont le bien, la vertu et le mérite étaient extraordinaires
[34]). But if we believe that the woman who learned "the news of
her husband's death the same day that she learned of the death of
Monsieur d'Orléans" (la nouvelle de la mort de son mari le même

---

[36] The emphasis on the visual, on verbs that emphasize the act of showing, does
suggest, as Lyons has argued, that Madame de Chartres bases her pedagogy on specific
examples and not on general rules: "The mother chooses the method of example over
the method of pure rule or discursive assertion. But by teaching in this way, by *showing*,
the mother is teaching the heroine how to *see* what she is looking at, or how to *look at*
what she sees. It is a lesson in how to draw from appearances a knowledge of what is"
(*Exemplum*, 222–23). The problem is precisely that this model breaks down.

jour qu'elle apprit celle de M. d'Orléans) is Madame de Chartres, then she herself is another example of lost virtue (54).[37] This reasoning is speculative, of course, but it follows the pattern of Madame de Chartres's instruction. It presents another case history that cannot be fixed, assigned a permanent place in the princess's education. Whatever her real identity, this woman has preserved a reputation for virtue despite her infidelities to her husband.

We see that the entire maternal pedagogy is consciously conceived in terms of an elaborate act of imitation: Madame de Chartres instructs her daughter to follow good examples; the princess is to remain faithful to her husband by following his positive example as it replicates the mother's own teachings, which are based on a faithful depiction of all that happens at court. But the novel fleshes out a fuller depiction of the court which confirms that the final emphasis of Madame de Chartres's pedagogy rests less with "examples" than with her art in representing them. What she shows is less compelling than what she infers. Her prescriptions are created, invented through the logic of her own speech, which derives one thing from its opposite (the happiness of virtuous women from an account of the unhappiness of unfaithful women), and not from any extant model. Thus, despite the rhetorical coherence of an argument that pretends, by omitting nothing, to model the truth, the mother's instruction in fact conceals a larger fallacy.[38] The princess is led not to follow examples but to reach beyond them, to find meaning in the ellipses of her mother's speech. It is telling that Madame de Chartres calculates her daughter's security according to her ability to entrust herself to her husband. As it is invoked in this passage to reflect the standards of prescribed behavior that work against the princess's own inclinations and self-directedness, the French verb *se défier de soi-même*, meaning literally to mistrust one's own abilities, to have no self-confidence, suggests the virtual eclipse of her desire and autonomy. This omission is by far the most significant.

The husband whom Madame de Chartres envisages, and ultimately secures, for her daughter is a censor. He extends the line of control initiated by the mother, who is empowered by her husband's death to assume full responsibility for the young princess.[39] Like Madame

---

[37] Hirsch, 85–86.

[38] For more on the rhetoric of examples, see Lyons, *Exemplum*, 3–34.

[39] For more on the dead father's role in this succession, see Kamuf, 70–71, and Greenberg, *Subjectivity*, 187–88.

de Chartres, the Prince de Clèves models a truth about the princess that differs from her self-knowledge. The princess's alienation is implicit in the idea that mother and husband are to form her; they substitute a fiction of fidelity and coherence for the real fragmentation produced when the princess is torn between duty and desire. Insisting that the princess "love her husband and be loved by him," Madame de Chartres, moreover, denies her daughter any real possibility of an identity independent of her role as wife and the obligations that this role imposes. The mother's position is an argument for "virtue as a self-created image and a self-willed relation to the world."[40] Within the world of the court, however, autonomy and emulation are exclusive terms. The princess cannot willfully adhere to her own desires and ideas by subscribing to her mother's notion of appropriate models. Clèves, the model husband appropriate for the princess, is selected by Madame de Chartres not because the princess loves him but because, unlike other suitors whom the mother would have preferred, he is available and because he promises to be able to fulfill the role of moral guide to the princess, after the mother's own example.

Though it speaks to her good intentions, the mother's pedagogy models a representational fallacy to the extent that it equates happiness with a "lack of trust in oneself" (*défiance de soi-même*). One does not need to cast Madame de Chartres in the villain's role to see that, though she means to protect her daughter by presenting a simple formula to imitate—the princess needs only to replicate the models highlighted for her—these lessons actually take the form of a prolegomenon, an opening rather than a closing of the world of possible interpretations. Although she intends to reduce the princess's choices, and thereby reduce the temptations for her to fall from grace, Madame de Chartres actually multiplies the available options. This proliferation of alternatives reflects the discrepancy between what Madame de Chartres purports to show (behavior present at court) and what she in fact shows (the possibility of behavior other than that which she can represent), as between a pedagogy lauded for its uncensored cultivation of the truth and its specific prescription that the princess cultivate a (false) image of fidelity to hide her real feelings in the event, believed likely, that

[40] Dalia Judovitz, "The Aesthetics of Implausibility: *La Princesse de Clèves,*" *MLN* 99 (1984): 1040.

her natural proclivities inform a different self-knowledge from that imposed by her mother. These are the gaps that inform our knowledge of the text.

Emphasizing the importance of ellipses, Joan DeJean has underscored the text's final valuation of all that eludes representation.[41] By locating the elliptical modeling in the mother's pedagogy, in the very technique that Lyons, with the novel's narrator, conversely calls showing, I mean to emphasize that knowledge is not a function of characters departing from examples, their failure to imitate, but rather a function of the very basic failure of representation to analyze in discourse without becoming the principal object of that discourse. As depicted in the mother's teachings and extended to the novel's *mises en abîme*, representation is but another drama, another fiction in the princess's life. Madame de Chartres wants to expose an unprecedented virtue, a virtue still absent from the court. She cannot, however, present this absence; she can only present herself representing it. Her representation of the court disguises her own pivotal role. Patterning knowledge as much by what she omits from her instruction as by what she tells, that is, by choosing not to censor in order to censor more effectively, Madame de Chartres is the exemplar of an epistemology wherein imitation is pure illusion. The real story, as it were, has been evacuated from the scene of representation, away from the court and in the mother, away from models and in the mother's interpretation of them.

Preferring speech to silence, confession to omission, Madame de Chartres appears to find assurance in the power of representation to structure reality. She is not wrong, but her representation is incomplete, and its gaps create a space in which appearance and reality continue to mirror each other. "Do what I say," she seems to counsel, "not what I say (show you) that others do." Yet one cannot simply translate from narrative to history. As Genette's analysis makes clear, one is indirect—it makes the self a character in a narrative scripted by others—while the other is a performance in which the character speaks in her own voice. The problem, as many critics have noted, is precisely how to go from one mode to the other. How can the princess mature into adulthood in such a way as to

[41] DeJean refers to the suppression of authorial identity, the elimination of proper names, and the princess's retreat from the court as ellipses which speak to the heroine's ultimate self-assertion ("Lafayette's Ellipses").

acquire autonomy, to be a player in the history of the court, without falling into the trap of self-denial?[42]

Certainly nothing in the mother's instruction facilitates a smooth transition to court life. Lyons has shown the inconsistencies that exist between the mother's lesson that "what appears is almost never the truth" (ce qui paraît n'est presque jamais la vérité [51]) and Diane de Poitiers's real, albeit unlikely, attachment to the king, as these are expressed in Madame de Chartres's own recounting of the couple's history.[43] Nothing in her account suggests that fidelity alone brings happiness. Moreover, her narrative equates appearance (the king loves Diane) with reality (he does indeed), thereby subverting her explicit message that appearances deceive. Thus, we find that it is not what Madame de Chartres says but the fact that she says it—not the logic of her discourse but the force of her own example—that best, albeit inconsistently, imposes itself on the princess here.[44]

That the mother should go on to perform in death her own ellipsis, to become an absent model for her daughter, is all the more significant because her death merely accentuates the tensions present in her counsel to the princess. In these tensions we see acted out Madame de Chartres's highly personal drama, a drama that is all the more striking because she devotes so much energy to telling not her story but court history. The mother's last words merely underscore all that her scrupulous cultivation of her daughter's conduct has let slip away, all that has escaped the careful control of language intended to "show" the truth. As if acknowledging this failure, the deathbed scene mixes discourses; it switches to dramatic representation, but in a speech that includes a narration of past events. Madame de Chartres moves back toward what should be a critical perspective, only to occult her strategy once again. Her last words are a warning to the princess that she is "on the edge of a precipice" (sur le bord du précipice) and must relinquish control to her husband in order to stay the course of virtue (64). The mother affirms that she knows the princess's attraction to Nemours: "I have been aware of your inclination for some time now; but I did not want to speak to you about it at first, for fear of making you aware of it yourself" (Il y a déjà longtemps que je me

---

[42] Miller; Lyons, *Exemplum*; and DeJean, "Lafayette's Ellipses" all make this point.

[43] Lyons, *Exemplum*, 225–26.

[44] Such inconsistency is further evident in Madame de Chartres's confirmation to Madame la Dauphine that the princess's publicly feigned but false claim of illness was the cause for her absence from Saint-André's ball (60).

suis aperçue de cette inclination; mais je ne vous en ai pas voulu parler d'abord, de peur de vous en faire apercevoir vous-même [64]). It is most significant that Madame de Chartres, whose claim to exceptional status rests on her "tell all" approach to education, here admits that she has deliberately concealed the truth. We might agree that she acts appropriately to protect her daughter. Yet in exercising her authority to furnish and suppress examples, to grant and withhold approval, and in exposing this manipulation to the princess, Madame de Chartres once again demonstrates the impossibility of separating out a path to virtue from her own role in modeling this path. The intended, and actual, effect of her deathbed speech is that the princess will never be free of the responsibility (and guilt) that it imposes. If Madame de Chartres is, as the passage about her pedagogy has revealed, the primary model through which all others are ordered, the linchpin of the mimetic process that she sets in motion, then her death can be said to model the elliptical virtue of all of her instruction. In death Madame de Chartres becomes the simultaneous absence/presence, the voice outside of history that continues to speak, the unfathomable model in pursuit of which the princess will remain.

Before examining the princess's response, I want to turn to other examples in the text that similarly underscore the function of representation as performance in order to suggest that Madame de Chartres's role, though primary, is by no means unique in this regard. The most intricate of these examples is one that has received substantial critical attention. I am referring to the scene at Coulommiers where we watch Nemours watch Madame de Clèves look adoringly upon his portrait, she unaware that he is watching her, just as he is unaware that Monsieur de Clèves's spy is watching him. This scene's "Chinese box of voyeurism," its "*mise en abîme* of the gaze," demonstrates how an entire history is fostered by representation.[45] In this performance of the mimetic act, this representation of representation, the capturing of court history in the portrait on which the princess's gaze is fixed is subordinate to the highly erotic history enacted through the multiple layers that make this scene the most sexually fulfilling encounter of the princess and Nemours's relationship. More than a prop, representation—the capturing of history as an image—is cele-

---

[45] These are terms employed by Joan DeJean, "Female Voyeurism: Sappho and Lafayette," *Rivista di Letterature Moderne et Comparate* 40 (July–September 1987): 210, and Greenberg, *Subjectivity*, 177, respectively.

brated as an event. Critics have noted that the princess is able in this scene to live out her "erotic longings."[46] She is empowered through an image of Nemours that she has had brought into the pavilion, an act that subordinates Nemours himself to her fantasy, that makes him a mere accessory to her desire.[47] If there is knowledge produced in or through this scene, therefore, it is the solipsistic knowledge that there is no model outside the self, no external history to be imitated. We have seen that Madame de Chartres's representations of the court intend to objectify history in order to suppress the princess's desire; their purpose is to elicit a cultural heritage that subsumes the individual into a larger social identity. Diametrically opposed to these examples, this scene locates identity in the princess because she is able to represent her desire to herself. "I think," Descartes has affirmed, and this representation constitutes the sole proof of my being. Nothing, however, proves a resemblance between consciousness and the world. Nothing signifies outside my representation and in the world of objects; there is no resemblance between my thoughts and the external world that ensures meaning. So knowledge in this scene is modeled not in the gaze as it originates in the male spy and lover but in the princess's projection of her own desire. Indeed, the princess does not know initially that Nemours is even there.

Three other episodes together represent a typology of representation whose primary function is likewise performative rather than mimetic, for they do more to add to court history than to document it. The first substitutes an ideal for the real; the second, offering a faithful representation save the attribution of names, is dismissed as "implausible" by the person to whom it most intimately applies; the third is an accurate testimony that fails to inform. Significantly, none of these instances conveys the truth; the referent in each case is representation itself—representation as the object of representation.

A brief sequence involving Madame de Clèves's portrait does more than allow Nemours to establish a rivalry with Monsieur de Clèves and to possess her via her image. This scene, a prelude to the one just described, offers a discrete commentary on the artifice of represen-

[46] Miller, 37–38. See also Michel Butor, "Sur *La Princesse de Clèves*," in *Répertoire* (Paris: Minuit, 1960), 74–78.

[47] DeJean, "Female Voyeurism," 210–14. See also Naomi Schor, "The Portrait of a Gentleman: Representing Men in (French) Women's Writing," in *Misogyny, Misandry, and Misanthropy*, ed. R. Howard Bloch and Frances Ferguson (Berkeley: University of California Press, 1989), 117–20.

tation. Representation serves the utilitarian purpose of making present an absence. Madame la Dauphine commissions portraits of all the court's prominent figures to send to her mother. These miniatures are likenesses, imitations of the real. Yet this scene, revealing a baroque preference for idealized rather than actual beauty, recounts the princess's efforts to rectify an earlier portrait of herself. Madame de Clèves asks the painter to improve the miniature belonging to Monsieur de Clèves. Ordering that her hair be adjusted, she alters what she once was, or what she was believed to be, in favor of what she would become:

> The Dauphiness asked Monsieur de Clèves for a miniature that he had of his wife, in order to compare it to the portrait that had just been completed; everyone offered an opinion of the one and the other, and Madame de Clèves told the painter to adjust something in the hair of the one that had just been brought in. The painter, in response, took the miniature from the box in which it lay and, after working on it, put it back on the table.

> Mme la Dauphine demanda à M. de Clèves un petit portrait qu'il avait de sa femme, pour le voir auprès de celui que l'on achevait; tout le monde dit son sentiment de l'un et de l'autre; et Mme de Clèves ordonna au peintre de raccommoder quelque chose à la coiffure de celui que l'on venait d'apporter. Le peintre, pour lui obéir, ôta le portrait de la boîte où il était et, après y avoir travaillé, il le remit sur la table.
> (92–93)

The action here is dictated by the technical necessity of situating the portrait within reach of Nemours.[48] Appropriately, it concerns an object soon destined to enter the court commerce (*commerce du monde*). For it is precisely the status of self as object that the princess must ultimately refuse.

The princess later acts with the knowledge, still beyond her grasp in this scene, that her image does not interpret so much as it takes the place of her own story. Representation takes on a life of its own. Just as this painting marks the rivalry between Nemours and Clèves,

---

[48] Genette characterizes such technical constraints as the narrative's paradoxical tendency to justify the means by the ends. Gérard Genette, *Figures II* (Paris: Seuil, 1969), 94.

so later the story of her confession to her husband, violated by Nemours, who overhears it while concealed in the bushes, will be exchanged as fodder for court gossip. The effects of this reification of her desire within the court economy are most poignantly registered in the princess's response to hearing her own story. Pronouncing the anonymous tale of a woman who confides to her husband that she loves another man "guère vraisemblable" (hardly plausible [140]), the princess not only registers the improbability of her confession's having been either overheard by a third party or repeated by Clèves, whose own authority in the marriage the confession calls into question. She expresses the alienation that results from having her privacy violated.[49] The princess does not identify with this Other who assumes her role in the representation that circulates at court.

In the third instance representation is the most directly mimetic of the series: this example is less supplemental than the first, since it offers no ornamentation, and less deficient than the second, since it names all parties. It suffers instead from a certain porosity, that is, an inability to resist, to rule out, other representations. The gentleman's account of what he has seen while spying on the princess enters the story as a palimpsest onto which Monsieur de Clèves is able to represent not what has been witnessed but the nightmare of his own imagination. The prince receives the explicitly qualified report of the gentleman only to conclude that Nemours is in fact involved with the princess:

—"I have nothing to tell you," the gentleman responded to him, "on the basis of which one could judge with certainty. It is true that Monsieur de Nemours entered the garden in the forest two nights in a row, and that the following day he was in Coulommiers with Madame de Mercoeur."

—"That's enough," responded Monsieur de Clèves, "that's enough," motioning him again to retire, "and I need no further elucidation."

—Je n'ai rien à vous apprendre, lui répondit le gentilhomme, sur quoi on puisse faire de jugement assuré. Il est vrai que M. de Nemours a entré deux nuits de suite dans le jardin de la forêt, et qu'il a été le jour d'après à Coulommiers avec Mme de Mercoeur.

---

[49] DeJean offers a detailed analysis of this episode ("Lafayette's Ellipses," 997–98).

—C'est assez, répliqua M. de Clèves, c'est assez, en lui faisant encore signe de se retirer, et je n'ai pas besoin d'un plus grand éclaircissement. (172)

Following on the heels of this account, Monsieur de Clèves's death may be considered an extinction by representation. Just as her earlier confession had brought forward a truth that exposed as much pain as it avoided, his wife's confident reassurances of scrupulous behavior now afford the prince an uneasy entry into death, proof that one representation is just as valid as the other in terms of motivating the action. Neither text alone offers an adequate epistemological map of the novel, for the prince's fiction has direct consequences, and thus as much truth value as the princess's honest attempt to dispel his fears by recounting her efforts to resist Nemours. Knowledge depends on one's ability to explain how both function together. If these representations are self-negating, then it is clear that the key to knowledge must be found outside representation.

I have been suggesting that such knowledge emerges from the princess's own behavior. It originates in her response to her mother, to the many layers of their relationship which would have her model something that simply is not there. Although the princess means to follow the letter of Madame de Chartres's advice—that is, to remain faithful to Monsieur de Clèves—she is constrained by the inconsistencies of the instruction she has received to look away from models and into herself, away from history and its representation and toward an idealized behavior that is neither imitated (modeled after examples) nor imitable (capable of being replicated). The princess's impulse is to fill the gaps, to penetrate the space left open by Madame de Chartres's own example—her pedagogy, her calculated misrepresentations, and her death. For the princess this exploration takes the form of a stoic recourse to silence. Silence marks a refusal to be subjected to the court, to lose her privacy in the court commerce. She distances herself from speech just as she closes herself off from society. And in this eventual separation the princess severs a vital link with her mother, a link to an empty virtue stipulated on submission and self-abnegation, even as she pursues the high moral ground that Madame de Chartres set out for her.

In a first phase the princess fails to give her mother a full account of her inclination for Nemours (56), an act repeated when she later withholds the true explanation for her absence from the Maréchal de Saint-André's ball (59). This quiet and perhaps not altogether conscious revolt prepares the crucial scene of her extraordinary confession to her husband. Even more remarkable, perhaps, than the princess's exceptional admission is her categoric refusal to identify Nemours: " 'It is useless to pressure me,' she replied, 'I have the strength to silence what I think I ought not say' " (Vous m'en presseriez inutilement, répliqua-t-elle; j'ai de la force pour taire ce que je crois ne pas devoir dire [130]).[50] The suppression of her lover's name is remarkable given the combined pressure of Monsieur de Clèves; echoes of her mother's counsel to confide everything, to mistrust her own inclinations (*se défier d'elle-même*); and her own need to unburden herself. By withholding Nemours's name, the princess isolates within herself a passion that identifies her as separate from her husband as from her mother, a passion that is hers alone.[51]

The same behavior marks the novel's conclusion. In an extraordinary final gesture, the widowed princess refuses her lover and withdraws from society and into silence. She does so without sacrificing her love, if by love one understands the desire that defines her. The end of the novel is notable for the exceptional quality of the princess's choice, for the inimitability of her example, and for a particular detail inserted into this brief description. The princess's rejection of Nemours is justified by Lafayette, who is careful, in a very brief account of the final years of the princess's life, to specify the limits of the duke's fidelity.[52] Nemours's devotion is not so strong as to survive indefinitely in the face of her rejection: "Finally, many years having passed, time and absence slowed his pain and extinguished his passion" (Enfin, des années entières s'étant passées, le temps et l'absence ralentirent sa douleur et éteignirent sa passion [195]). No man has arguably suffered a more severe test of his love; no man has done more to stay attached to the woman he loves. But the princess's one criterion for committing herself to the duke, a standard which I believe dominates her thinking here even more than her duties to Monsieur de Clèves's memory as intensified by her (unwitting) role in

[50] The hostile reaction of Valincour to this scene is well known. For more on the novel's critical reception, see DeJean, "Lafayette's Ellipses."

[51] This is a case of truth being imparted as a result of a failed mirroring within the couple's relationship. Nemours also suppresses the princess's name (along with his own) when he relates the story of her confession to the Vidame. Unlike the princess, who would preserve her intimacy, and whose self-knowledge is concealed in this secret, however, Nemours immediately circulates her story, clear evidence that he is "of the world." He represents himself as an anonymous lover in a story to be exchanged with those of others caught in a similar trap.

[52] Hirsch, 83.

precipitating his death, is that Nemours offer a lasting attachment. By walking away, however, the duke justifies, at least in symbolic terms, the princess's suspicions. Although they run counter to the expectations of the court and to her own passion, these suspicions ultimately validate her choice to remain alone. The princess has sought a higher fulfillment: a permanent, coherent, and therefore singular union. Singular, she learns, allows for no Other. Impelled to fulfill her mother's ambitions for her, as she is moved to flesh out the gaps in her mother's depiction of the court, the princess nonetheless acts in opposition to Madame de Chartres's vision that a woman should model herself after the history of others in order to suppress her own inner voice. The princess proceeds beyond the court's cycle of deceptions, outside the failed promise of an enduring love, away from the state spectacle that subjects all desire to public consummation/consumerism, and into a world whose virtue lies in its very capacity to exceed our ability to represent it, to penetrate its silence.

If we recognize a didactic function in the novel's construction of a story from within other stories, the purpose of the princess's education seems ill served. Viewed from this perspective, her isolation at the novel's close represents her failure to remain at court, her inability to survive as a social entity. This is the tragedy of suicide, the self's violation of the self. We cannot ignore the suppression involved in the princess's denial of society and her exclusion from public life and from all representation, that is, from all efforts to know the world by identifying herself with it. Still, we must recognize that the princess has been led consistently away from mimetic activity in order to supplement an absence, to fill a void. Beginning with Madame de Chartres's advice to her daughter, the prescription to learn by imitation and example is inscribed in the narrative as a blurring of ideas. Though structured through the specular play of multiple *mises en abîme*, Madame de Lafayette's novel does not build from microstructure to macrostructure. There is no mirroring of individual and collective stories, no minimal narrative whose re-presentation exposes the virtue of fidelity—be it diegetic, marital, or personal.[53] The refinement of representation lies less in analogy than in display, the ex-

---

[53] Erica Harth further suggests that Lafayette never entirely resolves the tension between the need to imitate history and the need to create an original love story: "Love does not so much revise history as it dehistoricizes fiction." The result, she concludes, "is a balanced compromise between the subversive and the acceptable" (*Ideology and Culture in Seventeenth-Century France* [Ithaca: Cornell University Press, 1983], 219, 220). For a detailed analysis of the specific relations between historical models and Lafayette's

tended reflection of the court's changing forms. The history of the court cannot, therefore, serve as a model for a young woman's self-restraint any more than for her self-knowledge. The narrative strategy of the novel leads, as a consequence of its own complex logic, beyond the pretense of a world captured in representation, as beyond the pretense of its capture. The last pages depict the heroine's passage to the other side of representation, her passage from discourse to silence and a meaning protected from all social and literary commerce. The princess leaves a life that is desperately in need of something exemplary, something deserving of emulation, for an obscure and isolated beyond wherein she herself will become an example of an extraordinary virtue.

With *La Princesse de Clèves* this study comes full circle, echoing with its multiple intercalated stories held up as models for the young heroine the (baroque) *mises en abîme* analyzed by Foucault in reference to the painterly quality of Velázquez's masterpiece. Consistent with Foucault's theory, in both novels studied here Lafayette accentuates the function of representation as representation through the historical displacement that separates her contemporary reader from the novel's internal audience. Moreover, she shows the capacity of the novel to embed within itself a model for representation that is a mirror of the text's own functioning as art, as this in turn implies disguise, occulting, and the promotion of a particular discourse at the expense of another. The elided subject nonetheless forms part of the knowledge made available to the reader. If the present chapter returns attention to Foucault's analysis of the classical episteme, therefore, it is to open rather than to conclude the debate about the capacity of representation to order knowledge through a specific model, however elaborate. In the chapter that follows I attempt to reframe the episteme outlined by Foucault from within the space ordered by literature.

---

fiction, see Faith E. Beasley, *Revising Memory: Women's Fiction and Memoirs in Seventeenth-Century France* (New Brunswick: Rutgers University Press, 1990), 194–243.

Chapter Five

The Art of Naming:
The Taxonomies of Descartes,
Furetière, and Pascal

In a *New York Times* article provocatively titled "Science in the Laboratory of the Imagination," George Johnson writes:

> To test the brain's power to detect the most elusive of patterns, psychologists give people strings of binary numbers and ask them to predict which digit—one or zero—will be next in line. Almost instinctively, the subjects come up with rules to explain the sequences. *Two zeroes are followed by three ones, three zeroes by two ones.* . . . And when the rules break down, they revise them. Then they revise the revisions. Little do they know that the digits are actually being generated at random by the electronic equivalent of flipping a coin. So strong is this hunger for pattern that we see it even when it isn't there.[1]

In my study of the classical model, I have emphasized that this very "hunger for pattern" is intrinsic to the literature of seventeenth-century France. Work after work demonstrates how efforts to pattern meaning, even the most artistic and refined, inevitably fail. This failure is not the result of an ability to see pattern when it "isn't there," as the modern-day example depicts. Rather, it stems from the converse strategy of eliding what is not patterned (different) even though this other meaning "is there." As it represents an interest in the clas-

---

[1] George Johnson, "Science in the Laboratory of the Imagination," *New York Times*, May 1, 1994, sec. 4.1.

sification of knowledge, the quest for patterns is not, of course, new to the classical period or unique to our own times.[2] But the new science of Descartes marks a milestone in this long history of classification, for, as we have seen, it locates knowledge in the scientist's own representation. Knowledge is shaped by the rigorous patterning of representation, the perfection of science's analytic tools, and not a preestablished order of things. Even though the seventeenth century believes that God created the universe, it remains the task of science to piece together information about the world in such a way as to make God's original table of elements part of man's own.

My reading of literary texts has suggested that the standards for classification are far less stable than Foucault would have us see through his insistence on language's power to dissect, partition, and repartition. Waxing nearly poetic, Foucault in *Les mots et les choses* describes how classical science bridges the gaps of time by erecting a logic that appears to offer the continuity of space: "Language gives the perpetual disruption of time the continuity of space, and it is to the degree that it analyses, articulates, and patterns representation that it has the power to link our knowledge of things together across the dimension of time" (113/129). Yet we are moved to ask whether Foucault's rhetoric does not in fact give the lie to his theory.

The soundness of the methodological underpinnings for Foucault's elaboration of the classical episteme notwithstanding, the probability of man's reaping the desired result of a fleshed-out scientific table is slight. This disappointing result is not simply a consequence of the fact that there is, as Foucault insists, always some unclassifiable content.[3] Nor is it an indication that one cannot, in a first instance, dis-

---

[2] Lorraine J. Daston observes: "Such classifications had been a scholarly pastime since late antiquity; they became a scholarly preoccupation in the early sixteenth century and continued to captivate original minds until the end of the nineteenth century" ("Classifications of Knowledge in the Age of Louis XIV," in *Sun King: The Ascendancy of French Culture during the Reign of Louis XIV*, ed. David Lee Rubin [London: Associated University Presses, 1992], 207).

[3] In *Les mots et les choses* Foucault is careful to stress the "inadequate" relation of classical man with regard to the infinite, the unknowable excess (316/327). In general, however, his analysis of the seventeenth century does more to accentuate the will of science to achieve an adequate representation of all things in the world than it does to acknowledge the deficiencies or complications implicit in the application of the method by individual writers. As the present chapter demonstrates, science itself is less sanguine. Or, rather, science knows well the burden of classification, a burden that literature has elaborately demonstrated in its depiction of meanings that refuse to stay in the space to which they have been assigned.

tinguish between like kinds and different kinds. The problem lies in the second layer of analysis, that of classification, the assignment of categories to the groups of things that one has identified. Literary texts are very close to science in their indication that the formation of a taxonomy is not a value-neutral process. Categories are bound to moral judgments, the privileging of certain contexts over others. A particular taxonomy is thus itself subject to modification, vulnerable to outside influences and reconfigurations. The refined network of relations that it articulates does not reflect the absolute precision of representation as an analytic tool.

My discussions in the previous chapters have shown that literature is an effective laboratory for representation, for it offers a study of the mind in situ as it uses language to figure the world. That is, fiction merely exaggerates the basic function through which science represents to the public what it discovers, and, even more important, how the discovery process is inseparable from representation itself. I have noted the uncertainty of meanings produced in literary texts through the operations of exclusion and inclusion. Inscribing and valorizing all that is the same (Horace, Titus) at the expense of all that is different (Camille, Bérénice), this model does suggest, consistently with Foucault, that the classical period is capable of elaborating a chain of identities not based on resemblances alone. We are nonetheless left with a conundrum. How do we explain why it is that in the theater of Corneille and Racine resemblances are believed to carry the day? All difference is evacuated from the space of representation, elided from the society that in the end ensures continuity through a modeling of the same. I have argued that what is different in these texts does not in fact just disappear. The other meaning recontextualizes the knowledge framed by representation, and in so doing it multiplies and diversifies the reader's perceptions. In Chapter 3 I suggested that even the precision of difference(s) does not ensure clarity. For one thing, differences are perceived in the context of what is the same: Sosie is not Mercure, yet they are mirror images of each other; the autobiographical "I" of the *Discours* is not the "I" of the cogito, a subject constituted in representation that can in turn be re-presented by every reader. Moreover, as La Rochefoucauld's maxims allow us to see, the text continually overwrites itself and any identities that it establishes. Each maxim is an act of naming that is a metamorphosis, a recontextualization of the model that assigns names. The maxims turn the initial model into a mere feint, a false structure that is annulled as soon as the maxim is read and new meanings are generated. Lafayette's novels go so far as to suggest a representational fallacy, a mirroring that is an occulting of the very process through which differences are established.

It appears, then, that the excluded matter cannot be equated with an absolute difference, or pure negation. Rather, this excess forms part of the act/art through which representation calls attention to its own power to signify. In the foregoing chapters I have indicated that more is at stake than the meaning framed by the text's model. One therefore wonders whether Foucault at times insists more on the literal statements of purpose of individual works than on the actual praxis of classical discourse, the meanings that texts "perform." In the scientific domain the question becomes: Does representation similarly signify more than it purports to show through its rigorous classification of elements? Is there more to the text than its content, more to the order of discourse than the explicit relations of equivalence, difference, exchange, repetition, and so on underlined by Foucault?

In the *Règles pour la direction de l'esprit* (Rules for the direction of the mind) Descartes observes that the imaginary is used to translate reason:

> But I have spoken of its envelope, not because I wish to shroud this doctrine and hide it in order to protect it from the public; I wish rather to clothe and adorn it so as to make it easier to present to the human mind.

> Mais j'ai parlé d'enveloppe, non que je veuille envelopper cette doctrine et la cacher pour en éloigner la foule, mais plutôt afin de l'habiller et de l'orner, en sorte qu'elle puisse être davantage à la portée de l'esprit humain.[4]

Descartes masks the hard truths of mathematics with numbers and figures to make them easier to understand. Even more dramatically, the fable in the *Discours* can be said to be a device for making clearer, or animating, the facts of the method that he relates.[5] The imaginary, or poetic, dimension, is thus consciously intended by Descartes to

---

[4] René Descartes, *Règles pour la direction de l'esprit,* in *Descartes: Oeuvres et lettres,* ed. André Bridoux (Paris: Gallimard, 1953), 48; published in English in *The Philosophical Writings of Descartes,* trans. John Cottingham, Robert Stoothoff, and David Murdoch, vol. 1 (Cambridge: Cambridge University Press, 1985), 17 (trans. modified). In subsequent citations the page number of the translation precedes that of the French edition.

[5] For more on the status of the fable as final determinant of meaning in the *Discours,*

convey the truth of his science, to translate it for the reader. But just as today we understand the concept of translation to be a creative process—the reproduction of another text that resembles but is not identical to the original, and that therefore always, inevitably, distorts the original—so this imaginary, which renders Descartes's meaning clear, does more than elucidate the meaning that he intends to convey, his explicit message. I refer not to the imaginary that is the object of scientific research—optical illusions, a belief that beings inhabit the moon, and so on—but the imaginary that is a function of representation itself. Just as in literature, there are ambivalences that occur in scientific writing, despite the fact that the latter is carefully constructed to restrict the flow of meaning. Science is subject to the same slippage of meaning in and out of the categories that it establishes to mark its discoveries. It is this other meaning that I want to underscore by examining the taxonomic systems of Descartes, Furetière, and Pascal. I refer to the literary or poetic function of these texts in order to distinguish their rhetorical power from the supposedly neutral scientific analysis that they offer. Once representation is seen to subvert the system of identities that it puts in place, it becomes clear that Foucault's analysis would have us interpret literally texts whose theorizing about classification invites closer scrutiny. The question then becomes: What do the texts do if in fact they do not do what they say?

The Artistry of Descartes

The question posed in this context is admittedly less important for a grammar, where the rules of syntax are boldly and baldly given, than for scientists' accounts of their discoveries.[6] In Chapter 3 I examined the problem of the autobiographical persona in the *Discours*, the "I" of the text who recounts his own history. What remains to be studied is the scientific component of the philosopher's text. Specifically, I want to investigate whether, beyond the autobiographical dimension, the scientific method represented by Descartes can be fully explained by his use of what I term the taxonomic model. This model refers to

---

see Jean-Luc Nancy, "Mundus est fabula," in *Ego sum* (Paris: Flammarion, 1979), 95–127.

    [6] Although he makes many references in *Les mots et les choses* to the *Logique de Port-Royal*, Foucault offers surprisingly few references to the *Discours de la méthode*.

identities and differences, as Foucault underscores, and also to the classification of identities and differences, that is, to representation as the inevitable vehicle of moral judgment, the imbuing of values.

I propose to explore how this frame structure to some extent contradicts the notion of an all-encompassing logical system of analysis which Descartes offers as the content of the *Discours*. Like literature, the scientific text can be seen also to contain within its own representation a resistance to what, in a paraphrase of Descartes, one might call the facile classification according to a few simple categories:

> Nor is it an immeasurable task to seek to encompass in thought everything in the universe, with a view to learning in what way particular things may be susceptible to investigation by the human mind. For nothing can be so many-sided or diffuse that it cannot be encompassed within definite limits or arranged under a few headings by means of the method of enumeration that we have been discussing.

> Ce n'est pas non plus un travail immense que de vouloir embrasser par la pensée tout ce qui est contenu dans l'univers, pour reconnaître comment chaque chose est soumise à l'examen de notre esprit; car il ne peut rien y avoir de si multiple ou de si dispersé qu'on ne puisse, au moyen de l'énumération dont nous avons parlé, circonscrire dans des limites déterminées et ramener à un certain nombre de chefs (*rubriques*).[7]

Descartes does appear to offer a virtual road map for the kind of analysis that Foucault offers, an explicit statement of the rules for forming knowledge. But in the *Discours* Descartes himself exemplifies the very problematic that I have sketched. We note a discrepancy between his ordering of knowledge through the perfection of his model, on the one hand, and the final knowledge that his text produces, on the other. That is, we perceive a difference between the method, which is a knowledge to be extracted from the narrative and applied by other scientists to their research, and Descartes's description of his formulation of the method, his own representation—parts of which are deliberately inimitable—of his findings. To point up this inconsistency is not to claim that Descartes ignores the relations I explore. I have suggested that Descartes intends his fable to make the method more accessible without distorting it as a fictional fable, or illusion,

[7] Descartes, *Règles*, 31/65–66.

might do. The attention that Descartes pays to his own representation and to the reception of his ideas suggests that he is aware of the kinds of questions I raise regarding the potential of his text to inform a more comprehensive knowledge than is framed by his method.

To test the theory of the science that lies behind the modeling process through which Descartes presumes to guide his reader, I now turn to Part 5 of the *Discours* in an effort to see if a more objective structuring of knowledge is possible. The statement about "good sense" which opens the *Discours*—"Good sense is the best-distributed thing in the world" (Le bon sens est la chose du monde la mieux partagée" [111/126])—is considered by some to be ironic. Yet this idea finds an echo in the more objective assessment offered in Part 5 that reason alone separates all humans—"even fools"—from all other things:

> For it is quite remarkable that there are no men so dull-witted or stu-pid—and this includes even madmen—that they are incapable of ar-ranging various words together and forming an utterance from them in order to make their thoughts understood.

> Car c'est une chose bien remarquable qu'il n'y a point d'hommes si hébétés et si stupides, sans en excepter même les insensés, qu'ils ne soient capables d'arranger ensemble diverses paroles, et d'en composer un discours par lequel ils fassent entendre leurs pensées. (140/165)

Descartes, however, does not appear to suffer fools gladly. As we saw in Chapter 3, he offers himself as unique exemplar of the method, the only one whose "good sense," though a universal human quality, suffices to order knowledge. One should have enough good sense to follow his example, and no other. The example itself, however, is anything but neutral. Not only does the text represent a clear strategy for evading his critics, but also it invites one to ask how the new sci-ence—the "what" of discovery—is connected to the "how."

Citing "certain considerations" that have prevented him from pub-lishing his ideas, notably on the earth's movement—a reference to the condemnation of Galileo by the Roman Inquisition—Descartes offers a treatise on light, the planets, and human anatomy (132/154). This portion of the *Discours* constitutes a summary of an unpublished treatise in turn consisting of ideas from *Le monde de M. Descartes ou le Traité de la lumière* (The world of Monsieur Descartes or the Treatise on light) and the *Traité de l'homme* (Treatise on man).[8] It would be an exaggeration to claim that this summary treatise within the treatise (Part 5) within the treatise that is the entirety of the *Discours* stands as a *mise en abîme* of the latter text, if only because the exposition of the method is elided here. The fifth part does, however, offer an encapsulated version not of the method itself but of the representation of Descartes's documentation of his science, his own representation of representation. This portion of the *Discours* therefore offers rather spectacular testimony, even within this largely testimonial piece of writing, to the art of composition and analysis. Part 5, moreover, presents what is arguably the most complex taxonomy developed by Descartes in the *Discours*, and therefore merits special attention here.

Descartes's argument extends from considerations about the universe to a description of inanimate bodies and plants, and then to animals, with special attention placed on man, whose superior reasoning capacity is underscored. In the final phase of his presentation, Descartes uses a detailed description of the circulatory system in order to distinguish between the mechanical systems of all living organisms and the uniquely human ability to represent thoughts in language. We see in this organization of Descartes's presentation—in the systematic movement from largest to smallest, from the universe to the heart—a parceling of information that parallels the elaboration of a taxonomic table.

It is no mere coincidence that Descartes frames his account, which describes the general truths that he deduces from those already presented, with an analogy to the painter's art and an emphasis on the importance of perspective:

> My aim was to include in it everything I thought I knew about the nature of material things before I began to write it. Now a painter cannot represent all the different sides of a solid body equally well on his flat canvas, and so he chooses one of the principal ones, sets it facing the light, and shades the others so as to make them stand out only when viewed from

---

[8] Written in French between 1629 and 1633—that is, before the publication of the *Discours* in 1637—these works appeared posthumously in 1664 as separate texts. A Latin translation based on a copy of the original *Traité de l'homme*, then called *L'homme de René Descartes*, was published in 1662 in Leiden. Sylvie Romanowski notes that Part 5 of the *Discours* "represents [its] *raison d'être*. . . . This entire work was undertaken for the sole purpose of discussing *Le monde*" (*L'illusion chez Descartes: La structure du discours cartésien* [Paris: Klincksieck, 1974], 128).

the perspective of the chosen side. In just the same way, fearing that I could not put everything I had in mind into my discourse, I undertook merely to expound quite fully what I understood about light. Then, as the occasion arose, I added something about the sun and fixed stars, because almost all light comes from them; and about the heavens, because they transmit light; about the planets, comets, and the earth, because they reflect light; about terrestrial bodies in particular, because they are either coloured or transparent or luminous; and finally about man, because he observes these bodies.

J'ai eu dessein d'y comprendre tout ce que je pensais savoir, avant que de l'écrire, touchant la nature des chose matérielles. Mais, tout de même que les peintres, ne pouvant également bien représenter dans un tableau plat toutes les diverses faces d'un corps solide, en choisissent une des principales, qu'ils mettent seule vers le jour, et, ombrageant les autres, ne les font paraître qu'autant qu'on les peut voir en la regardant; ainsi, craignant de ne pouvoir mettre en mon discours tout ce que j'avais en la pensée, j'entrepris seulement d'y exposer bien amplement ce que je concevais de la lumière; puis, à son occasion, d'y ajouter quelque chose du soleil et des étoiles fixes, à cause qu'elle en procède presque toute; des cieux, à cause qu'ils la transmettent; des planètes, des comètes et de la terre, à cause qu'elles la font réfléchir; et en particulier de tous les corps qui sont sur la terre, à cause qu'ils sont ou colorés ou transparents ou lumineux; et enfin de l'homme, à cause qu'il en est le spectateur. (132/154)

The reference to Renaissance perspective, which does not correct the subject's view by presenting what he cannot see, can be said in this context to correlate with a principle of selection, and, in certain contexts, with censorship.[9] That the sides of objects are held in obscurity reinforces Descartes's need to avoid controversy with "the learned" (*les doctes* [131/153]). If the narrative that he offers in place of a more direct enumeration provides a comfortable veil against controversy, however, it models a problematic science. The account serves the didactic purpose of telling how one conveys knowledge to the reader. This text is the philosopher's representation of representation; we might well hear its echoes in Lafayette's account of Madame de Char-

---

[9] Erwin Panofsky observes that Renaissance perspective is often considered to favor the subjectivity of the viewer, since it does not correct his partial, oblique, and proximate vision (*La perspective comme "forme symbolique,"* trans. M. Joly [Paris: Minuit, 1975], 170).

tres's pedagogy. Descartes's elaboration of the scientist's writing technique shows how science proceeds deductively from one cause to another effect, with this effect in turn serving as the cause of the next effect, and so on, in an effort to account for the workings of the universe, that is, all of physics. Descartes's description of the celestial bodies as they extend across the heavens to earth and into the mind's eye of man, who stands at the end of this chain in the observer position, links macrocosm and microcosm. Significantly, however, this mirroring does not produce a fleshed-out taxonomy of either resemblances or differences. On the contrary, the text describes how representation provides only a subset of knowledge: there exists more than the painting shows; I cannot present here all that I know.

We can assume that Descartes would have us accumulate all of the pieces of knowledge that he could present in this text and elsewhere. That is, we are intended to multiply these pieces of information cumulatively, if not simultaneously. What we see is precisely how the system that Descartes elaborates functions as a continuous process. His text points to the unfolding of knowledge, to an absolute order whose totality is to some extent denied by the fact that it cannot be grasped at one glance, in one moment, but is instead continually, perhaps infinitely, in the state of being formed. Descartes's representation of this knowledge itself forms part of the knowledge that he conveys, and his stance both outside (as external narrator) and inside the knowledge system (as its principal agent) has its problems. We cannot know the system without knowing Descartes's role in representing it. This situation might well be a cumulative gain from the strictly taxonomic point of view, for we come to know two categories of things rather than simply one: the method and its representation. Yet Descartes's giving and withholding of information in this text reveals him once again to demonstrate what critics such as Jean-Luc Nancy, John Lyons, and Dalia Judovitz have shown to be the autobiographical foundation of his science. The primacy of Descartes's own history suggests how knowledge has begun to be distanced from the real object (the world) which he claims to know and in the text of his own representation.

Science, we believe, knows the limits of what it knows. Still, it is important to signal how this passage confirms a tension between method as a process of experimentation and method as constituting a final knowledge. The effect is similar to that of the spectator who wants to believe that the order modeled by the king at the play's close ensures harmony by stabilizing relationships, but who understands that this knowledge reflects the arbitrary stopping place of the play-wright, the perfection of his art. So, too, science, like literature, pros-pers under state support. Yet history shows that some research is compromised by pressures to meet the practical needs of the mon-archy as it wages war and confronts illness and commercial challenges. Why research is supported and the kinds of research that receive fund-ing are determining factors in what scientists discover. As a disicipline, moreover, science serves as its own arbiter. For although it intends to be a neutral purveyor of factual information, it knows that this infor-mation is conceived within, and therefore to some extent determined by, the particular framework that it has devised.

Descartes's classification appears solid enough. In its more intricate detail his logic is consistent with a physics constructed according to a geometric model.[10] Yet his insistence on what is elided from represen-tation precludes the reader's full and accurate knowledge. Or, more precisely, the truth of his science, dependent as it is on perspective, mirrors the specific relation that literature captures by showing how meaning shifts as the context shifts. This relation is reinforced in what follows, for Descartes now invents a new context to clarify his science. Further separating representation and the real, Descartes substitutes an imaginary world for the real one, once again in an ostensible effort to elude his critics:

> But I did not want to bring these matters too much into the open, for I wished to be free to say what I thought about them without having either to follow or to refute the accepted opinions of the learned. So I decided to leave our world wholly for them to argue about, and to speak solely of what would happen in a new world. I therefore supposed that God now created, somewhere in imaginary spaces, enough matter to compose such a world; that he variously and randomly agitated the different parts of this matter so as to form a chaos as confused as any the poets could invent; and that he then did nothing but lend his regular concurrence to nature, leaving it to act according to the laws he established.

[10] Etienne Gilson cites the reference to "the whole chain" in Descartes's opening sentence—"I would gladly go on and reveal the whole chain of other truths that I have deduced from these first ones" (Je serais bien aise de poursuivre, et de faire voir ici toute la chaîne des autres vérités que j'ai déduites de ces premières [131/153])—as an image familiar to Descartes which clearly illustrates "the deductive nature of a physics constructed a priori as a Geometry" (Etienne Gilson, ed., *Discours de la méthode*, by René Descartes [Paris: Vrin, 1925], 370).

Même, pour ombrager un peu toutes ces choses, et pouvoir dire plus librement ce que j'en jugeais, sans être obligé de suivre ni de réfuter les opinions qui sont reçues entre les doctes, je me résolus de laisser tout ce monde ici à leurs disputes, et de parler seulement de ce qui arriverait dans un nouveau, si Dieu créait maintenant quelque part, dans les espaces imaginaires, assez de matière pour le composer, et qu'il agitât diversement et sans ordre les diverses parties de cette matière, en sorte qu'il en composât un chaos aussi confus que les poètes en puissent feindre, et que par après il ne fît autre chose que prêter son concours ordinaire à la nature, et la laisser agir suivant les lois qu'il a établies. (132/154–55)

Although the cause of protection from censure is served by this thinly veiled fiction, the very thinness of the veil suggests that Descartes's art of categorization, its deliberate and self-styled order, protects but does not disguise the importance of his own role as author responsible for imparting the truth. That is, the imaginary world sketched by Descartes serves finally to support our understanding that knowledge is a product of the scientist's own ordering and measuring, his representation. Meaning depends on his interpretation of what God would do if He supported Descartes in his fictional enterprise.

Interpretation and creation are tightly connected here, with regard to both the scientist's relation to God and his own relation to his work. Descartes attempts to make a tabula rasa of his initial exposition in the earlier "unpublishable" work. We hear echoes of Part 1, where he rejects the ideas of his teachers and vows to look away from custom and within his own capacity to model the truth through reason. Descartes in fact aims to erase the "table" of any science other than his own, to bypass the tradition of scholarship whose work he challenges. Is it really a tabula rasa, though, when the imagined world has all the properties of the real world, which is the subject of the original document from which he now claims to distance himself? Referring to comparable passages about a fictional world in *Le monde*, Sylvie Romanowski observes that although Descartes appears to set up an imaginary realm to identify our own, in the end the text eludes such a descriptive explanation and allows the philosopher's language to become a subject in its own right. The theme of illusion gains in importance, for Descartes deals with science indirectly, through the veils of writing and in discourse which, now that they are released from their objects, can "function freely, without constraints, and can free up all of their riches."[11] Significantly, what is erased as this fable becomes an element of representation in the *Discours* is not Descartes's own theory of the properties of the world so much as all that would impinge on his ability to initiate in representation, by his own ordering of information, the truth about the world that he wishes to communicate to his reader.[12] Representation offers an interpretation of the world that is, at some fundamental level, an origin of meaning.

In making him the author of his own world, Descartes's narrative parallels the Genesis account of Creation.[13] Not that he would take—or, perhaps more to the point, be caught taking—God's role: "Without basing my arguments on any principle other than the infinite perfections of God, I tried to demonstrate . . ." (sans appuyer mes raisons sur aucun autre principe que sur les perfections infinies de Dieu, je tâchai à démontrer . . . [132/155]); "Still, I did not want to infer from all these things that this world was created in the way that I was proposing; for it is much more likely that, from the beginning, God made it exactly as it should be" (Toutefois je ne voulais pas inférer de toutes ces choses que ce monde ait été créé en la façon que je proposais; car il est bien plus vraisemblable que, dès le commencement, Dieu l'a rendu tel qu'il devait être [133/156; trans. modified]). What, then, constitutes proof? Is it the philosopher's representation or God's Creation? Or is it something in between these categories as sketched by Descartes?

To justify, or minimalize the radical nature of, what he presents, Descartes cites the theological principle that God conserves the world through the same action whereby He originally made it: "But it is certain, and it is an opinion commonly accepted among theologians, that the act by which He now conserves it is exactly the same as that

[11] Romanowski, 99. Romanowski further observes: "Whereas *Le monde* aimed directly at Science, and indirectly at its opposite [illusion], in the *Discours*, Illusion is treated both indirectly and directly: science takes a back seat, and the persuasion of the reader locked in error becomes the writer's principal goal" (132). See also Timothy J. Reiss, "Cartesian Discourse and Classical Ideology," *Diacritics* 6 (Winter 1976): 24.

[12] Dalia Judovitz argues that in *Le monde* Descartes offers an interpretation "more radical than Galileo's, since he openly assumes a new role as the author and creator of a fable of a new world. Man as the subject of knowledge is the creator of a new order that imitates and challenges God's creative capacities" (*Subjectivity and Representation in Descartes: The Origins of Modernity* [Cambridge: Cambridge University Press, 1988], 94).

[13] Gilson notes that "it is believed that Descartes, who, in writing *Le monde* and the *Discours*, made his way rather easily through the various snags of *Genesis*, but who contented himself with working around them without pretending to suppress them, subsequently conceived a much more ambitious plan: to show that his explanation agreed more than that of scholasticism with the literal meaning of the biblical narrative" (382).

by which He created it" (Mais il est certain, et c'est une opinion communément reçue entre les théologiens, que l'action par laquelle maintenant il le conserve est toute la même que celle par laquelle il l'a créé [133/156; trans. modified]). Descartes may act "in good faith" here by shifting from illusion to an idea of divine perfection and protection; or he may instead be writing simply to appease his critics. More consequential for evaluating his science is the fact that even in this justification there is evidence of a certain tautological reasoning: things are as they are because God would will them thus. From this rationale we can conclude, moreover, that things are best understood through cause-and-effect relations because this is how we best understand them. For it would be equally logical, if less desirable from both the religious and the scientific standpoints, that things generated in one way subsequently develop in another. In the scientist's mind the randomness of life is made to conform to the standards that he sets in order to achieve a degree of control, to acquire what is the knowledge of probability and predictability. From the point of view of a cumulative knowledge that affords human beings a greater mastery of the elements, there is nothing wrong in this conception; science does indeed acquire more and more information by proceeding in this manner. Nonetheless, we see here an illustration of what modern philosophers describe as science's inevitable inscription of values into its research, for the method designed to objectify the world reflects the limits of what science already knows.

We create the categories—smallest to largest, part to whole—because we understand them to facilitate our perceptions of the world. The imperative that things "need to be this way" is thus as anthropocentric as it is devout. Yet this is the rationale for Descartes, who concludes the quoted passage with the claim that there has always been, even in the initial chaos of Creation, an order to the material things in nature. This concept is cited in support of the scientist's method as much as in honor of God:

Even if in the beginning God had given the world only the form of a chaos, provided that he established the laws of nature and then lent his concurrence to enable nature to operate as it normally does, we may believe without impugning the miracle of creation that by this means alone all purely material things could in the course of time have come to be just as we now see them. And their nature is much easier to conceive if we see them develop gradually in this way than if we consider them only in their completed form.

De façon qu'encore qu'il ne lui aurait point donné, au commencement, d'autre forme que celle du chaos, pourvu qu'ayant établi les lois de la nature il lui prêtât son concours pour agir ainsi qu'elle a de coutume, on peut croire, sans faire tort au miracle de la création, que par cela seul toutes les choses qui sont purement matérielles auraient pu, avec le temps, s'y rendre telles que nous les voyons à présent. Et leur nature est bien plus aisée à concevoir lorsqu'on les voit naître peu à peu en cette sorte, que lorsqu'on ne les considère que toutes faites. (133–34/156–57)

Descartes believes that the human organism functions according to the same laws as matter, like a machine. But the idea of mechanics, systems, is a logical construct for which man, as much as nature, is responsible. Descartes himself readily asserts the fallibility of any system that mimics God's own:

Even though such machines might do some things as well as we do them, or perhaps even better, they would inevitably fail in others, which would reveal that they were acting not through understanding but only from the disposition of their organs. For whereas reason is a universal instrument which can be used in all kinds of situations, these organs need some particular disposition for each particular action; hence it is for all practical purposes impossible for a machine to have enough different organs to make it act in all the contingencies of life in the way in which our reason makes us act.

Bien [que des machines] fissent plusieurs choses aussi bien ou peut-être mieux qu'aucun de nous, elles manqueraient infailliblement en quelques autres, par lesquelles on découvrirait qu'elles n'agiraient pas par connaissance, mais seulement par la disposition de leurs organes. Car, au lieu que la raison est un instrument universel qui peut servir en toutes sortes de rencontres, ces organes ont besoin de quelque particulière disposition pour chaque action particulière; d'où vient qu'il est moralement impossible qu'il y en ait assez de divers en une machine, pour la faire agir en toutes les occurrences de la vie de même façon que notre raison nous fait agir. (140/165)

Descartes affirms that man alone among all of God's creatures is capable of representing his thoughts. The text indicates, moreover, that representation creates and then undercuts its own framework for structuring ideas. Science, too, is subject to manipulation, to the "particular disposition" required for it to do its work.

Like the artist who positions his objects to expose their most revealing side, so the scientist shifts in and out of proof through systematic deduction in the initial phase; to proof through demonstration which depends on the invention of a new world, a fable, in the next stage; and then, in a third sequence, to proofs based on empirical observation with his analysis of the circulatory system. Descartes prefaces this last analysis with the advice that those not versed in anatomy should dissect the heart "of some large animal with lungs" (de quelque grand animal qui ait des poumons) in order to follow his discussion (134/158). Ironically, to reinforce the depiction of his imaginary world, an account situated in the past, he resorts, in the present, to describing his discoveries about the heart:

> But so that you might see how I dealt with this subject, I shall give my explanation of the movement of the heart and the arteries. Being the first and most widespread movement that we observe in animals, it will readily enable us to decide how we ought to think about all the others.

> Mais, afin qu'on puisse voir en quelle sorte j'y traitais cette matière, je veux mettre ici l'explication du mouvement du coeur et des artères, qui étant le premier et le plus général qu'on observe dans les animaux, on jugera facilement de lui ce qu'on doit penser de tous les autres. (134/157)

We see clearly that the fable is now a representation of the real.[14] With this visual observation through dissection, moreover, the position of man as a witness to the universe—"and finally about man, because he observes these bodies"—switches to that of an active participant in representation, scalpel in hand. Even more significant is the fact that in his role as author/creator of meaning, Descartes indicates that dissection and anatomical study confirm what man already contains and, by extension, must eventually know to preexist within himself: "For, examining the functions which could occur in such a body in consequence of this, I found precisely those which may occur in us without our ever thinking of them" (Car, examinant les fonc-

---

[14] Romanowski's discussion of the use of direct discourse reinforces this notion (131–32).

tions qui pouvaient en suite de cela être en ce corps, j'y trouvais exactement toutes celles qui peuvent être en nous sans que nous y pensions [134/157; trans. modified]). All that he discovers in animals is believed to reflect what is in man, who retains his central position in the chain of being. The point, of course, is not that Descartes is wrong but that something might elude him should it not correspond to the model, to the range of possibilities that he sets for himself.

This finding, in its privileging of I-centeredness, is perfectly consistent with the fable of the entire project in the *Discours*. The autobiographical, or literary, representation that makes Descartes the hero of his own narrative creates a highly subjective environment in which to generate the impersonal "I," subject of the cogito. It is impossible to separate radically the impersonal from the personal, objective from subjective, even in this text dedicated to promoting the emergence of subjectivity through a unique reliance on representation, on the capacity of the mind to reason, rather than on any external source. All meaning is a function of the fable that the philosopher creates, a projection of his mind's eye.

It is arguably the case that Descartes in Part 5 is layering his story for purely didactic purposes and that such representation in no way qualifies the actual ordering of the scientific information that he has accrued. One can suppose that if the need to bring this material to the public were less constrained by circumstances, Descartes would have presented a more straightforward representation that would reveal his taxonomy to be a more objectively efficient device for ordering knowledge. But if we turn now to what might be considered just such a taxonomy minus the narrative dimension, to Furetière's dictionary, we find an example of how the method for classification played out over the course of the century. Significantly, the classification that organizes the dictionary presents the same proclivity toward ambiguity and indifferentiation noted throughout this study.

Furetière: The Art of Method

Furetière's *Dictionnaire universel* (Universal dictionary) appeared in 1690, two years after his death.[15] The history of the publication of this work is important, for it helps to situate the more normative, and

[15] Antoine Furetière, *Dictionnaire universel, contenant généralement tous les mots français tant vieux que modernes, & les termes de toutes les sciences et les arts . . . recueilli et compilé par*

therefore comprehensive, usage represented by Furetière in opposition to the official language sanctioned by the Académie française. Having been expelled from this institution for his theories about lexicography, Furetière persisted in compiling a dictionary of "universal" linguistic usage which challenged the elitism of the *Dictionnaire de l'Académie française* (Dictionary of the Académie française). Owing largely to the lawsuit between Furetière and the Académie over issues concerning the dictionary, we have in the form of the *Factums* his defense of a language that belongs to no one, not even Louis XIII, who sanctioned the Académie's dictionary, or his son, who received that dictionary with far less enthusiasm than he did Furetière's.[16] Published in Holland, Furetière's work was presented to Louis XIV on August 24, 1694, a date that coincided with the Académie's own presentation of its dictionary to the monarch. That the latter event occurred a full fifty-nine years after the inception of the project did not go unnoticed by Louis.[17]

Furetière maintained that the Académie expropriated for imperial purposes what belongs to the public domain. He felt that "by claiming a monopoly on language, the Académie, in the name of the king, usurped the place of the universal."[18] Exactly what Furetière intends by "universal" is apparent in his title, which specifies that his is a dictionary "containing generally all French words, old as well as modern, & the terms for all the sciences and the arts" (contenant généralement tous les mots français tant vieux que modernes, & les termes de toutes les sciences et des arts). This list of subjects to be found in the dictionary includes fourteen entries for the sciences; three for jurisprudence; twenty-one for mathematics; sixteen for the arts (a term including poetry and rhetoric as well as falconry and the mechanical arts); plus seven other categories that range from terms relating to the Orient and the Occident to the origin of proverbs and their relation to other languages; and a final grouping that begins

---

feu Messire Antoine Furetière, Abbé de Chalivoy, de l'Académie française, 3 vols. (The Hague: Arnout and Reinier Leers, 1690). I have modernized the spelling in all citations.

[16] Antoine Furetière, *Recueil des factums d'Antoine Furetière, de l'Académie française, contre quelques-uns de cette académie, suivi des preuves et pièces historiques données dans l'édition de 1694, avec une introduction et des notes historiques et critiques*, ed. M. Charles Asselineau (Paris: Poulet-Malassis et de Broise, 1859).

[17] For more on this history, see Alain Rey, introduction to *Le dictionnaire d'Antoine Furetière* (Paris: Robert, 1978), and "Linguistic Absolutism," in *A New History of French Literature*, ed. Denis Hollier (Cambridge: Harvard University Press, 1989), 373–79.

[18] Jean-Charles Darmon, "Furetière et l'universel," *Stanford French Review* 14 (Winter 1990): 15.

with the names of authors whose work helps to define usage and ends with a general reference to information that likewise illustrates the meaning of words. This taxonomy of the dictionary provides us with the beginnings of a grid for cultural identity.[19] For it not only structures a comprehensive list of things in the world but also indicates how they signify in relation to specific categories. The categories for normative language are not entirely objective, or neutral, however.[20] Curiously absent from this enumeration of subject headings is any reference to history, religion, or ethics, although the dictionary does provide definitions for history, religion, God, and the like. In its dedication to the "arts and sciences," to what man produces, this classification therefore signals an effort to establish through representation an order of things independent of any fixed narrative, be it that of official history or divine origin.

Science is opposed to art (meaning both craftsmanship and the fine arts), as the first entry under "science" confirms: "Knowledge of things, acquired by extensive reading, or long meditation" (Connaissance des choses, acquise par une grande lecture, ou une longue méditation). But the second definition blurs the distinction between knowledge and the practice or skill (mastery) of that knowledge, its art: "Is said more specifically of a particular art, of the effort made to deepen the knowledge of a particular subject, to reduce it to rules and methods in order to perfect it" (Se dit plus spécifiquement d'un art particulier, de l'application qu'on a eue à approfondir la connaissance d'une matière, de la réduire en règle & en méthode pour la

---

[19] Cf. Louis Marin's observation that Furetière's dictionary "is, in many respects a genuine treatise on cultural anthropology" ("Classical, Baroque: Versailles, or the Architecture of the Prince," trans. Anna Lehman, in *Baroque Topographies: Literature/History/Philosophy*, ed. Timothy Hampton, *Yale French Studies* 80 [1991]: 169).

[20] Timothy J. Reiss indicates that explicit claims about the neutrality of classificatory systems were not made until the second half of the eighteenth century ("Espaces de la pensée discursive: Le cas Galilée et la science classique," *Revue de Synthèse* 85–86 [1977]: 5–47). Still, it is difficult not to interpret Furetière's "universal" system, which eschews the exclusive usage of the elite class, as an effort not simply to broaden the dictionary— to make it more inclusive—but to objectify it, that is, to make it more neutral by making it less aristocratic. Cf. Michael Moriarty: "The lexicographer is not . . . disinterested. . . . The 'common culture' his work embodies is a sectional one: no less than the individual author he is socially, culturally, ideologically positioned. But part of this positioning is a conscious subjection to discourse in general rather than to the particular and competing discourses that seek to purvey a certain truth not universally recognized. He must incorporate, in his individual position, the sum of all the other individual positions deemed to merit consideration (although it is he who does the deeming)" (*Taste and Ideology in Seventeenth-Century France* [Cambridge: Cambridge University Press, 1988], 54).

perfectionner). The reference to rules and method relates, of course, to efforts to use the scientific method. Nonetheless, the general reference to any systematic practice or skill within a discipline—"the application made to deepen the knowledge of a particular subject"— considerably broadens the scope of the definition. It includes philosophy, which refers to "all sciences" (toutes les sciences) as well as the "human sciences, the knowledge of Languages, Grammar, Poetry, Rhetoric, and other things that one learns in the Humanities" (sciences humaines, la connaissance des Langues, de la Grammaire, de la Poésie, de la Rhétorique, & autres choses qu'on apprend dans les Humanités). In fact, it is the association of both terms—science as proof of a certain *savoir* (knowledge) or content, and method as the art of representing the scientist's discovery—that the dictionary underscores in multiple ways.

If we look under "art," we find that this term is situated in relation to standards of good taste and against science, whose sole activity, it claims, is proof—*demonstration*:

> Art is principally an accumulation of precepts, rules, inventions, and experiments, which, once observed, allow one to succeed in the things that one undertakes, making them useful and agreeable. In this sense *Art* is divided into two branches: one, the Liberal *Arts*, the other the Mechanical *Arts*: and in this sense it is opposed to *Science*, whose principle consists of demonstrations.

> Art, est principalement un amas de préceptes, de règles, d'inventions & d'expériences, qui étant observées, font réussir aux choses qu'on entreprend, les rendent utiles & agréables. En ce sens l'*Art* se divise en deux branches: les uns sont les *Arts* Libéraux, les autres sont les *Arts* Mécaniques: & en ce sens il est opposé à *Science*, dont le principe consiste en démonstrations.

Yes, science, we learn under "experiment" (*expérience*), privileges proof over speculation: "Descartes said that he had a higher opinion of the Artisans' experiments, than of all the speculations of the Learned" (Descartes disait qu'il faisait plus de cas des *expériences* des Artisans, que des spéculations de tous les Doctes).[21] In his privileging

---

[21] In another entry we discover that for the artisans themselves *expérience*, which in French has the double sense of "experiment" and "experience," represents a kind of trial project, a lesser final project: "*Experiment*, among the Artisans and the trade Guilds,

of the artisan over the learned man, the humble over the doctrinaire, Descartes clearly posits truth on the side of normalizing relations; he prefers those who have acquired real, practical knowledge outside the academy, whose traditions he finds deficient. Valorizing the artisan at the expense of the scholar, Descartes proves an apt model for Furetière's insistence that universal usage replace the Académie's efforts to identify artificially a language for *les grands*. But is there a clear order to this normalization? Is the scientist not impressed by artistry as much as by proof?

When we turn to "method," we see the merging of art and science posited in terms of a taxonomic problem:

> Method. n. fem. Art of arranging things in such a manner that one can make, or teach, or retain them with greater facility. Descartes's *Method* is a wonderful work. What is most productive in the sciences is to learn them with *Method*. At the College one disagrees whether Logic is an Art, a Science, or a *Method*.

> Méthode. subst. fém. Art de disposer les choses d'une manière qu'on les puisse faire, ou enseigner, ou les retenir avec plus de facilité. La *Méthode* de Descartes est un ouvrage merveilleux. Ce qui profite le plus dans les sciences, c'est de les apprendre avec *Méthode*. On dispute au Collège, si la Logique est un Art, une Science, ou une *Méthode*.

In this reference "method" clearly refers to Descartes's *Discours* and to its content (the "how to" part of the text). The second definition—to learn with method, or application—refers either to Descartes's method alone, that is, to the practice of ordering and measuring, or perhaps more logically, to the "art of science." According to this interpretation, one does best in scientific pursuits when one masters the discipline, referring in a nonrestrictive way not to method alone but to all the skills employed within a given field. The academic debate about what constitutes an art, a science, or a method is mirrored in the dictionary itself. For in its parceling of information the dictionary

---

means a 'half masterpiece,' or minor project. Journeymen aspiring to become Masters are required to do a major work; those working under the Master are required only to make a simple *experiment*, a light *experiment*" (*Expérience*, parmi les Artisans & les Corps de métier, signifie un demi chef-d'oeuvre. Les compagnons aspirant à la Maîtrise sont obligés de faire un chef-d'oeuvre: les fils de Maître ne font qu'une simple *expérience*, une légère *expérience*).

suggests differences where there are affinities; it blurs the categories that it devises for identifying specific usage. It is perhaps for this reason, moreover—this sorting of information that in the end fails to separate things—that Furetière includes in his definition of the encyclopedia the observation that "it is foolhardy for a man to want to possess the *Encyclopedia*" (C'est une témérité à un homme de vouloir posséder *l'Encyclopédie*), since this work represents "universal science, the collection or linking of all the sciences together" (science universelle, recueil ou enchaînement de toutes les sciences ensemble).

Jean-Charles Darmon argues that Furetière's use of the concept "universal" is not only epistemological "but also juridical, social, political, economic, even aesthetic: the 'beauty' of the *Dictionnaire universel*, its 'connection' [*liaison*] its 'cohesion' [*suite*], its 'energy' can be said to derive from the intersection of these lines of force."[22] Furetière clearly attempts to expand knowledge by going beyond the restricted lexicography of the Académie and toward what he believes is a universal and more comprehensive record of usage and cultural achievement. Yet, as Darmon convincingly argues, Furetière does not so much fix as multiply relationships between words. For the value that Furetière ascribes to the dictionary relates not only to word usage but also to the network of relations established from entry to entry.

If we look now to terms that refer to patterning, or the ordering of logical systems, we find evidence that the proliferation of meanings signaled by Darmon reflects a problematic taxonomy. In particular, the division into categories or classes shows the inscription of cultural values to occur in such a way as to suggest the limits of representation's capacity to posit the truth:

Class: n. fem. Distinction of persons or of things, in order to rank them according to their merit, or their value, or their nature. Homer, Virgil, & Corneille are Poets of the first *class*. Lucan, Claudian are of an inferior *class*. It is not known in what *class* to put Hermaphrodites; it is not known whether they are male or female. This Author studies natural bodies; in order to have a greater facility he arranged them into several *classes*: metals, minerals, vegetables, etc. This word comes from *classis*, which comes from the verb *kalo, congrego, convoco. Class* is nothing other than a group of things assembled separately.

[22] Darmon, 16.

Classe: subst. fem. Distinction de personnes, ou de choses, pour les ranger selon leur mérite, ou leur valeur, ou leur nature. Homère, Virgile, & Corneille sont des Poètes de la première *classe*. Lucain, Claudian sont d'une *classe* au-dessous. On ne sait en quelle *classe* ranger les Hermaphrodites, on ne sait s'ils sont mâles ou femelles. Cet Auteur traite des corps naturels, & pour plus grande facilité il les a rangés en plusieurs *classes*, en métaux, minéraux, végétaux, etc. Ce mot vient de *classis*, qui vient du verbe *kalo, congrego, convoco*. *Classe* n'est autre chose qu'une multitude assemblée à part.

The division of literary figures into greater and lesser achievers merely confirms the importance of the assignment of value to any order of things. The reference to the scientific table which concludes this definition, however, appears to be neutral. But the efficacy of this science in naming the things of this world breaks down with the hermaphrodite.[23] The dependence of Furetière's sentence on an *either-or* construction implies, and most self-consciously, an inherent weakness in the classification system. He does not challenge the existence of hermaphrodites, their difference. Rather, he acknowledges the inability of the division into male and female to account for this sex that is not one but two, and therefore neither. In this statement of confusion we find a lexicographical equivalent of the sign that signifies outside the frame of representation. Camille, too, is ambivalently gendered— too aggressive for a woman, too sentimental for a man.

Turning now to a specific kind of patterning, or order, namely law, we see repeated references to the idea of submission to a superior authority. One entry in particular, the second of fourteen, is especially interesting in light of the examination in previous chapters of the function of Orientalism in Racine's and Lafayette's texts:

[Law] is used in this sense for Religions. The ancient *Law*, or the *Law* of Moses, was the *Law* of God, the one that he gave to his people through the mouth of his Prophet. The *Law* of grace, or the Christian *Law*, is that which was given to us by our Lord Jesus Christ; it is the true *law*.

[23] It is interesting in the present context to note Foucault's study of hermaphroditism. The original French version of *Herculine Barbin, dite Alexina B. présenté par Michel Foucault* (Paris: Gallimard, 1978) lacks Foucault's introduction to the English edition. See Michel Foucault, introduction to *Herculine Barbin, Being the Recently Discovered Memoirs of a Nineteenth-Century Hermaphrodite*, trans. Richard McDougall (New York: Colophon, 1980).

The Turks follow the *law*, the Religion of Muhammad, their false Prophet. One says the Tables of the *law*, referring to God's ten commandments; on this depend the *law* and the Prophets.

[Loi] se dit en ce sens des Religions. L'ancienne *Loi*, ou la *Loi* de Moïse a été la *Loi* de Dieu, celle qu'il a donnée à son peuple par la bouche de son Prophète. La *Loi* de grâce ou la *Loi* Chrétienne est celle qui nous a été donnée par notre Seigneur Jésus-Christ, c'est la vraie *loi*. Les Turcs suivent la *loi*, la Religion de Mahomet leur faux Prophète. On dit les Tables de la *loi*, parlant des dix commandements de Dieu, de là dépend la *loi* & les Prophètes.

The existence of a body of laws and the communication of these divine principles through the prophets is posited on the side of truth, whereas the Turks are said to follow a false prophet and to be in error.

The definition of law here is certainly accurate; Furetière describes two different kinds of legal codes: the Christian and the Islamic. Neither type, however, is presented independently of the European context. The cultural prejudices evident in this exposition are transparent to us; it is an example of knowledge conceived along clear national, racial, and religious lines. What is even more striking from the point of view of method, however, is that farther down the list of definitions Furetière cites an example of an exception to the rule that is still true. Referring to natural law, he observes:

It is a general *law* that the weak object obeys the stronger, that the light object yields to the heavier. The Solar Eclipse that appeared at the time of the passion of Jesus Christ occurred against the ordinary *laws* of nature.

C'est une *loi* générale, que le faible objet obéit au plus fort, que le léger cède au plus pesant. L'Eclipse du Soleil qui parut au temps de la passion de Jésus-Christ, se fit contre les *lois* ordinaires de la nature.

The eclipse is the extraordinary event in nature that is believed to reinforce the exceptional moment of Christ's death. Whatever the historical accuracy of this example, the fact that Furetière cites it suggests his awareness of the need to preserve a certain fluidity within any taxonomic system. The eclipse is the break in the pattern that proves the randomness of experience. It thus indicates the limits of any "law" that represents knowledge through paradigms that exclude rare or unique events, that is, any new information which is inconsistent with the knowledge already patterned.

The point is not that science in the seventeenth century cannot yet claim to predict an eclipse, for it can.[24] The example of the eclipse allows us to extract a general rule of representation. Any adequate account of nature must include the regular motion of the planets and the comparatively irregular occurrence of an eclipse. Yet the same reasoning is not applied to cultural differences: Turks are not accorded, in a way that is not pejorative, the status of merely being different. Their status as an exception to the Christian rule is viewed as a sign of error and inferiority. Furetière accurately records information as it has been coded by his own culture; his claim to universal (normative French) representation is not challenged by my analysis. Still, it is interesting to note how Furetière's examples both indicate that it is impossible to perceive difference independently of a predetermined system, whether it be the astronomers' charts or a set of values based on religious beliefs. The eclipse, like the Turk, has its own order. Eclipses do occur at regular intervals, and the Turks are not Others within the Orient. But we must go outside of what is known, what is defined here as the truth of law, in order to identify them.[25] Examined as a representation of representation—as a display

[24] Under "eclipse" Furetière notes: "Longitude can be detected with certainty only by means of eclipses. There are sure means for predicting eclipses, & for knowing on what horizon they will appear. Römer discovered a machine, or a sort of planisphere and clock, which, by means of a handle that one turns, marks all the *eclipses* of the Planets that have occurred or that will ever occur. It is a marvelous invention" (On ne sait point certainement les longitudes que par le moyen des *éclipses*. Il y a des voies sûres de prédire les éclipses, & de savoir sur quel horizon elles paraîtront. Römer a trouvé une machine ou espèce de planisphère & de montre, qui par le moyen d'une manivelle qu'on tourne, marque toutes les *éclipses* des Planètes qui ont été ou qui seront jamais. C'est une invention merveilleuse).

[25] Not surprisingly for these times, the entry under "Turk" in the dictionary does nothing to alleviate the problem. Although it appears at first to be more objective, the initial definition includes a reference to the Turks' religion as a sect: "subject of the Oriental Emperor who professes himself a member of the Sect of Muhammad" (sujet de l'Empereur d'Orient qui fait profession de la Secte de Mahomet). More revealing is the subsequent reference to what "is said proverbially" (*on dit proverbialement*): "that a child is strong as a Turk, when he is big and strong for his age. One also says, to treat someone *'like a Turk treats a Moor'* [arrogantly], in order to say that he is treated harshly and as a declared enemy. One also says, in order to insult a man, to accuse him of barbarism, cruelty, irreligion, that he is a *Turk*" (qu'un enfant est fort comme un *Turc*, quand il est grand est robuste pour son âge. On dit aussi, traiter de *Turc* à More, pour dire, à la rigueur & en ennemi déclaré. On dit aussi en voulant injurier un homme, le taxer de barbarie, de cruauté, d'irréligion, que c'est un *Turc*).

of method and not simply as the content that it orders—Furetière's taxonomy allows us to see that the breakdown into categories implies the corresponding need to look at the restrictions to meaning implicit in the categories themselves.

Under "order" Furetière includes an interesting reference to a standard utilized in his own work:

> Is also said of the arrangement that is made of things having no advantage, rank, or natural precedent over each other, about which one nevertheless wants to avoid confusion. Words are placed in a Dictionary according to Alphabetical *order*.

> Se dit encore de l'arrangement qu'on fait des choses qui n'ont point d'avantage, de rang, ni de préséance naturelle les unes sur les autres, dont on veut pourtant éviter la confusion. On range les mots dans un Dictionnaire suivant l'*ordre* Alphabétique.

No single dictionary entry serves as a key to explaining all the others; the alphabetical listing precludes the hierarchization of entries according a prescribed set of values. These examples indicate, however, that one does not succeed entirely in avoiding confusion (ambiguity) or privilege. To do so implies the rigid separation of categories that, according to the present reading of the dictionary, need instead to be associated for their full meaning.

Pascal: Reading the New Science

There is no way out of this dilemma. Classification is so complex that, to use Descartes's terms, the division of a problem into its simplest parts multiplies rather than reduces the possibilities of signification. If anything, the taxonomy demonstrates that the whole of analysis is far more than the sum of its parts. I submit in this final investigation that it is Pascal, another figure whose career spans both science and literature, and whose *Pensées* move between an informative prose style and a rapturous poetry, who best represents the final complexity of classical representation.[26]

---

[26] All references to the *Pensées* are to Blaise Pascal, *Pensées*, ed. Léon Brunschvicg (Paris: Garnier-Flammarion, 1976). The second *pensée* number refers to the Lafuma classification.

Not the least of the paradoxes of the *Pensées* is that Pascal's Jansenist apology has become the symbol of a certain discontinuity which critics have alternately described as fragmentation (Marin, Stanton), difference (Melzer), and defamiliarization (Lyons).[27] The inscrutable contours of Pascal's argument evade the grasp of the critic who would take hold of the text, intending to shape it neatly under his or her pen, to mold a final meaning for this work by releasing its underlying tension. Pascal himself seeks to locate meaning in God, in a "transcendental signifier" that explains the relation of things in this world. He exposes this larger meaning by rejecting science, by thwarting all endeavors to explain or reason one's way into knowledge.[28]

Consistent with all modern science, Pascal's writing evinces a strong tendency toward nominalism, a belief that ideas are but names and that there are no absolute truths, simply the arbitrary and controvertible truths expressed in language.[29] Arguably, for the modern

[27] Louis Marin refers to the "fragmentary discourse whose unending [*interminée*] succession and aleatory order are capable of engendering the infinite distances covered by the commentary [*l'infinité des parcours du commentaire*], and thus an infinity of meanings" (*La critique du discours: Sur la "Logique de Port-Royal" et les "Pensées" de Pascal* [Paris: Minuit, 1975], 124). Arguing that discrepancies between the various editions of the *Pensées* reveal a historic resistance to the imposition of a definitive formal arrangement and interpretation, Domna C. Stanton also underscores the text's proclivity toward "dis-order predicated on fragmentariness and discontinuity" ("Pascal's Fragmentary Thoughts: Dis-order and its Overdetermination," *Semiotica* 51, nos. 1–3 [1984]: 212). Sara E. Melzer argues that the *Pensées* attempt "to subvert the semiological code by showing that all language is inherently figural (rhetorical). Rhetorical language is irredeemably fallen because figures disrupt the one-to-one relationship between words and things by introducing alternative and contradictory meanings. Meaning is always other than what language directly states" (*Discourses of the Fall: A Study of Pascal's "Pensées"* [Berkeley: University of California Press, 1986], 10). John D. Lyons asserts that all examples in Pascal are in fact counterexamples: "Despite an apparently simple binary system in which things are classified within a differential grid of clarity and obscurity, such opposition cannot provide a key to the semiotics of society. What is clear and what is unclear change places unpredictably. . . . Pascal uses the effects of proximity to make the clear obscure and to defamiliarize the everyday through an excessive and unexpected magnification" (*Exemplum: The Rhetoric of Example in Early Modern France and Italy* [Princeton: Princeton University Press, 1989], 173).

[28] Stanton observes: "It is one of the text's most effective, paradoxical strategies that readers both determinedly seek and never definitively find a rational order of meaning that would fill the signifying gaps and bridge the elliptical fragments" ("Pascal's Fragmentary Thoughts," 220).

[29] Marin refers to this text from "De l'esprit géométrique: De l'art de persuader": "For definitions are devised only to designate the things that one names and not to show their nature" (Car les définitions ne sont faites que pour désigner les choses que l'on nomme et non pas pour en montrer la nature). Blaise Pascal, *Opuscules et lettres*, ed. Louis Lafuma (Paris: Aubier-Montaigne, 1955), 126; quoted in Marin, *Critique*, 125n42. Nominalism is central to Bacon, Descartes, Galileo, and Hobbes.

mind at least, this insistence on what I call the context-dependency of meaning—the shifting of meanings that occurs as the context shifts—is Pascal's science, the system that allows us to understand his thoughts. Indeed, it is in his insistence on the arbitrariness of categorization and classification that Pascal has most to contribute to our understanding of how knowledge is constituted within the classical period.[30]

The *Pensées* fall outside the purview of Foucault's analysis of the episteme.[31] I mean, however, to restore Pascal's fragments to a discussion of the conditions that make knowledge possible in the seventeenth century. Critics have used Pascal to refute Foucault's archaeology.[32] My intent, however, is not to negate but to flesh out the notion of the classical episteme through a reading of Pascal that includes the effects of his poetic discourse.

In many important respects Pascal appears to be a retrograde philosopher within the system that Foucault elaborates, a throwback to a seemingly outmoded model of signification. For much of Pascal's thinking depends on the explicit geometry of a plenitudi-

[30] The arbitrariness of classification has been noted by Virginia K. Howe, "*Les Pensées*: Paradox and Signification," *Yale French Studies* 49 (1973): 120–31. Citing Howe, Stanton observes: "Even a basic division into the general and particular, a proposition and its supporting evidence is arbitrary" ("Pascal's Fragmentary Thoughts," 216). Hugh M. Davidson argues that Pascal establishes an agreement about propositions and then moves, seemingly backwards, to the presuppositions: "We should ordinarily be inclined to say that a proof is an organism consisting of two parts, an antecedent and a consequent. However, as Pascal uses the word, *preuve* refers to the former, the presupposition, rather than to the latter, to the certifying part rather than to the whole instance of reasoning" (*The Origins of Certainty: Means and Meanings in Pascal's "Pensées"* [Chicago: University of Chicago Press, 1979], 5). See also Davidson's discussion of verification in *Pascal and the Arts of the Mind* (Cambridge: Cambridge University Press, 1993), 76. For an analysis of the imprecise nature of proof in the *Pensées*, see Buford Norman, *Portraits of Thought: Knowledge, Methods, and Styles in Pascal* (Columbus: Ohio State University Press, 1988), chap. 7.

[31] For a different probing of the relations between Foucault's definition of the episteme and Pascal, see Jan Miel, "Les méthodes de Pascal et l'épistémè classique," in *Méthodes chez Pascal: Actes du colloque tenu à Clermont-Ferrand 10–13 juin 1976* (Paris: Presses Universitaires de France, 1976), 27–36, and "Pascal, Port-Royal, and Cartesian Linguistics," *Journal of the History of Ideas* 30 (1969): 261–71.

[32] Stanton opposes Foucault's view in *L'ordre du discours* that there is a fear of disorder. She refers to the work of Barthes, Butor, Blanchot, and Derrida to suggest a modern reorientation toward disorder that is consistent with contemporary readings of Pascal ("Pascal's Fragmentary Thoughts," 214). Melzer uses both Foucault and Derrida to explain how the *Pensées* defy the notion of classical language as clear, transparent, and concise. She does so, however, without problematizing the relations between Foucault and Derrida as I do. I maintain that the tension between these modern philosophers is critical for explaining how the *Pensées* structure knowledge.

nous and symmetrical model of resemblances, what he terms dispro-
portion:

> What is a man in infinity? . . . Let a mite offer in the smallness of his
> body incomparably smaller parts, legs with joints, veins in these legs,
> blood in these veins, humors in this blood, drops in these humors, vapors
> in these drops; let him, dividing these last things further, exhaust his
> ability to conceive these things, and let the last object to which he now
> comes be that about which we speak; he will think perhaps that this is
> the limit of smallness in our world. I want to make him see a new abyss
> in this. I want to depict for him not only the visible universe but the
> immensity of nature that one is capable of conceiving as being contained
> within this smallest atom. Might he see there an infinity of universes,
> each one of which having its firmament, its planets, its earth, in the same
> proportion as in the visible world; on that earth, animals and finally
> mites, in which he will discover again the same results that the first pro-
> duced; and find in other worlds the same thing yet again without end
> and without repose, such that he becomes lost in these marvels, which
> are as astonishing in their smallness as the others are by their amplitude.
> For who will not admire the fact that our body, which just before was
> not perceptible in the universe, itself imperceptible within the whole, be
> at present a colossus, a world, or rather a whole with regard to the noth-
> ingness beyond our grasp?

> Qu'est-ce qu'un homme dans l'infini? . . . Qu'un ciron lui offre dans la
> petitesse de son corps des parties incomparablement plus petites, des
> jambes avec des jointures, des veines dans ces jambes, du sang dans ces
> veines, des humeurs dans ce sang, des gouttes dans ces humeurs, des
> vapeurs dans ces gouttes; que, divisant encore ces dernières choses, il
> épuise ses forces en ces conceptions, et que le dernier objet où il peut
> arriver soit maintenant celui de notre discours; il pensera peut-être que
> c'est là l'extrême petitesse de la nature. Je veux lui faire voir là-dedans
> un abîme nouveau. Je lui veux peindre non seulement l'univers visible,
> mais l'immensité qu'on peut concevoir de la nature, dans l'enceinte de
> ce raccourci d'atome. Qu'il y voie une infinité d'univers, dont chacun a
> son firmament, ses planètes, sa terre, en la même proportion que le
> monde visible; dans cette terre, des animaux et enfin des cirons, dans
> lesquels il retrouvera ce que les premiers ont donné; et trouvant encore
> dans les autres la même chose sans fin et sans repos, qu'il se perde dans
> ces merveilles, aussi étonnantes dans leur petitesse que les autres par
> leur étendue; car qui n'admirera que notre corps, qui tantôt n'était pas

perceptible dans l'univers, imperceptible lui-même dans le sein du tout, soit à présent un colosse, un monde, ou plutôt un tout, à l'égard du néant où l'on ne peut arriver? (72/199)

Pascal here appears to be but another case of what Foucault describes with regard to the epistemological configuration of the Renaissance as proof that "everything will find its mirror and its macrocosmic justification on another and larger scale," and, inversely, that "the visible order of the highest spheres will be found reflected in the darkest depths of the earth" (31/46).

According to Foucault, in the seventeenth century man's own capacity to codify, to order the world in language, comes to predominate over the previous century's notion of a universal order predetermined by God. The divine order was believed to be discernible in all the elements of Creation, that is, in the things of this world themselves. This theory holds that the finite conceptualization of the Renaissance in which the microcosm—man—is reflected in, and hence bound by, the macrocosm—the cosmos—gives way in the seventeenth and eighteenth centuries to a representation that is infinite in its potential to signify. Classical writers are freed from the constraint that meaning precedes and thus determines representation; they are released from the idea that interpretation is an infinite reworking of the same master narrative of God's plenitudinous universe. Instead, the seventeenth century perceives the world in terms of an infinitely expanding table of elements that man conceives and orders.[33]

Foucault undoubtedly shortchanged the Renaissance when he insisted on this model. As a heuristic device, however, it enables us to situate Pascal more accurately within the classical episteme. In spite of some holdover similarities with the Renaissance model, we find in this *pensée* the same insistence on classical representation's implicit link to the verb *to be* (*être*) which Foucault underscores. The main task of the classical episteme, Foucault insists, "is *to ascribe a name to things,*

---

[33] One need not adopt Foucault's idea of a radical severing with the Renaissance to appreciate how the history of ideas was evolving to separate out the cause of faith from that of science. Foucault specifies that in the classical period the infinite is posited as much on the side of him who represents God as on that of Him who is God. The two realities, however, are never perceived to be coterminous: the text is never confused with the real, or representation with God. The real knowledge maker is man, though his capacity to make knowledge is a divine gift: "Though God still employs signs to speak to us through nature, he is making use of our knowledge, and of the relations that are set up between our impressions, in order to establish in our minds a relation of signification" (59/73).

and in that name to name their being" (120/136). In his depiction of the great chain of being, Pascal is in effect attributing a name to things. Consistent with Foucault's theory of the new episteme, Pascal demonstrates that meaning is dependent on the order of things in representation. Thus, the mite is tiny in relation to a human, but gargantuan when considered in relation to the atoms of which it is composed. Its meaning ultimately depends not on some inherent quality in itself, its essence, but on how it is situated as a sign within language, which functions as a system of signs.

In this *pensée* Pascal informs us that what we see and can represent may be equal to all that we cannot see or represent; he makes us understand that science blinds us to all that it cannot yet conceive but that may well exist. Identities change as knowledge is fleshed out and the position of things relative to other things is altered. Knowledge thus depends on our being able to determine the right perspective; to know we must recognize the appropriate context for evaluating the relation of things. Since the great chain of being is infinitely expandable, our perspective, Pascal insists, is always a matter of speculation, modification:

> If one is too young, one does not judge well; too old, the same thing.
> . . . So it is for paintings seen from too far away and too close. And there
> is only one indivisible point which is the right place. The others are too
> close, too far away, too high, or too low. Perspective assigns it in the art
> of painting, but who will assign it in truth and in ethics?

> Si on est trop jeune, on ne juge pas bien; trop vieil, de même. . . . Ainsi
> les tableaux, vus de trop loin et de trop près. Et il n'y a qu'un point
> indivisible qui soit le véritable lieu: les autres sont trop près, trop loin,
> trop haut ou trop bas. La perspective l'assigne dans l'art de la peinture,
> mais dans la vérité et dans la morale, qui l'assignera? (381/21)

The changes in perspective delineated by Pascal suggest, in effect, that knowledge is vulnerable to paradigm shifts. That is, meanings are products of a particular frame structure; knowledge is altered as the frame model is reconceived by the subject who ascribes a new context or perspective to what he views.[34]

---

[34] For an analysis of the specific values that inform Pascal's writing, see Lucien Goldmann, *Le Dieu caché: Etude sur la vision tragique dans les "Pensées" de Pascal et dans le théâtre de Racine* (Paris: Gallimard, 1959).

Throughout Pascal's work the incompleteness of knowledge is similarly represented through shifts along a signifying chain that situates the subject within a geometric space. I cite but two additional examples:

> I see these terrifying spaces of the universe that enclose me, and I find myself attached to a corner of this vast expanse, without my knowing why I am in this place rather than in another, nor why this short time which is given me to live is assigned at this point rather than at another in all of the eternity that preceded me and all that follows me. I see only infinities on all sides, which enclose me like an atom and like a shadow that lasts only an instant and then disappears forever.

> Je vois ces effroyables espaces de l'univers qui m'enferment, et je me trouve attaché à un coin de cette vaste étendue, sans que je sache pourquoi je suis plutôt placé en ce lieu qu'en un autre, ni pourquoi ce peu de temps qui m'est donné à vivre m'est assigné à ce point plutôt qu'en un autre de toute l'éternité qui m'a précédé et de toute celle qui me suit. Je ne vois que des infinités de toutes parts, qui m'enferment comme un atome et comme une ombre qui ne dure qu'un instant sans retour. (194/427)

> When I consider the short duration of my life, absorbed into the eternity preceding and following the little space that I occupy and even that I see, sunken into the infinite immensity of spaces of whose existence I know nothing and which know nothing of me, I am frightened and I am amazed to see myself here rather than there, because there is no reason why it should be here rather than there, why in the present rather than then. Who put me here? By whose order and action have this place and this time been destined to me?

> Quand je considère la petite durée de ma vie, absorbée dans l'éternité précédant et suivant le petit espace que je remplis et même que je vois, abîmé dans l'infinie immensité des espaces que j'ignore et qui m'ignorent, je m'effraie et m'étonne de me voir ici plutôt que là, car il n'y a point de raison pourquoi ici plutôt que là, pourquoi à présent plutôt que lors. Qui m'y a mis? Par l'ordre et la conduite de qui ce lieu et ce temps a-t-il été destiné à moi? (205/68)

All of these examples suggest—beyond the religious content of a fall from grace and what Pascal claims is the illusion that Cartesian science produces a complete knowledge—the very process through which representation represents its own capacity to signify without restricting the field of signification. As the subject contemplates his proximity to all that is near and his alienation from all that is far—as these signifiers slip closer to and then farther away from any center of signification posited by the text—we see the precariousness of meaning that is continually subject to reconfiguration. As the context shifts, identities are fragmented and reassigned.[35]

In another *pensée* Pascal makes the leap from perspective in painting to what today we would call the semiotics of language. A given object looks like *x* until we approach and see that it is more than *x:*

> A city, a countryside, from far away is a city and a countryside; but as one approaches, they are houses, trees, tiles, leaves, grass, ants, ants' legs, to infinity. All this is enveloped in the name countryside.

> Une ville, une campagne, de loin est une ville et une campagne; mais à mesure qu'on s'approche, ce sont des maisons, des arbres, des tuiles, des feuilles, des herbes, des fourmis, des jambes de fourmis, à l'infini. Tout cela s'enveloppe sous le nom de campagne. (115/65)

Here the viewing subject, like the reader, is in fact suspended. Pascal underscores our limited vision, our inability to perceive and to analyze all that is. Suggesting that the word *countryside* (*campagne*) functions as an analytic tool, and that he can find an infinite number of composite parts of this noun, Pascal signals how meaning is not only arbitrary, limited by the final label or name that man ascribes to it, but also context-dependent. That is, meaning is a function not so much of being as of knowledge itself, the system (language) that assigns identities. A name has been assigned to account for all that man sees in the countryside. Countryside, like all paradigms produced by science, has fixed dimensions; any facet of the country that cannot be explained by this term has no meaning, no value. To see more—and Pascal by his sustained deconstruction of the paradigm urges us to do just this—one has to reconceive the paradigm; one needs to diversify,

---

[35] The act of framing meaning, moreover, does not ensure in Pascal, any more than in La Rochefoucauld, that there is anything but a false bottom to all the various paradigms that one invokes to order knowledge. Cf. Melzer: "What one uses to decide the proper interpretation of signs are more signs. The effort to lift the veil of signs thus leads only to their proliferation, so that we can never be sure whether we are face-to-face with the bare truth or with our (mis)representations of truth" (110).

broaden the category of nouns into something much more fluid and indeterminate. By structuring the naming process as an infinite regress—the search for the more and more that we cannot see—Pascal in effect sets up a model of infinite progress, a model of an episteme that is characterized more by the state of becoming (*devenir*) than by being (*être*).[36] Thus I would argue that Foucault's analysis of the classical episteme nonetheless falls short of explaining Pascal's ultimate contribution to our understanding of the conditions that made it possible to order knowledge in the seventeenth century.

Foucault enables us to see in the *pensée* about the country, and others like it, the same devotion to analysis, the same possibility of structuring meaning through an arbitrary system of signs that is, he writes, "able to make nature visible from its primary elements right to the simultaneity of all their possible combinations" (62/76). For in its insistence on the unfolding of the sign countryside, this *pensée* demonstrates exactly the phenomenon that Foucault describes as typical of the classical episteme: its capacity to structure thoughts in language based on techniques of analysis and the recombination of elements.

One might be tempted nonetheless to dismiss Pascal as a retrograde example, as offering a defense of what Foucault negatively terms "the primitive text of a discourse sustained, and retained, forever," an old master narrative.[37] One could easily argue that Pascal attempts to debunk the rational method, to substitute for it the old

---

[36] Marin offers an extensive analysis of this fragment (*Critique*, chap. 4). Invoking Roman Jakobson's model, he examines the question of the *pensée*'s fragmentation in terms of a signified whose totality can never be captured by the signifier. He posits a metonymic chain of signifiers that extends indefinitely toward infinity, in contrast to the signified chain, which leads toward zero as the infinite division of meaning is spun out by the text: "The signifier will never coalesce with the signified, since this being which the signifier designates in the signified flows infinitely toward nothingness without ever being annulled there. . . . Man is in this way disappropriated of his language since he retains only a general and distant idea of the meaning of what is being pronounced in it; and since, surreptitiously, this meaning is dissolved in the infinite substitutive game of the parts into the whole" (*jeu substitutif infini des parties dans le tout* [*Critique*, 125]).

[37] Foucault writes "In the Classical age, to make use of signs is not, as it was in preceding centuries, to attempt to rediscover beneath them the primitive text of a discourse sustained, and retained, forever; it is an attempt to discover the arbitrary language that will authorize the deployment of nature within its space, the final terms of its analysis and the laws of its composition. It is no longer the task of knowledge to dig out the ancient Word from the unknown places where it may be hidden; its job now is to fabricate a language, and to fabricate it well—so that, as an instrument of analysis and combination, it will really be the language of calculation" (62–63/76–77).

cause of religious faith. Although this is undoubtedly Pascal's avowed purpose, the *pensée* about the countryside nonetheless makes us know not the divine (which is, after all, by Pascal's own admission an act of faith in a *deus absconditus,* a God whom we cannot see) but the potential for knowledge. It does so by virtue of the very "calcul," or analytic power of Pascal's own representation here. For what Pascal demonstrates in insisting on a city that, like the countryside, can be reconceived as so many houses, trees, and so on is not the failure of the rational method—we can indeed identify cities and country-side—so much as how this method is dependent on a persistent effort to erect categories that are themselves limited in their useful-ness, vulnerable to recombinations, epistemological shifts. Cities would be valorized differently if the political landscape were factored into the equation, for example. In such circumstances would the city appear more like the country or less so? Such questions imply that knowledge is knowledge not because it correctly describes the true state of the natural world but because it has been framed within a particular paradigm. These enabling structures ultimately determine what the "facts" of science can mean. Thus, if Foucault's analysis justifies our inclusion of Pascal in the new episteme, if he helps us to understand Pascal's nominalism, Pascal's *Pensées* in turn suggest that the episteme is less rigorously contained, less universal in its or-der, than Foucault would allow.

"Nature has placed all of its truths individually, each inside itself" (La nature a mis toutes ses vérités chacune en soi-même), Pascal af-firms. To this he adds: "Our art encloses them one inside the other, but this is not natural: each one occupies its own place" (Notre art les renferme les unes dans les autres, mais cela n'est pas naturel: cha-cune tient sa place [21/684]). Analogies, he claims, blind us from seeing the truth of things; they prevent us from valuing differences. And what Pascal makes us see, consistent with Foucault, is that such identities depend on how they are ordered "one inside the other" in language. Admittedly, for Pascal, this is all art, and as such is inferior to nature, God's creation. Representation, by this account, is itself a failed effort to get at the truth. But by making us see this failure, by calling attention to all that we miss if we insist on certain paradigms into which identities are funneled one atop another, Pascal uses lan-guage to inform us about representation in ways that are perfectly consistent with Foucault's analysis of the science of this period. Pascal, too, shows the meaning of a thing to depend on "its place" in rep-resentation. Pascal, however, in his tireless dialectic, posits meaning that escapes the text's model, that is out there in nature, knowable only as an unknowable, unidentified in representation.

Foucault emphasizes more the act of naming than the context for naming, placing final emphasis on a unitary language: "One might say that it is the Name that organizes all Classical discourse; to speak or to write is not to say things or to express oneself, it is not a matter of playing with language, it is to make one's way towards the sovereign act of nomination, to move, through language, towards the place where things and words are conjoined in their common essence, and which makes it possible to give them a name" (117/133). He goes on to characterize the naming process—*nomination*—as an act that leads to an eventual point of completion, whereby the name, and with it the classical episteme, reaches its end: "But once that name has been spoken, all the language that has led up to it, or that has been crossed in order to reach it, is reabsorbed into it and disappears. So that Classical discourse, in its profound essence, tends always toward this boundary" (117/133).[38]

Foucault describes globally the dialectical process whereby one paradigm exhausts itself and gives way to another. Pascal, however, demonstrates the effect of many paradigm shifts occurring simultaneously without exhausting the possibilities for structuring new meaning. Rather, many paradigms—as many as there are nouns—all reverberate and regenerate as experience is accumulated. Experience causes our perspective to shift and the thing named to be other than what it seemed when we first named it. To Foucault's emphasis on "nomination" Pascal allows us to add another layer of analysis which relates specifically to an act of encoding that is a representation suspended in time and space. The latter functions like a grid through which all identities are filtered. But the grid is itself unstable; it floats within language. Foucault conceptualizes that at certain points in history meanings are deferred to a new paradigm in a sustained evolution toward a distinct but unattainable end. He concludes the passage just cited by insisting that classical discourse never fulfills its ambition of completing its table, never speaks the name that fixes the full order of things: "but in surviving [this boundary, classical discourse] pushes the boundary still further away. It continues on its way in the perpetually maintained suspension of the Name" (117/133). Pascal suggests why the deferral of meaning is so pervasive.

[38] See also Foucault's commentary on the analysis of the sign in the *Logique de Port-Royal* (61/75).

It is, of course, Derrida and not Foucault who consistently talks of texts as functioning through deferral.[39] Foucault in the end makes a claim for the solidity of classical discourse in the form of a fleshed-out taxonomy. This important difference notwithstanding, his emphasis on meanings that are substituted for one another, and on a limit of language that remains forever unattainable, poses an interesting problem for the modern reader of Pascal. The acrimonious debates between Foucault and Derrida are well known. The battle was fought over Descartes. By shifting the focus to Pascal, I hope to recontextualize not the specifics of their debate over madness but the issue of classifying difference in the age of absolutism.

Without rehearsing the intricacies of their dispute, let me clarify simply that Foucault in *L'histoire de la folie* attempts to posit an Other that is not determined by reason, by the language in which we order our thoughts. Therefore the Other is not tainted by the order already assigned to things. Derrida, by contrast, claims that it is impossible to conceive of meaning, even the antithesis of meaning as madness represents it, outside of language.[40] Edward Said was later to characterize the terms of their debate as a struggle between the "mise en discours" (putting into discourse) of Foucault and the "il n'y a pas de hors texte" (there is no outside the text) of Derrida's *mise en abîme*.[41]

In a brief evocation of classical literature, Foucault posits a first, seemingly premature end to the process of deferral. Literature, he claims, takes the process of naming to a dead-end conclusion: silence. Aphonia is the final result of a process of naming that is consistently deferred, for literature may well strive to reach "a name that remains always formidable because it exhausts, and thereby kills, the possibility of speech" (118/134). The case of Pascal illustrates, however, that literature does not, as Foucault's hasty reference to the Princesse de Clèves's "restrained confession" (*aveu si retenu*) (118/134) implies, lead to silence as the point of completion, or exhaustion, of the naming process. Rather, in the silences of Pascal's text, in the gaps formed by paradigm shifts, meanings echo and resound. Even as we identify the things of this world, we are told that their identity is context-

---

[39] For more on the importance of Derrida's concept of *différance* in elucidating Pascal's work, see Melzer, 9–10 and 91.

[40] See Jacques Derrida, *L'écriture et la différence* (Paris: Seuil, 1967), chap. 2. For a lucid recapitulation of the Foucault-Derrida debate, see Roy Boyne, *Foucault and Derrida: The Other Side of Reason* (London: Unwin Hyman, 1990).

[41] Edward W. Said, "The Problem of Textuality: Two Exemplary Positions," *Critical Inquiry* 4 (Summer 1978): 673.

dependent, dependent on our particular vantage point. In this artful obscuring of the act of naming, we see a release not from the efforts of representation to unify, organize, and analyze—all qualities that Foucault believes shape the classical episteme—but from the claim that representation succeeds in its efforts to fix a rigid taxonomy. Pascal's poetry informs us, against Foucault's insistence, that there is no "solid and tightly knit . . . unity of language . . . in the Classical experience" (120/135), unless that unity be found in the very process through which various elements are combined and recombined, tested and retested, that is, in an activity of naming that is unending.

Foucault was not a literary critic by training, and his analysis of the princess's "restrained confession" is arguably oriented more toward the theme of desire than toward the structure of desire. The novel, in any event, is more complex on both levels than Foucault's summary discussion allows us to see. Ultimately, as the example of Pascal serves to illustrate, the effect of including literary as well as scientific discourse in an analysis of the classical episteme is that we come to appreciate the episteme as a fluid configuration of paradigms, frame structures, in which meanings continue to vacillate. Indeed, the episteme is less an archaeology of the sign in all of its transparency than one of paradigms, clusters of signs that frame meaning, and that themselves shift over time.

I do not mean to imply that Derrida was right and Foucault was wrong, however. Derrida, in his uncovering of the privileging of speech over writing, does not provide an answer to the kinds of historically rooted questions that Foucault has posed and that are the subject of my own investigation. In Pascal's *Pensées* we see that silences do speak, and that they do so as a function of writing, the discursive activity so integral to the cultural experience of the seventeenth century, part of the documented representation of the period. Where Foucault and Derrida do come together is not in a taxonomy conceived as a monument to history (Foucault's "discours"), nor in a text that functions outside this history (Derrida's "*il n'y a pas de hors texte*"). What connects the outside and the inside of the classical period's structuring of knowledge is writing in general, and the elements that escape the text's model in particular. In its self-conscious design, its deliberate construction of paradigms, the texts studied in this book all model the modeling process that is, I believe, what shapes the classical episteme. The *Pensées* suggest once again a difference between method on the one hand and the process of experimentation which leads to and from the method on the other. The classical episteme constitutes the name, extended into an elaborate taxonomy, as an ideal. But to the degree that representation performs meaning—that it frames its own framing of identities as opposed to simply celebrating this frame as a milestone achievement that fixes knowledge—the concept of the episteme must be reconceived to emphasize experimentation over method. It is the history of this performance that is expressed in Pascal's writing.

If it is possible to find a point of tolerance between Foucauldian and Derridean claims about textuality, it is because in the seventeenth century, to a greater extent than ever before, history literally becomes a history of representation. More precisely, the external history—the *hors texte* that are the events of history as lived by real people—mirrors the internal history—the *mise en abîme*, the representation of these events—in this period because the external history is, as Foucault argues, a history of the breaking out of the divine mold, the secularization of society through representation. Even as it multiplies proofs and, in Pascal's *Pensées*, multiplies affirmations of God's infinite wisdom, knowledge in the classical age is released from the master narrative of God's Creation and into man's own hands as he writes the world into existence by testing his power to name first the angle of his vision—the particular perspective that I have been calling the text's model—and then the object that he holds in view. As he defines a context for his writing and uses this particular context to shape an order of things, he exposes the rigid constraints of a world ordered through what, in an adaptation of Derridean terminology can be called the transcendental tale of the resemblance of man and the cosmos. This tale gives way to the new science in which all models, including, most notably, that of science itself, yield before the knowledge that some meanings always surpass the model's capacity to name them. The history of the classical period is, in short, the history of the deconstruction of a master model. But this act of deconstruction is one in which even the science that offers itself in place of the old model is shown to exceed itself, that is, to float within the vast space that Pascal designates as divine and that we, in a more secular vein, might call the yet-unrealized potential for meaning, the other knowledge still to be mastered. Whereas Foucault in a dialectical view of history looked to the eighteenth century to postulate the end point of classical representation, I have looked to the art of Pascal's representation to show how no final end, no exhaustion of a paradigm, but rather a continual series of rebeginnings, a continual reconfiguration of ideas, marks the classical period's great experiment with the method that has become its hallmark.

Meanings in the classical period are, as Foucault has brilliantly detailed, produced through man's efforts to order and measure, to codify. I have been suggesting, however, that in this notion of calculation (*calcul*) we come to see not so much the championing of the scientific method, of another master discourse, as the championing of the modeling process itself. We discover the experiment through which the rational model, like all other paradigms, is created, contextualized by science, and in turn recontextualized by the literature, as this term refers both to fictional texts and to the occulted elements of nonfictional texts devoted to the exposition of taxonomic systems. That is, the literary component of writing reflects not the literal meaning of scientific texts so much as the activity through which science demonstrates how in representation all meanings are framed, all facts dependent on the models in which they are conceived. Pascal's proclamation of faith itself serves to advance the cause of knowledge; his contestatory logic informs us about the possibilities of a language that speaks to us of the signifying power of representation even as he would speak to us of God.

The revolution in science that takes place in the classical period, and with it the increased separation of religion and science, makes especially poignant the interconnections between science and literature. For both fields show how a culture conceives itself in representation. Tensions between religious and secular beliefs began well before the classical period, and continue even through the present day. But in the striking confluence of the scientific and literary patterning of knowledge which the seventeenth century evidences by isolating religion from method, we discover a burgeoning of a new worldview in which man begins to write his own story. He begins to identify himself and his world in a representation that depends not on a preexistent, God-given order but on his own ability to conceptualize his experience in language. Perhaps more than anything else, this history of representation is a study in the relations that Pascal, through his emphasis on the fluidity of our position with regard to knowledge and the consequent suspension of meaning, shows to be a refusal of "rational complacency."[42] By this I mean a refusal to

[42] Ronald Levao, "Francis Bacon and the Mobility of Science," *Representations* 40 (Fall 1992): 17. Studying the work of Francis Bacon, Levao uses this term in a different sense

conceal the very structures that frame and contextualize meanings and an urge to push beyond existing paradigms to new ones. Knowledge is always subject to a greater knowing, whether it be in the form of faith in God's wonder or an understanding of the limits of what man is able to discern.

Determined to examine the rise of classical science in all of its many facets, Foucault nevertheless includes no reference to Pascal in the chapters he devotes to this subject. The omission is telling—of a deficiency not in *how* Foucault analyzes but in *what* he analyzes to constitute the classical episteme. Believing, no doubt, that Pascal represents the cause of faith—in contrast to the devout rationalism of Descartes—he sees fit to elide the philosopher whose *Pensées* likewise give shape to the ordering of knowledge in the classical period. In this selection of one philosopher's writings over the other, we see a proclivity toward taking the content at face value, and ignoring the more telling praxis through which both Descartes's science and Pascal's religiosity reveal a similar tendency to perform a knowledge independent of their stated purpose. Each author formally structures a knowledge that goes beyond the explicit message that he directs toward his readers.

It bears repeating that Descartes himself went to great lengths to affirm the existence of God, and that it would be inappropriate to situate him, any more than Pascal, within a tradition of nonbelievers. Instead, it has been my intent to show how, despite protestations of faith, both Descartes and Pascal, like Furetière, reveal the ordering of knowledge in seventeenth-century France to be independent of the will to truth that marks their writing, their desire to affirm the irrefutable accuracy of what they represent. The grid of categories that determines the order of things, and that thus supersedes the act of naming individual objects, is, as all three writers show, suspended, vulnerable to what I have called shifts in context. Though he calls attention to the representation of representation in Velázquez's paint-

---

but similarly underscores the tension between knowing and unknowing, order and disorder: "Science borrows from theology the subversion of rational complacency: even as the contemplation of God produces 'wonder, which is broken knowledge,' so the contemplation of nature produces 'knowledge broken.' Although one marks the limit of thought when facing the infinite and the other 'invites men to enquire farther' into the finite, each produces a *docta ignorantia*, a complex state of knowing and unknowing, self-consciousness and self-abnegation, fulfillment and hunger" (17–18; Levao cites Francis Bacon, *Of the Proficience and Advancement of Learning Divine and Humane* and *New Organon.*).

ing, and though he returns periodically to the idea of a meaning that escapes the grid for knowledge whose construction he meticulously studies, Foucault does not sufficiently explain the art of science as it is understood by Descartes, Furetière, and Pascal. These three writers allow us to see that in the taxonomy through which it celebrates itself as Other to art, as to faith and to ignorance, science in the end exposes precisely how it substitutes a cultivated knowledge for the Truth.

Conclusion

Final Perspectives

Descartes completes his exposition of the scientific method by declaring his intention to omit nothing. The fourth precept of the *Discours* specifies that he will consistently "make enumerations so complete, and reviews so comprehensive, that [he] could be sure of leaving nothing out" (faire partout des dénombrements si entiers, et des revues si générales, qu'[il fût] assuré de ne rien omettre [120/138]). With this principle Descartes launches what history has come to see as the symbolic beginning of a vast experiment with taxonomy. Much of the present study, however, has been dedicated to showing that something is in fact always omitted. More precisely, I have endeavored to explain that for each thing that is named there is some other meaning which, although relegated to a signifying space outside that framed by representation, continues to speak to us. As readers and spectators, we come to know representation as representation. We understand the process through which the text's exclusionary model establishes a restricted knowledge—one whose parameters it artificially determines—within a broader epistemological field. This field includes not only the meaning ordered by the model but all that the model sloughs off as it concentrates its own energies, thereby reinforcing—arbitrarily—all that the author would have us know about the perfectibility of forms and the certainty of identities. My purpose, however, has not been to certify the failure of Cartesian science to reach its stated goal. Rather, I have refocused attention on this broader knowledge in order to explore the historical implications of the rise of science in conjunction with the absolutist rule of seventeenth-century France. In this culturally conceived context for observing how meanings are formulated, to err is also to know. It is to know otherwise and more than what the master teaches through his programmatic, official discourse as played out in the proclamations of science and the state, as well as those of a mother instructing her daughter.

Today philosophers of science contend that the "eureka," or serendipitous, event is fundamental to scientific discovery. Adopting the concept of tinkering, introduced by Claude Lévi-Strauss in *La pensée sauvage* to describe the thought processes of savages, Aharon Kantorovich argues that "scientific creation is not method-governed and that science has no predetermined goal."[1] The seemingly anecdotal quality of science is now recognized as an essential component in the formation of knowledge. With this concept modern philosophy justifies retrospectively a focus on the epistemological evolution in the classical period as it includes all that authors would write off in order to assert the authority of a particular discourse, whether it be the narrative component of the *Discours* or the differences that literature brings to light in its effort to model a knowledge of fixed identities.

Each of the works studied in this book has suggested the limits weighing on the classical period's efforts to know absolutely. The pursuit of a finite and absolute knowledge is collapsed by representation into the production of lesser truths. This production is always skillful, however; it displays how the process of experimentation is an end in and of itself. This process is responsible for formulating a knowledge that is no less rich, no less revealing about the cultural climate of the times and the possibilities for structuring ideas, than is the knowledge gleaned from the perfectibility of the scientific method or, in literature, what I have called the model ordering the text. The theater teaches us that tragedy is never without its cathartic effects. Classical writers cannot satisfy completely their desire to empower themselves, a desire expressed in the present study as the will to knowledge. But each step an author takes toward identifying that elusive excess that escapes his or her control—each reformulation of an idea—is productive in that it shows the responsibility for knowing the world to be the author's own.

Science shows how writers shape knowledge through the careful elaboration of categories, the meticulous determination of identities

---

[1] Aharon Kantorovich, *Scientific Discovery: Logic and Tinkering* (Albany: State University of New York Press, 1993), 3.

and differences. In its reliance on systematic analysis, literature in its own way emerges as an authority on the science of representation. Like science, literature has dedicated itself to exploring how meanings are encoded and embedded within a text. Elaborating the process that I have labeled contextualization, literature calls attention to the fact, implicit in science, that any paradigm is a construct. The model ordering knowledge is a device for containing experience, for taking the unknown and making it predictable by subjecting it to a system that man invents and refines. I have used Foucault's commentary about classical science without adopting his theory of ruptures in an effort to save the baby as I threw away the bath water. I have shown that literature speaks to Foucault's science to the degree that it accentuates how representation itself becomes a factor in representation. Literary works display how information is filtered through a model or grid for establishing identities. Although it is impossible for meaning to be conceived outside the model, as it is impossible to step outside language, it is important to know that any knowledge structured through the model is necessarily limited, framed by the already known. This model is always susceptible to being reconfigured, for it opens up onto the still unnamed but authentic experience of ambivalence typified by the marshal in Velázquez's *Las meninas*. To know what is still undetermined is the future of science. The weight of discovery is always balanced by the knowledge that all systems are provisional and that the identities they fix are solidified at the expense of others which represent the potential for new knowledge. Literature codes this experience, identifying what elides the model as a difference that is not negated, as a meaning that is not merely Other to the model's Same. Literature thus does not so much fill a void created by science as flesh out the same experiment with method.

It is possible to argue, against Foucault, that sixteenth-century literary texts in one important respect function in essentially the same way as literary texts from successive periods: language was then, as it is now, separate from the things that it named. Even if Renaissance theory had not yet formulated the specific idea of the transparency of language or of the ability of language to create the phenomena of which it speaks, we today are wary of any concept that does not show the text to substitute the signs that it creates for the real it describes. Whatever vestiges of an Aristotelian ideology remained intact in the Renaissance—whatever beliefs were held regarding essences contained within things themselves, put there by God—the literature of this period was by no means limited to showing a chain of being that extended from microcosm to macrocosm. Nor can texts by Rabelais or Montaigne, to take just the most obvious examples, be said to signify without recourse to the disturbing ambivalences of the kind underscored in this book with regard to their seventeenth-century successors.

What does happen between the sixteenth and the seventeenth centuries relates more to the cultural phenomenon of the increased secularization of ideas. For Descartes God is necessary to create the natural world and, as part of this originary act, to beget man's soul. But from the moment of Creation onward, man is a rational being, and in the seventeenth century man's exercise of reason makes the order of the world a product of his representation. We witness a world in which, historically, the encoding of meaning assumes a new priority, since the rise of an absolutist court and the revolution in science both serve to deny religion its unique role as purveyor of truth. This difference is important because it allows us to maintain an idea of a consistent linguistic function—language used to fashion a worldview—while noting that the new emphasis on method, and, correspondingly, on language as an analytic tool, defines an epistemological evolution that is in turn contingent on a variety of cultural influences. Specifically, the development of a method that permits the elaboration of extensive taxonomies—these models which man constructs himself—fills a gap created when the belief in a predetermined order subsides. The point is not to determine whether science opened the door for an absolutist state or whether the reverse is true, but to appreciate the possibilities for knowledge as these emerge more or less simultaneously in science, in the politics of church and state, and in the arts. This convergence of discourses reflects the broad dimensions of an epistemological evolution; it shows codification to assume a pride of place because God, framer of meaning, has yielded his fired torch to man's pen. History and science both evince an epistemological tightening, a "classical" composition around a central model of finite and predictable knowledge, which literature in its own exemplary way also celebrates. But literature opens this model in such a way as to expose the assumptions implicit in the ordering of method itself.

Classical society moves away from religion's master narrative of God's Creation and toward man's own absolutist claims. Yet in the wake of this historic evolution we witness an order of things that is anything but monolithic, anything but fixed. No one specific content or method but rather the freedom to experiment explains the epistemology of this period. It is this enlightened discourse that propels itself into the next century. If Foucault links the classical period with the eighteenth century, it is undoubtedly on account of the milestone achievement of the *Encyclopédie,* a taxonomic feat of unprecedented proportions. I turn once again to Diderot and the *Encyclopédie* in order to open the frame of my own representation to a model that, though it would complete the experiment in method, displays the complexities of representation I have underscored throughout my study of seventeenth-century texts. For not only does Diderot recognize the problems inherent in transcribing a particular object such as the machine for making stockings. He also knows full well the problems inherent in the system designed to order the encyclopedia, its intricate web of articles.

Diderot devises a complex genealogy, or table, for specifying the extensive network of relations enumerated by the philosophers. If the *Encyclopédie* has the merit of offering a system ordered independently of God, it cannot escape manifold problems of classification, particularly as they concern the establishment of cross-references (*renvois*). Jacques Proust notes that the system adopted by Diderot, for all its systematic detail and precision, ultimately fails to satisfy him. Diderot, Proust asserts, sees text succumb to the hierarchization of values that man assigns in less than objective fashion:

> Nature offers us only individual things, infinite in number and with no fixed and determined division between them. All things in nature follow one another with no perceptible difference. And on this sea of objects that surrounds us, if there appear certain ones, like the tips of rocks, which seem to pierce the surface and dominate the others, they only owe this advantage to particular systems, to vague conventions, and to certain events that are foreign to the physical arrangement of beings and to the true institutions of philosophy.

> La nature ne nous offre que des choses particulières, infinies en nombre et sans aucune division fixe et déterminée. Tout s'y succède par des nuances insensibles. Et sur cette mer d'objets qui nous environne, s'il en paraît quelques-uns, comme des pointes de rochers, qui semblent percer la surface et dominer les autres, ils ne doivent cet avantage qu'à des systèmes particuliers, qu'à des conventions vagues, et qu'à certains évé-

nements étrangers à l'arrangement physique des êtres, et aux vraies institutions de la philosophie.[2]

Here we discover Pascal's perspective minus the religion, a model for representation that insists on the relativity rather than the universality of all that it names. But if the encyclopedists' vast classification system fails to complete the task set by Cartesian science, if it fails to identify all things in the world, it cannot be said not to signify. Indeed, the experiment with taxonomy itself constitutes a new knowledge.

To recognize that any of the various systems devised to classify things produces the same rewards and the same complications is to know precisely how much more is knowable than can ever be represented.[3] In this fragmentation of information, not only Descartes but also Pascal and all the literary writers from Rotrou to Lafayette speak to us about a knowledge formed by the perspective that allows us to view the frame of representation from a distance sufficient to appreciate it as a whole entity, and thus to see more than what this model contains within itself. The reader's knowledge is not limited to what is fixed by the frame of the text, be it scientific or literary. It records as well the author's hand which sets the model in motion.

Descartes invented an evil genius (*mauvais génie*) to keep him from falling into error by forcing him to be absolutely certain that he had overlooked nothing. He believed that it was better to err on the side of caution than to assign a value mistakenly to something whose identity eluded him. It is admittedly to distort his system to ask, in light of the present study, how to compare two false positives. But how do we assess the relative merits of science and literature if, on the one hand, science claims to be true but is not because its taxonomy is incomplete, alterable, and inexhaustible and, on the other hand, literature claims to be an illusion but also speaks the truth about representation? In its basic structuring the Cartesian system makes no

---

[2] Jacques Proust, "Diderot et le système des connaissances humaines," *Studies on Voltaire and the Eighteenth Century* 256 (1988): 124. Proust cites Denis Diderot, "Prospectus du dictionnaire," in *Oeuvres complètes*, ed. Herbert Dieckmann, Jacques Proust, and Jean Varloot (Paris: Hermann, 1975–), 5:91.

[3] Proust observes that all classificatory systems (whether they order information alphabetically; discipline by discipline; or in a table following Bacon's design of an encyclopedic tree) are more or less interchangeable: "It matters not which grid is used, only that there be one and that it be constructed by a human mind" (118). He argues that, although the encyclopedists give the best possible representation, a space emerges between image and text which continues to speak (123). We see here the same overriding of the model I have analyzed in classical texts.

place for these ambiguities. In this book I have shown, however, that such indifferentiation does indeed inform us about the possibilities for structuring knowledge in the classical period. Such is the case because, as Foucault has argued in *Les mots et les choses*, one of the consequences of the emphasis on a finite or absolute knowledge in the classical period is that man is always inadequate with regard to the infinite (316/327). We have seen, moreover, that to disavow the significance of all that breaks the frame of representation is to create an inferior knowledge, a false idol of a text in which to mirror our own desire for completeness in flagrant disregard of all that the text produces but disavows. Descartes, we can presume, would not have us beg the question posed here if to do so would mean sacrificing the certainty of ambiguity for the illusion of a greater truth. And in this persistent need to correct the error that occurs when the method fails to produce its desired effects, we discover how experimentation in the classical period brings about its own rewards.

Bibliography

Aijaz Ahmad. *In Theory: Classes, Nations, Literatures.* London: Verso, 1992.

Apostolidès, Jean-Marie. *Le prince sacrifié: Théâtre et politique au temps de Louis XIV.* Paris: Minuit, 1985.

——. *Le roi-machine: Spectacle et politique au temps de Louis XIV.* Paris: Minuit, 1981.

Austin, J. L. *How to Do Things with Words.* Ed. J. O. Ormson and Marina Sbisà. Cambridge: Harvard University Press, 1975.

Balandier, Georges. *Le pouvoir sur scènes.* Paris: Balland, 1980.

Barthes, Roland. "La Rochefoucauld: Réflexions ou sentences et maximes." In *Le degré zéro de l'écriture suivi de Nouveaux essais critiques.* Paris: Seuil, 1972.

——. *Sur Racine.* Paris: Seuil, 1963.

Beasley, Faith E. *Revising Memory: Women's Fiction and Memoirs in Seventeenth-Century France.* New Brunswick: Rutgers University Press, 1990.

Behdad, Ali. *Belated Travelers: Orientalism in the Age of Colonial Dissolution.* Durham: Duke University Press, 1994.

Bénichou, Paul. *L'écrivain et ses travaux.* Paris: Corti, 1967.

Bersani, Leo. *A Future for Astyanax: Character and Desire in Literature.* Boston: Little Brown, 1976.

Boyne, Roy. *Foucault and Derrida: The Other Side of Reason.* London: Unwin Hyman, 1990.

Bridoux, André, ed. *Descartes: Oeuvres et lettres.* Paris: Gallimard, 1953.

Brockliss, L. W. B. *French Higher Education in the Seventeenth and Eighteenth Centuries: A Cultural History.* Oxford: Clarendon, 1987.

Brody, Jules. "*La Princesse de Clèves* and the Myth of Courtly Love." *University of Toronto Quarterly* 38 (1969): 105–35.

Bruneau, Marie-Florine. *Racine: Le jansénisme et la modernité.* Paris: Corti, 1986.

Burke, Peter. *The Fabrication of Louis XIV.* New Haven: Yale University Press, 1992.

Butor, Michel. "Sur *La Princesse de Clèves.*" In *Répertoire.* Paris: Minuit, 1960.

Corneille, Pierre. *Horace.* In *Oeuvres complètes.* Ed. André Stegmann. Paris: Seuil, 1963.

Culler, Jonathan. "Paradox and the Language of Morals in La Rochefoucauld." *Modern Language Review* 68 (January 1973): 28–39.

Dällenbach, Lucien. *Le récit spéculaire: Essai sur la mise en abyme.* Paris: Seuil, 1977.

Darmon, Jean-Charles. "Furetière et l'universel." *Stanford French Review* 14 (Winter 1990): 15–46.

Daston, Lorraine J. "Classifications of Knowledge in the Age of Louis XIV." In *Sun King: The Ascendancy of French Culture during the Reign of Louis XIV.* Ed. David Lee Rubin. London: Associated University Presses, 1992.

Davidson, Hugh M. *The Origins of Certainty: Means and Meanings in Pascal's "Pensées."* Chicago: University of Chicago Press, 1979.

———. *Pascal and the Arts of the Mind.* Cambridge: Cambridge University Press, 1993.

Defaux, Gérard. *Molière, ou les métamorphoses du comique: De la comédie morale au triomphe de la folie.* Lexington, Ky.: French Forum, 1980. 2d ed. Paris: Klincksieck, 1992.

DeJean, Joan. "Female Voyeurism: Sappho and Lafayette." *Rivista di Letterature Moderne et Comparate* 40 (July–September 1987): 201–15.

———. "Lafayette's Ellipses: The Privileges of Anonymity." *PMLA* 99 (October 1984): 884–902.

———. *Tender Geographies: Women and the Origins of the Novel in France.* New York: Columbia University Press, 1991.

Derrida, Jacques. *L'écriture et la différence.* Paris: Seuil, 1967.

Descartes, René. *La dioptrique.* In *Descartes: Oeuvres et lettres.* Ed. André Bridoux. Paris: Gallimard, 1953.

———. *Discours de la méthode pour bien conduire sa raison.* In *Descartes: Oeuvres et lettres.* Ed. André Bridoux. Paris: Gallimard, 1953.

———. *The Philosophical Writings of Descartes.* 2 vols. Trans. John Cottingham, Robert Stoothoff, and Dugald Murdoch. Vol. 1. Cambridge: Cambridge University Press, 1985.

———. *Préambules.* In *Oeuvres philosophiques.* 3 vols. Ed. Ferdinand Alquié. Paris: Garnier Frères, 1963–73.

———. *Règles pour la direction de l'esprit.* In *Descartes: Oeuvres et lettres.* Ed. André Bridoux. Paris: Gallimard, 1953.

Diderot, Denis. *Oeuvres complètes.* 33 vols. Ed. Herbert Dieckmann, Jacques Proust, and Jean Varloot. Paris: Hermann, 1975–.

Doubrovsky, Serge. *Corneille et la dialectique du héros.* Paris: Gallimard, 1963.

———. "*La Princesse de Clèves:* Une interprétation existentielle." *La Table Ronde* 138 (1959): 36–51.

———. "Vingt propositions sur l'amour-propre: De Lacan à La Rochefoucauld." In *Parcours critique.* Paris: Galilée, 1980.

Felman, Shoshana. *Le scandale du corps parlant: Don Juan avec Austin ou La séduction en deux langues.* Paris: Seuil, 1980.

Forestier, Georges. *L'esthétique de l'identité dans le théâtre français (1550–1680): Le déguisement et ses avatars.* Geneva: Droz, 1988.

Foucault, Michel. *Herculine Barbin, dite Alexina B. présenté par Michel Foucault.* Paris: Gallimard, 1978.

——. *Histoire de la folie à l'âge classique.* Paris: Gallimard, 1972.

——. Introduction to *Herculine Barbin, Being the Recently Discovered Memoirs of a Nineteenth-Century Hermaphrodite.* Trans. Richard McDougall. New York: Colophon, 1980.

——. *Les mots et les choses: Une archéologie des sciences humaines.* Paris: Gallimard, 1966.

——. *The Order of Things: An Archaeology of the Human Sciences.* Trans. Alan Sheridan. New York: Vintage, 1973.

——. *L'ordre du discours.* Paris: Gallimard, 1971.

——. *Surveiller et punir: Naissance de la prison.* Paris: Gallimard, 1975.

Freud, Sigmund. "Screen Memories." In *The Complete Psychological Works of Sigmund Freud.* 24 vols. Ed. and trans. James Strachey. Vol. 3. London: Hogarth Press and the Institute of Psycho-Analysis, 1953–74.

Furetière, Antoine. *Dictionnaire universel, contenant généralement tous les mots français tant vieux que modernes, & les termes de toutes les sciences et les arts . . . recueilli et compilé par feu Messire Antoine Furetière, Abbé de Chalivoy, de l'Académie française,* 3 vols. The Hague: Arnout and Reinier Leers, 1690.

——. *Recueil des factums d'Antoine Furetière, de l'Académie française, contre quelques-uns de cette académie, suivi des preuves et pièces historiques données dans l'édition de 1694, avec une introduction et des notes historiques et critiques.* Ed. M. Charles Asselineau. Paris: Poulet-Malassis et de Broise, 1859.

Gearhart, Suzanne. *The Interrupted Dialectic: Philosophy, Psychoanalysis, and Their Tragic Other.* Baltimore: Johns Hopkins University Press, 1992.

Genette, Gérard. *Figures II.* Paris: Seuil, 1969.

——. *Figures III.* Paris: Seuil, 1972.

Gilson, Etienne, ed. *Discours de la méthode.* By René Descartes. Paris: Vrin, 1925.

Girard, René. *Mensonge romantique et vérité romanesque.* Paris: Grasset, 1961.

Goldmann, Lucien. *Le Dieu caché: Etude sur la vision tragique dans les "Pensées" de Pascal et dans le théâtre de Racine.* Paris: Gallimard, 1959.

Goodkin, Richard. "A Choice of Andromache's." *Yale French Studies* 67 (1984): 225–47.

Gossman, Lionel. *Men and Masks: A Study of Molière.* Baltimore: Johns Hopkins University Press, 1963.

Goux, Jean-Joseph. *Les iconoclastes.* Paris: Seuil, 1978.

Greenberg, Mitchell. *Canonical States, Canonical Stages: Oedipus, Othering, and Seventeenth-Century Drama.* Minneapolis: University of Minnesota Press, 1994.

——. *Corneille, Classicism, and the Ruses of Symmetry.* Cambridge: Cambridge University Press, 1986.

——. *Subjectivity and Subjugation in Seventeenth-Century Drama and Prose: The Family Romance of French Classicism.* Cambridge: Cambridge University Press, 1992.

Greenblatt, Stephen J. *Renaissance Self-Fashioning: From More to Shakespeare*. Chicago: University of Chicago Press, 1980.

——. *Shakespearean Negotiations: The Circulation of Social Energy in Renaissance England*. Berkeley: University of California Press, 1988.

Gutwirth, Marcel. *Molière ou l'invention comique: La métamorphose des thèmes et la création des types*. Paris: Minard, 1966.

Hampton, Timothy. "Introduction: Baroques." *Baroque Topographies: Literature/ History/Philosophy*. Ed. Timothy Hampton. *Yale French Studies* 80 (1991): 1–9.

Hanson, Norwood Russell. *Patterns of Discovery: An Inquiry into the Conceptual Foundations of Science*. Cambridge: Cambridge University Press, 1958.

Harootunian, H. D. "Foucault, Genealogy, History: The Pursuit of Otherness." In *After Foucault*. Ed. Jonathan Arac. New Brunswick: Rutgers University Press, 1988.

Harth, Erica. *Cartesian Women: Versions and Subversions of Rational Discourse in the Old Regime*. Ithaca: Cornell University Press, 1992.

——. *Ideology and Culture in Seventeenth-Century France*. Ithaca: Cornell University Press, 1983.

Held, Julius S., and Donald Posner. *Seventeenth- and Eighteenth-Century Art: Baroque Painting, Sculpture, Architecture*. Englewood Cliffs, N.J.: Prentice-Hall, 1979.

Hirsch, Marianne. "A Mother's Discourse: Incorporation and Repetition in *La Princesse de Clèves*." *Yale French Studies* 62 (1981): 67–87.

Horowitz, Louise K. *Love and Language: A Study of the Classical French Moralist Writers*. Columbus: Ohio State University Press, 1977.

Howe, Virginia K. "*Les Pensées*: Paradox and Signification." *Yale French Studies* 49 (1973): 120–31.

Hubert, Judd D. *Molière and the Comedy of Intellect*. Berkeley: University of California Press, 1962.

Jansen, H. W. *History of Art: A Survey of the Major Visual Arts from the Dawn of History to the Present Day*. Englewood Cliffs, N.J.: Prentice-Hall, 1973.

Johnson, George. "Science in the Laboratory of the Imagination." *New York Times*. May 1, 1994. Section 4.1.

Judovitz, Dalia. "The Aesthetics of Implausibility: *La Princesse de Clèves*." *MLN* 99 (1984): 1037–56.

——. *Subjectivity and Representation in Descartes: The Origins of Modernity*. Cambridge: Cambridge University Press, 1988.

Kamuf, Peggy. *Fictions of Feminine Desire: Disclosures of Heloise*. Lincoln: University of Nebraska Press, 1982.

Kantorovich, Aharon. *Scientific Discovery: Logic and Tinkering*. Albany: State University of New York Press, 1993.

Kantorowicz, Ernst H. *The King's Two Bodies: A Study in Mediaeval Political Theology*. Princeton: Princeton University Press, 1957.

Keller, Evelyn Fox. *Reflections on Gender and Science*. New Haven: Yale University Press, 1985.

Kristeva, Julia. *Pouvoirs de l'horreur: Essai sur l'abjection*. Paris: Seuil, 1980.

Kuhn, Reinhard. "The Palace of Broken Words: Reflections on Racine's *Andromaque.*" *Romanic Review* 70 (1979): 336–45.

Kuhn, Thomas S. *The Structure of Scientific Revolutions.* 2d ed. Chicago: University of Chicago Press, 1970.

Lacan, Jacques. *Ecrits.* Paris: Seuil, 1966.

Lafayette, Marie-Madeleine Pioche de La Vergne, Comtesse de. *La Princesse de Clèves.* Ed. Antoine Adam. Paris: Flammarion, 1966.

———. *Zaïde.* In *Romans et nouvelles.* Ed. Alain Niderst. Paris: Bordas, 1990.

La Rochefoucauld, François, Duc de. *Maximes et Réflexions diverses.* Ed. Jacques Truchet. Paris: Garnier-Flammarion, 1977.

Levao, Ronald. "Francis Bacon and the Mobility of Science." *Representations* 40 (Fall 1992): 1–32.

Lévi-Strauss, Claude. *La pensée sauvage.* Paris: Plon, 1962.

Lewis, Philip E. *La Rochefoucauld: The Art of Abstraction.* Ithaca: Cornell University Press, 1977.

Locke, David. *Science as Writing.* New Haven: Yale University Press, 1992.

Longino, Helen E. *Science as Social Knowledge: Values and Objectivity in Scientific Inquiry.* Princeton: Princeton University Press, 1990.

Longino, Michèle. "The Staging of Exoticism in Seventeenth-Century France." Unpublished manuscript.

Lyons, John D. "The Dead Center: Desire and Mediation in Lafayette's *Zayde.*" *Esprit Créateur* (Summer 1983): 58–69.

———. *Exemplum: The Rhetoric of Example in Early Modern France and Italy.* Princeton: Princeton University Press, 1989.

———. "Speaking in Pictures, Speaking of Pictures: Problems of Representation in the Seventeenth Century." In *Mimesis: From Mirror to Method, Augustine to Descartes.* Ed. John D. Lyons and Stephen G. Nichols, Jr. Hanover, N.H.: University Press of New England, 1982.

———. "Subjectivity and Imitation in the *Discours de la méthode.*" *Neophilologus* 66 (1982): 508–24.

Mandrou, Robert. *Des humanistes aux hommes de science: XVIe et XVIIe siècles.* Vol. 3 of *Histoire de la pensée européenne.* Paris: Seuil, 1973.

Marin, Louis. "Classical, Baroque: Versailles, or the Architecture of the Prince." Trans. Anna Lehman. In *Baroque Topographies: Literature/History/Philosophy.* Ed. Timothy Hampton. *Yale French Studies* 80 (1991): 167–82.

———. *La critique du discours: Sur la "Logique de Port-Royal" et les "Pensées" de Pascal.* Paris: Minuit, 1975.

———. *Le portrait du roi.* Paris: Minuit, 1981.

———. *Portrait of the King.* Trans. Martha Houle. Minneapolis: University of Minnesota Press, 1988.

Mauron, Charles. *L'inconscient dans l'oeuvre et la vie de Racine.* Paris: Corti, 1969.

Mauss, Marcel. *Essai sur le don: Forme et raison de l'échange dans les sociétés archaïques.* Paris: Alcan, 1925.

Melzer, Sara E. *Discourses of the Fall: A Study of Pascal's "Pensées."* Berkeley: University of California Press, 1986.

Mesnard, Jean. *Les "Pensées" de Pascal.* Paris: Société d'Edition d'Enseignement Supérieur, 1976.

Miel, Jan. "Les méthodes de Pascal et l'épistémè classique." In *Méthodes chez Pascal: Actes du colloque tenu à Clermont-Ferrand 10–13 juin 1976.* Paris: Presses Universitaires de France, 1976.

——. "Pascal, Port-Royal, and Cartesian Linguistics." *Journal of the History of Ideas* 30 (1969): 261–71.

Miller, Nancy K. "Emphasis Added: Plots and Plausibilities in Women's Fiction." In *Subject to Change: Reading Feminist Writing.* New York: Columbia University Press, 1988.

Molière. *Amphitryon.* In *Oeuvres complètes.* Ed. Pierre-Aimé Touchard. Paris: Seuil, 1962.

Morel, Jacques. *Jean Rotrou: Dramaturge de l'ambiguïté.* Paris: Armand Colin, 1968.

Moriarty, Michael. *Taste and Ideology in Seventeenth-Century France.* Cambridge: Cambridge University Press, 1988.

Murray, Timothy. *Theatrical Legitimation: Allegories of Genius in Seventeenth-Century England and France.* New York: Oxford University Press, 1987.

Nancy, Jean-Luc. *Ego sum.* Paris: Flammarion, 1979.

Nelson, Robert J. *Immanence and Transcendence: The Theater of Jean Rotrou, 1609–1650.* Columbus: Ohio State University Press, 1969.

Norman, Buford. *Portraits of Thought: Knowledge, Methods, and Styles in Pascal.* Columbus: Ohio State University Press, 1988.

Panofsky, Erwin. *La perspective comme "forme symbolique" et autres essais.* Trans. M. Joly. Paris: Minuit, 1975.

Pascal, Blaise. *Opuscules et lettres.* Ed. Louis Lafuma. Paris: Aubier-Montaigne, 1955.

——. *Pensées.* Ed. Léon Brunschvicg. Paris: Garnier-Flammarion, 1976.

Popper, Karl. *The Logic of Scientific Discovery.* 3d ed. London: Hutchinson, 1968.

Porush, David. "Voyage to Eudoxia: The Emergence of Post-Rational Epistemology in Literature and Science." *SubStance* 71/72 Special Issue: *Epistémocritique* (1993): 38–49.

Poulet, Georges. *Etudes sur le temps humain.* 5 vols. Vol. 1. Paris: Plon, 1952.

Proust, Jacques. "Diderot et le système des connaissances humaines." *Studies on Voltaire and the Eighteenth Century* 256 (1988): 117–27.

Racine, Jean. *Andromaque.* In *Oeuvres complètes.* Ed. Luc Estang. Paris: Seuil, 1962.

——. *Bérénice.* In *Oeuvres complètes.* Ed. Luc Estang. Paris: Seuil, 1962.

Ranum, Orest. *Paris in the Age of Absolutism: An Essay.* New York: John Wiley, 1968.

Reiss, Timothy J. "Cartesian Discourse and Classical Ideology." *Diacritics* 6 (Winter 1976): 19–27.

——. "The 'Concevoir' Motif in Descartes." In *La cohérence intérieure: Etudes sur la littérature française du XVIIe siècle, offertes à J. D. Hubert.* Ed. Jacqueline Van Baelen and David Lee Rubin. Paris: Jean-Michel Place, 1977.

——. *The Discourse of Modernism.* Ithaca: Cornell University Press, 1982.

————. "Espaces de la pensée discursive: Le cas Galilée et la science classique." *Revue de Synthèse* 85–86 (1977): 5–47.

————. *The Meaning of Literature.* Ithaca: Cornell University Press, 1992.

Relyea, Suzanne. *Signs, Systems, and Meanings: A Contemporary Semiotic Reading of Four Molière Plays.* Middletown, Conn.: Wesleyan University Press, 1976.

Rey, Alain. Introduction to *Le dictionnaire d'Antoine Furetière.* Paris: Robert, 1978.

————. "Linguistic Absolutism." In *A New History of French Literature.* Ed. Denis Hollier. Cambridge: Harvard University Press, 1989.

Romanowski, Sylvie. *L'illusion chez Descartes: La structure du discours cartésien.* Paris: Klincksieck, 1974.

Rotrou, Jean. *Le véritable Saint Genest.* Ed. E. T. Dubois. Geneva: Droz, 1972.

Rousset, Jean. *Forme et signification: Essais sur les structures littéraires de Corneille à Claudel.* Paris: Corti, 1962.

————. *La littérature de l'âge baroque: Circé et le paon.* Paris: Corti, 1954.

Said, Edward W. *Orientalism.* New York: Vintage, 1979.

————. "The Problem of Textuality: Two Exemplary Positions." *Critical Inquiry* 4 (Summer 1978): 673–714.

Schor, Naomi. "The Portrait of a Gentleman: Representing Men in (French) Women's Writing." In *Misogyny, Misandry, and Misanthropy.* Ed. R. Howard Bloch and Frances Ferguson. Berkeley: University of California Press, 1989.

————. *Reading in Detail: Aesthetics and the Feminine.* New York: Methuen, 1987.

Skenazi, Cynthia. "La représentation du théâtre dans *Le véritable Saint Genest* de Rotrou." *Papers in French Seventeenth-Century Literature* 17, no. 32 (1990): 75–84.

Stanton, Domna C. "The Ideal of 'Repos' in Seventeenth-Century French Literature." *Esprit Créateur* 15 (1975): 79–104.

————. "Pascal's Fragmentary Thoughts: Dis-Order and Its Overdetermination." *Semiotica* 51, nos. 1–3 (1984): 211–35.

Starobinski, Jean. *L'oeil vivant.* Paris: Gallimard, 1961.

————. "La Rochefoucauld et les morales substitutives." *NRF* 163–64 (July–August 1966): 17–34; 211–29.

Stone, Harriet. *Royal DisClosure: Problematics of Representation in French Classical Tragedy.* Birmingham, Ala.: Summa, 1987.

Stroup, Alice. "Louis XIV as Patron of the Parisian Academy of Sciences." In *Sun King: The Ascendancy of French Culture during the Reign of Louis XIV.* Ed. David Lee Rubin. London: Associated University Presses, 1992.

Todorov, Tzvetan. "La comédie humaine selon La Rochefoucauld." *Poétique* 53 (February 1983): 37–47.

Ubersfeld, Anne. "Le double dans l'*Amphitryon* de Molière." In *Dramaturgies: Langages dramatiques; mélanges pour Jacques Scherer.* Ed. Jacqueline de Jomaron. Paris: Nizet, 1986.

Valincour, J.-B. de. *Lettres à Mme la Marquise . . . sur le sujet de "La Princesse de Clèves."* Ed. Jacques Chupeau et al. Tours: Université François Rabelais, 1972.

Van Baelen, Jacqueline. *Rotrou: Le héros tragique et la révolte.* Paris: Nizet, 1965.

Van Delft, Louis. *Le moraliste classique: Essai de définition et de typologie.* Geneva: Droz, 1982.

Veeser, H. Aram, ed. *The New Historicism.* New York: Routledge, 1989.

——. *The New Historicism Reader.* London: Routledge, 1994.

Vernet, Max. *Molière: Côté jardin, côté cour.* Paris: Nizet, 1991.

Viala, Alain. *Naissance de l'écrivain: Sociologie de la littérature à l'âge classique.* Paris: Minuit, 1985.

Weinstein, Arnold. *Fictions of the Self: 1550–1800.* Princeton: Princeton University Press, 1981.

Zanger, Abby Elizabeth. "Classical Anxiety: Performance, Perfection, and the Issue of Identity." In *L'âge du théâtre en France/The Age of Theater in France.* Ed. David Trott and Nicole Boursier. Edmonton: Academic Printing and Publishing, 1988.

Index